supported by

the good
Financial
Management
guide
for the voluntary sector

by Paul Palmer, Fiona Young
and Neil Finlayson

giving voice and support to voluntary and commur

The National Council for Voluntary Organisations (NCVO) is the umbrella body for the voluntary sector in England, with sister councils in Wales, Scotland and Northern Ireland. NCVO has a growing membership of over 3,700 voluntary organisations, ranging from large national bodies to community groups, volunteer bureaux and development agencies working at a local level. We work to support the voluntary sector and to create an environment in which voluntary organisations of all kinds can flourish by providing a wide range of information, advice and support services and by representing the views of the sector to government and policy makers.

Our vision
NCVO's vision is of a society in which people are inspired to make a positive difference to their communities.

Our mission
A vibrant voluntary and community sector deserves a strong voice and the best support. NCVO aims to be that support and voice.

Published by NCVO Publications (incorporating Bedford Square Press), imprint of the National Council for Voluntary Organisations, Regent's Wharf, 8 All Saints Street, London N1 9RL

First published in 1999. Revised 2002. Updated with new text and format in 2005 by Professor Paul Palmer, and Fiona Young supported by Neil Finlayson, Cass Business School, City University, London.

2002 revisions by Professor Paul Palmer, Jackie Severn and Stephen Williams, London South Bank University.

Typeset by JVT Design
Printed by Latimer Trend

British Library Cataloguing in Publication Data
A catalogue record for this book is available from the British Library

ISBN: 0 7199 1662 3

Every effort has been made to trace or contact the copyright holders of original text or illustrations used. The publishers will be pleased to correct any error or omissions brought to their attention in future editions of this book.

Acknowledgements

Author's Acknowledgements

We would like to thank the following for allowing us to use their material in the text:
Mark Salway, Finance Director, Cats Protection League and formerly of KPMG for his contribution on Full Cost Recovery.

Mark Freeman, Chief Executive of Charity Business for his assistance on Outsourcing.

Mark Davies, Andrew Jessen and Nigel Price of Unity Trust Bank for their assistance on banking.

Paul Mitchell, Andrew Pitt, David Rowe and John Harrison of UBS for their assistance on investment.

John Tate for his assistance on IT and computerising the accounts.

Sue Douthwaite for the fund raising problem exercise in Chapter 2.

We also acknowledge with thanks the assistance given by NCVO, and acknowledge the respective contributions of Haroon Bashir, the author of the first edition, Jackie Severn and Stephen Williams for revisions to the second edition, much of whose work remains valid in this update.

NCVO's Acknowledgements

We would like to thank HBOS for their ongoing support of NCVO's financial management project which provides financial management resources for the voluntary sector. Our particular gratitude is due for their support for the publication of this update to the *Good Financial Management Guide*.

Contents

Author's Introduction

When I was asked to revise the *Good Financial Management Guide* in 2002, I said that it would not be a simple task. If the period of change to voluntary organisation finance for the years 1999-2002 had been fast moving, the last three years 2002-2005 has been like a hurricane. In addition to the new Charity SORP, there has been in a shift in understanding how voluntary organisations should tender, charge for their services and recover overheads when contracting with statutory authorities. The 'governance revolution' has continued with roll-over in good practice from the private sector and much more, including the need for registered charities to be more transparent and accountable for their activities. When I first revised this book I wrote of a 'climate change' in attitude, which acknowledges that the financial management of voluntary organisations goes beyond simple bookkeeping to voluntary organisations becoming social businesses. While some business practices are not appropriate for voluntary organisations, the need to demonstrate that the organisation is economic and efficient with resources has become recognised. But the pace of change continues to move on. Voluntary organisations now need to be transparent and clearly demonstrate that they are seeking and obtaining the best value from their resources and delivering appropriate, effective services. This book continues to be unashamedly about promoting best practice and is therefore full of prescriptive advice obtained from experts, practitioners and research. I would like to thank my new co-authors, Fiona Young, who brings experience as both a practitioner and someone who worked on 'the other side' as an auditor to charities, and Neil Finlayson who acted as a professional reviewer, and whose commitment to the sector, since I first met him as the audit manager to the charity I worked for in the mid 1980s, has never ceased.

Paul Palmer, Professor of Voluntary Sector Management, Cass Business School, City University, London and Consultant on Charities at UBS.

Fiona Young, Director of Resources, Crisis and Visiting Lecturer in Charity Accounting, Cass Business School, City University, London.

Neil Finlayson, Charities Partner, Kingston Smith Chartered Accountants and Guest Lecturer in Charity Auditing, Cass Business School, City University, London.

Introduction

This book is a non-specialist's guide to the financial management of voluntary organisations. It aims to meet the needs of a wide range of voluntary organisations, regardless of their constitution, size, areas of activity and area of remit.

Why is a guide to financial management necessary?

Widespread changes are taking place in the voluntary sector that will affect every organisation within it. These include:

- The report of the Commission on the Future of the Voluntary Sector initiated a far-reaching debate on voluntary action in the UK. The growth of funding from government into the sector through service contracting has had financial implications. The micro-finance of that relationship has required voluntary organisations to understand both the complexity of that relationship and their cost structures. We cover in detail overheads and full cost recovery.
- In 2005 the income mix of voluntary organisations reflects four very different sources of finance. Income from the public; income from statutory authorities, increasingly linked to service contracts; a growing but still very small income from corporate sources; and investment income, which is recovering after the fall in capital markets from 2002-2004. Each of these sources requires different forms of financial management.
- According to the NCVO Almanac (published every two years and containing detailed research on the voluntary sector) there are signs of very modest growth in smaller organisations, but it is middle-sized organisations – those with an annual income between £100,000 and £10 million – that are being squeezed. These organisations are not investing in fundraising, are heavily reliant on generating earned income, and do not have significant investment assets.
- The legal framework within which voluntary action takes place has also continued to evolve, as a result of national legislation. With a new Charities Bill scheduled to be introduced, European legislation affects voluntary organisations as employers through, for example, the National Minimum Wage and the Working Time Directive, and as service providers through human rights.

- The Charity Accounting Statement of Recommended Practice (SORP) was revised in 2005 with an emphasis on transparency and accountability. This is covered in detail later in this book.
- Complexity of charity taxation. The voluntary sector is by no means exempt from tax, although exemptions exist for direct taxation (income tax), indirect taxation in the shape of VAT is a complicated and specialist area.

Everyone involved in the voluntary sector should be aware of the impact these factors can have on their organisations:

- The trustees, who are charged with the stewardship and governance of the organisation.
- The management team, who must work with the trustees to formulate policy and deliver services.
- The staff and volunteers, who need to be motivated by a clear mission and clear values to carry out their day-to-day functions.
- The finance officer (professionally qualified or otherwise), whose role is being transformed from 'police officer and score-keeper' to 'business partner', working across organisational boundaries to deliver a strategic and value-adding finance service.

This guide will enable the reader to understand how these changes are affecting voluntary organisations and in particular, their impact on financial management at a strategic and operational level.

An issue that has received much attention recently is the role of trustees in financial management and the division of responsibility between the trustee board and management.

Chapter One, 'Structuring the organisation for financial strength', looks at governance across all three sectors and addresses the question of responsibility, specifically the responsibility of trustees in relation to financial management. How this question is answered can mean the difference between financial success or failure for a voluntary organisation.

Chapter Two, 'Financing the mission', looks at strategic intent: how to strike the balance between the mission of the organisation and the resources it has available. It proposes a framework for long-term strategic planning that will help managers and trustees to decide which charitable programmes to adopt. Only when the strategic objectives have been decided can the wider question of management information and budgeting be addressed. This is the point at which any inadequacies in financial planning, control and monitoring become evident.

Chapter Three, 'Budgeting', translates the mission into financial terms and comes up with a financial blueprint for achieving mission-orientated goals. This chapter also looks at how to prepare (and revise) budgets and how to enable staff to participate in the process. The aim of budgeting is to allocate an organisation's current resources so that it achieves its programme goals, and effective asset management will maximise the value of those resources.

Chapter Four, 'Resource management', looks at strategic options such as forming alliances and outsourcing; at cash flow planning and investments; and tackles the tricky issues of restricted funding and charity reserves.

Chapter Five, 'Special financial procedures', shows how the financially astute voluntary organisation will use techniques such as ratio analysis – which will enable it to assess performance and identify trends so as to ensure liquidity – and cost accounting, which allows management to make informed decisions based on a proper analysis of costs and to understand and recover overhead costs.

These chapters are followed by three chapters which clarify some of the bigger issues in charity accounting. Chapter Six deals with 'Charity accounts and financial management' and outlines the issues brought up by the Statement of Recommended Practice (SORP).

Chapter Seven, 'Key issues', covers recent developments including risk assessment, performance indicators, banking and investment management.

Chapter Eight, 'Taxation' outlines the position surrounding taxation and VAT in particular.

Finally, a new chapter nine looks at the special issues relating to the accounting of smaller voluntary organisations.

Where appropriate, each chapter of the guide begins with a summary of the contents and concludes with case studies or examples showing how theory has been translated into practice.

References to further reading and resources can be found towards the back of the book.

1 Structuring the organisation for financial strength

1.1 The governance debate
1.2 The trustee board
1.3 The financial management role of trustee boards
1.4 Exercises and case studies

1.1 The governance debate

Governance can be defined as 'the system by which organisations are directed and controlled'. Institutions of every kind – government, public bodies, voluntary organisations and commercial companies – are under increasing pressure to be more transparent about what they do and more responsive to the people they serve. This has led to demands for higher standards of accountability, behaviour and performance. Commercial practices that were condoned in the past – such as insider trading – are no longer acceptable, and accounting rules are becoming tighter. A similar tightening up is taking place in government and in public life in general.

This section looks briefly at the main developments in governance in the private, public and voluntary sectors. It will be of particular interest to the trustees of voluntary organisations, given the increasing professionalisation of the voluntary sector and the renewed emphasis being placed on the legal obligations of trustees.

In any voluntary organisation, a precondition for financial strength is the clear definition of the roles and responsibilities of trustees, paid staff and volunteers. Without this clarity of roles, responsibility for income generation and expenditure will be dissipated; and with it, any hope of control.

Developments in the private sector
In the 1990s there was a shift of attention away from how organisations are managed to how they are governed. This was partly the result of a series of prominent corporate failures and frauds in the late 1980s and 1990s. To prevent such failures happening

again there has been a series of Committees and Codes into corporate and public life – the first and most prominent being the 1992 Cadbury Committee on the Financial Aspects of Corporate Governance. Against this backdrop of prominent corporate failures, the Cadbury Committee set out to address the low levels of confidence in company financial reporting and auditing, which have often been blamed for enabling the abuses of executive directors to go undiscovered. The Cadbury Report, however, goes beyond financial audit procedures to examine board structures and models of corporate governance. The committee developed a Code of Best Practice in Corporate Governance which is based on principles of openness, integrity and accountability. In addition, the position of non-executive directors has been strengthened by the establishment of audit committees that report directly to them.

The Hampel Report (1996) reviewed Cadbury and noted that few companies gave effectiveness opinions and concluded that this was because:

- Effectiveness was hard to define.
- It opened the auditors and directors to unreasonable legal claims.
- It implied that controls can offer absolute assurance against misstatement or loss; in fact no system of control is proof against human error or deliberate override.

The Hampell Committee incorporated previous reports and produced the 'Combined Code' which requires public company directors to report on all internal controls, not just financial ones. The Turnbull committee in 1999 provided more detailed guidance in this area, linking governance to risk management and a system of internal control. Features of the Turnbull Code state:

- The Board should maintain a sound system of internal control to safeguard shareholders' investment and the company's assets.
- The Board should, at least annually, conduct a review of the effectiveness of the group's system of internal control and should report that they have done so.
- The review should cover all controls, including financial, operational and compliance controls and risk management.
- Companies which do not have an internal audit system should from time to time review the need for one.
- The Board, in its annual report, should summarise the process it has applied in reviewing the effectiveness of the system of internal control – in essence this important point is

about the transparency of what has been done and provides the focus for internal audit's role with the audit committee.

The combined code recognises the need to ensure a risk-based approach to developing sound business practices in order to protect the shareholders' interests. It states that all companies need clear systems of internal controls that are part of the normal management and governance processes of the organisation, embedded within the organisation's operations, and not treated as a separate exercise undertaken to meet regulatory requirements. The guidance also recommends that companies should be able to respond promptly to risks arising from both within and outside the company. Although the combined code is only applicable to listed companies, its message is applicable to all organisations and has been embraced in both the public sector, through for example the CIPFA *Good Governance Standard for Public Service*, and for charities by the Charity Commission in the Charity SORP which requires a statement on risks and internal controls.

Updates and current reviews

On 1 November 2003 a new combined code was issued which derived from a review of the role of non-executive directors by Derek Higgs, and a review of audit committees by Robert Smith. Both of these reviews were prompted by concerns that the principles outlined by Cadbury on corporate governance were not being adhered to and to give clear guidance to boards on what was expected. Non-executive directors were expected to take an active role in their companies, for example, in relation to setting remuneration levels to executive management and providing an effective review to curb any management excesses, including undesirable behaviour and excessive risk taking. Smith focused on the role and effectiveness of audit committees giving clear guidance on their role and composition, including their relationship with the board and with internal audit. In July 2004 the Financial Reporting Council set up a review of the Turnbull guidance lead by Douglas Flint.

The main aim of these codes has been to find ways of making executive directors more accountable for their actions to a group of stakeholders (in this case the shareholders). Similar focuses on acountability in the public sector began with the Nolan Committee, and NCVO and Charity Commission have promoted best practice in Charity Governance. These developments in private sector governance have had, and will continue to have, a major influence on how the public and voluntary sectors develop their own governance structures.

Developments in the public sector

The public sector has often had a bad press too, particularly over its supposedly inappropriate use of public money. The 1979-97 Conservative administration began a process of reform and restructuring that has had a major effect on the way governance has been addressed.

The central theme of these reforms was the need to improve efficiency through greater competition, as pressure to reduce public expenditure and local taxation became politically fashionable. This policy was implemented by introducing private sector management practices – for example, performance indicators to assess the quality of services, and multiple audits to ensure best value for money – and by removing elected members and replacing them with appointees who had business experience.

The reforms culminated in widespread structural change during the 1980s and 1990s, when many public services were removed from the direct control of local authorities and run instead by quangos, operating under contracts with central government.

This growth in quangos, coupled with the increase in central government control, has raised concerns about the membership of such bodies and their accountability. There is talk of a 'governance gap', of the danger of creating a closed professional elite that would ultimately control these quangos. The third Nolan Committee report, *A Report on Standards of Conduct in Local Government* (Nolan III), published in July 1997, set out to consider an overall ethical framework for local government, and how this framework might be adapted to different circumstances.

The code elaborates on the types of written agreements that should exist, including the relationship statement; job description and reciprocation; reporting arrangements; and liability and responsibility statement.

To sum up, the public sector has been deeply involved in the governance debate and continues to be with fresh initiatives. In 2005 a new standard for the governance of public services was issued. This new standard presents six core principles of good governance. Each principle has supporting principles that explain what is involved in putting good governance into practice. The six principles are:

1. Good governance means focusing on the organisation's purpose and outcomes for citizens and service users.
2. Good governance means performing effectively in clearly defined functions and roles.

3. Good governance means promoting values for the whole organisation and demonstrating the values of good governance through behaviour.
4. Good governance means taking informed transparent decisions and managing risk.
5. Good governance means developing the capacity and capability of the governing body to be effective.
6. Good governance means engaging stakeholders and making accountability real.

The standard is intended to help all organisations in the public sector but also some in the voluntary and community sector as well as registered social landlords who receive public money to provide specific services.

The widespread structural changes – and the concerns over accountability arising from those changes have resulted in codes of conduct seeking to establish good governance. At the same time, the push to make local authority services more economic and effective has introduced many private sector management practices into the public sector.

Developments in the voluntary sector

Section 97 of the Charities Act 1993 defines trustees as 'the people responsible under the charity's governing document for controlling the management and administration of the charity, regardless of what they are called'. In fulfilling this responsibility, trustees may delegate the management of the organisation's day-to-day affairs to an executive committee (a committee of paid staff in this instance) whilst they themselves concentrate on governance. This delegation of duties does not, however, absolve trustees from being held accountable in law for the activities of the voluntary organisation. Given these legal responsibilities, governance issues and practices are therefore particularly relevant to trustees. Beyond the question of probity, the professionalism of trustees is leading them to seek greater accountability and effectiveness.

The voluntary sector economy has, until recently, experienced a period of rapid growth, driven initially by the Conservative administration's decision to contract out the provision of local services to the voluntary sector in 1988. Social housing has moved from being the responsibility of the local authority to being that of housing associations, who have been encouraged to take a commercial approach to managing the housing stock and finances. Further growth of the sector has been fuelled by the care in the community programme. The Labour Government of 1997 adopted the main recommendations of the Commission on the Future of the Voluntary Sector, and in particular introduced the Compact to provide a best practice context for how statutory authorities should contract with voluntary organisations. Government funding to the voluntary sector has increased year on year and now approaches some 40 per cent of total sector income.

Inefficiencies in the public and voluntary sectors are bound to cause public concern, and both sectors rely on the good faith of the general public. NCVO research into public trust and confidence in charities has revealed:

- A very limited understanding amongst the public of what charities are doing.
- Concern about the voluntary sector's relations with the state (amongst some respondents).
- A fear that gap-filling 'lets the state off the hook'.
- That lottery publicity has opened up the debate about what is a deserving cause.
- That many see the voluntary sector as being full of competing charities.
- A demand for greater transparency, for example, about administration costs.
- A perceived lack of information on which to base giving decisions.

The above results, together with the revelation of failings in certain 'household name' charities, has shaken public confidence and forced the Charity Commission to tighten up its regulatory procedures.

The Joseph Rowntree Foundation introduced a code of practice on the governance of voluntary organisations. This code is intended for voluntary bodies that deliver services with the benefit of public funding, and that seek to be effective and accountable. Such organisations will, the code states, be clear and open about their work and conscious of their social responsibilities. The code covers:

- *Effectiveness*: showing clarity of purpose, being explicit about the needs to be met and ways in which resources are managed.
- *Accountability*: evaluating effectiveness and performance, dealing with complaints fairly and communicating to all stakeholders how responsibilities will be fulfilled.
- *Standards*: having clear operating standards.
- *User involvement*: making arrangements to involve users of services.

- *Governance*: having a systematic and open process for making appointments to the governing body, setting out the roles and responsibilities of members.
- *Volunteers*: having clear arrangements for involving, training, supporting and managing volunteers.
- *Equality and fairness*: ensuring that policies and practices do not discriminate unfairly.
- *Staff management*: recruiting staff openly, remunerating them fairly and being a good employer.

NCVO has supported a series of initiatives on improving charity governance as has the Charity Commission which published *Hallmarks of a Well-run Charity*. These respective initatives are constantly being updated and the reader should consult the respective websites:

www.ncvo-vol.org.uk
www.charity-commission.gov.uk
www.opm.co.uk/ICGGPS/

SORP 2005 – Trustee Annual Reports and Governance

The new Charity SORP discussed in detail in Chapter 6 and only applicable to registered charities with an income greater than £250,000 has become prescriptive in now requiring charities to provide distinct information about the organisation as follows:

Content of the Trustees' Annual Report
Reference and administrative details of the charity, its trustees and advisers.

The report should provide the following reference and administrative information about the charity, its trustees and advisers:

(a) The name of the charity, which in the case of a registered charity means the name by which it is registered. Any other name by which a charity makes itself known should also be provided;

(b) The charity registration number (in Scotland the Scottish Charity Number) and, if applicable, the company registration number;

(c) The address of the principal office of the charity and in the case of a charitable company the address of its registered office;

(d) The names of all of those who were the charity's trustees (Glossary GL 7) or a trustee for the charity (Glossary GL 59) on the date the report was approved. Where there are

> The new Charity SORP is only applicable to registered charities with an income greater than £250,000.

more than 50 charity trustees, the names of at least 50 of those trustees (including all the officers of the charity, e.g. chair, treasurer) should be provided. Where any charity trustee disclosed is a body corporate, the names of the directors of the body corporate on that date must be disclosed

(e) The name of any other person who served as a charity trustee (Glossary GL 7) or as a trustee for the charity (Glossary GL 59) in the financial year in question.

(f) The name of any Chief Executive Officer or other senior staff member(s) to whom day to day management of the charity is delegated by the charity trustees.

(g) The names and addresses of any other relevant organisations or persons. This should include the names and addresses of those acting as bankers, solicitors, auditor (or independent examiner or reporting accountant) and investment or other principal advisers.

Source: The Charity Commission SORP 2005

It should be noted that the Charity Commission can give dispensation not to provide such details, for example if a person would be deemed to be in danger. While the details identified in the SORP are only applicable to larger charities they are an example of best practice and should be followed by all voluntary organisations.

Quality standards

It is well established that there is a clear link between governance and quality assurance. A voluntary organisation's reason for existence is to deliver the best possible services to beneficiaries. However, sometimes it all goes wrong. It has been suggested that this happens because voluntary organisations lack the bottom line of profit and have to rely on softer, less quantifiable and measurable performance monitors and goals. These issues also confront the public sector and the search for value for money has often been linked to what have been termed the three Es – these can be defined for voluntary organisations as:

It is well established that there is a clear link between governance and quality assurance.

- **Economic:** not spending 95p to raise £1; essentially minimising waste.
- **Efficient:** getting the best use of what money is spent; a high output to input ratio.
- **Effective:** spending funds so as to achieve the organisation's objectives; getting things done.

The pursuit of quality and continuous improvement is not new to the voluntary sector: the commitment to deliver the best possible services to beneficiaries has been a major driving force for many years, and most voluntary organisations are highly motivated to deliver high standards of service. But in the absence of the criteria used in the private sector – such as profit or return on investment – trustees, management and staff need other ways of measuring their performance. There are, however, various obstacles:

- Market or customer satisfaction is rarely a measure of quality – in the words of one charity representative: "It is possible to give very bad advice very nicely."
- Voluntary organisations often have a monopoly on providing certain services; therefore continued high demand is not necessarily an indicator of quality.
- Many end users are 'silent': for example, elderly or mentally disabled people may not be able to make an informed view of quality.

For the last ten years, voluntary organisations have been under pressure to show that they have achieved, and maintained, verifiable quality standards. This has increasingly been at the insistence of the purchaser of services, especially local authorities, or the donors who fund activities. There has also been concern among the wider public about the probity and performance of the voluntary sector.

The Quality Standards Task Group was set up at NCVO in July 1997. After wide consultation, the Group recommended that the voluntary sector should:

- *Establish quality principles*. These would describe an organisation's fundamental beliefs that form the basis for its whole management ethos.
- *Commit to the concept and practice of continuous improvement*. This would provide for the systematic and methodical enhancement of an organisation's capabilities and performance.

The proposed principles for the voluntary sector state that a quality voluntary organisation:

- Strives for continuous improvement in all it does.
- Uses recognised standards or models as a means to continuous improvement and not as an end.
- Agrees requirements with stakeholders, and endeavours to meet or exceed these the first time and every time.

- Promotes equality of opportunity through its internal and external conduct.
- Is accountable to stakeholders.
- Adds value to its end users and beneficiaries.

1.2 The trustee board

Given the huge range of requirements and best practice guidelines, an effective, well-structured trustee board of committed individuals is of paramount importance, and the vital first step in ensuring the organisation's financial strength. In this section, we take a brief look at some of the issues to consider when recruiting trustees.

What are you looking for in a board member? Ideally you will want to find people whose skills, experience and personal qualities will complement those of your current board.

Thinking about any existing skills gaps could give you ideas about where to look, and could help to improve the composition of your board. After carrying out a skills audit (see Appendix A ot this chapter), the board needs to decide on a strategy to attract new trustees and to utilise the range of skills which are already available.

The board may wish to set up a nominating committee with the specific task of recruiting new trustees (as well as implementing board development/induction programmes). It is important to write a job description and person specification for trustees: these not only help the organisation to clarify the role of its trustees, but also serve as useful aids for people thinking about becoming trustees, and help those considering nominating others for trusteeship to put forward suitable candidates. It may also be useful to draw up a code of conduct, spelling out the relationship between trustees and the organisation; this can help to clarify expectations on both sides, making obligations plain to potential trustees. The code should state, for example, that expenses may be claimed, and should give an honest estimate of the amount of support the organisation can give new trustees and the time commitment required of them.

> Ideally you will want to find people whose skills, experience and personal qualities will complement those of your current board.

Finding new trustees

Here are some ideas of where to look:

> Organise an event that will enable people to learn about your organisation.

- Consider your volunteers, supporters, donors, service users/beneficiaries and colleagues in partner organisations, or those involved in related areas of work.
- Organise an event that will enable people to learn about your organisation.

- Do any local firms have employee volunteering schemes? If not, why not encourage them to start one? Contact your local Chamber of Commerce for ideas on who to contact.
- Use a newsworthy event as a lever to obtain free publicity in the media.
- Advertise in national or local newspapers, professional journals, community centres or libraries.
- Try using a trustee brokerage service. These draw their potential trustees from a variety of different sources – retired people, professionals, business people, black and minority ethnic people etc – and offer levels of service varying from basic introductions to full recruitment.

Induction of trustees

In order to be effective, trustees must be given all the information they need to understand the organisation – its aims, beneficiaries, the boundaries within which it operates – and their own role as trustees.

An induction pack should be compiled, containing information about the organisation and the role and responsibilities of trustees. Here are some suggestions about what it should include:

- A brief history of the organisation.
- The governing document.
- Standing orders.
- Roles and responsibilities of trustees, including trustee job descriptions.
- The annual report and accounts for the previous three years.
- Sets of recent board papers and minutes, including management accounts.
- Board and committee structures.
- Terms of reference for the board of trustees and all committees.
- Dates of forthcoming meetings.
- Names, addresses, telephone and fax numbers of trustees.
- Major policy documents.
- If staff are employed, the organisation's staff structure and the Chief Executive Officer's job description.
- A manual (such as NCVO's *Good Trustee Guide*).
- A self assessment form to enable recruits to indicate their own support needs: for example, pairing, debriefing meetings.
- An effective induction should not only prevent new trustees from becoming disillusioned and leaving, but should also mean that they quickly become a useful member of your board.

SORP 2005 requires charities to disclose in their annual reports the induction programme of new trustees.

The governing structure

Recruits will need to know whether the main board of trustees has any sub-committees, and if so, what their terms of reference are. If the trustees have powers to delegate work to sub-committees, all decisions of those sub-committees should be reported to the full board of trustees, who must take ultimate responsibility for them. Recruits must also be told whether there are any advisory groups and how they fit into the governing structure and whether there are any additional working parties or ad hoc committees.

The structure of the organisation

An organisation chart, together with a list of the names of key staff with their job titles and responsibilities, will provide a useful overview of the structure of the organisation. Staff are normally accountable through a line management structure to the chief executive, who is in turn answerable to the trustees. To avoid blurring these lines of accountability, trustees may need guidance on when it is appropriate to contact a member of staff directly and when they should go through the chair or chief executive.

Annual reports and accounts

Each year trustees should be given a copy of the organisation's annual report and accounts. They should keep these copies for at least three years.

Conflicts of interest

Conflicts of interest arise when the personal or professional interest of a board member is potentially at odds with the best interest of the organisation: for example, when a board member performs professional services for an organisation, or suggests that a friend or relative be considered for a staff position. These decisions are perfectly acceptable if the board makes them in an objective and informed manner, and if they benefit the organisation. Even if they do not meet these criteria, such decisions are not usually illegal – but they are vulnerable to legal challenges and public misunderstanding.

A damaged reputation is the most likely result of a poorly-managed conflict of interest. Because public confidence is so important to voluntary organisations, boards should take steps to avoid even the appearance of impropriety. These steps may include:

- Adopting a conflict of interest policy that prohibits or limits business transactions with board members and requires board members to disclose potential conflicts.
- Disclosing conflicts when they occur so that board members who are voting on a decision are aware that another member's interests are being affected.
- Requiring affected board members to withdraw from decisions that present a potential conflict.
- Establishing procedures, such as competitive bids, that ensure that the organisation is receiving best value in the transaction.

Connected persons

The Charities Act 1993 states that:

'Connected persons' are persons who at any time during the relevant accounting period, or the previous accounting period, are or were:

(a) trustees of the charity;

(b) persons who hold or held the title to property or investments of the charity;

(c) donors of material assets to the charity (whether the gift was made on or after the establishment of the charity);

(d) any child, parent, grandchild, grandparent, brother or sister of any person mentioned in (a) to (c);

(e) any officer, employee or agent of the charity (which would include an organisation which provides management services);

(f) the spouse of any person mentioned in (a) to (e);

(g) any firm or institution controlled by any one or more persons mentioned in (a) to (f), or in which any such person is a partner;

(h) any corporate body in which any 'connected person' mentioned in (a) to (g) has a substantial interest, or in which two or more such persons taken together have a substantial interest.

Sample form

Conflicts of Interest

As a trustee, you are required to act in the best interests of 'X' charity. However, inevitably, trustees have a wide range of interests in private, public and professional life and these interests might, on occasions, conflict, (i.e. director of

---

supplier or consultant to charity). We are obliged to review any possible conflicts when preparing our annual report so ask you to supply the following details:

Has 'X' charity made any loans to you? No ☐   Yes ☐

Have you, or people connected with you through family, business or another charity, an interest in a contract or transaction with 'X' charity? No ☐   Yes ☐

Have you or any person connected with you derived any pecuniary benefit or gain from 'X' charity? No ☐   Yes ☐

Signed: _____ Date: _____

Self-assessment for the board

Evaluation is a central function of any board. The trustees must assess whether the organisation is carrying out its mission effectively. In addition, they should carry out an annual evaluation of the chief executive. Unfortunately, many voluntary sector boards pay too little attention to these types of evaluation.

At least once a year the board should also review its own performance. Trustees should stand back and ask themselves what role the board is playing in the governance of the organisation, what its strengths and weaknesses have been, and use this evidence to plan for the years ahead. This review can strengthen the board by:

> *At least once a year the board should also review its own performance.*

- Identifying the criteria for an effective board.
- Identifying important areas where improvement is needed.
- Measuring progress towards the goals set by the board.
- Shaping the future make-up and structure of the board.
- Building trust and enabling members to work more effectively as a team.

A self-evaluation by individual trustees is also helpful. This can identify areas of strength and recognise weakness; support needs; and highlights those board programmes to which the trustee feels best able to contribute. This exercise can also lead a trustee to conclude that it is time for him or her to leave the board!

Another useful part of the learning process could be a one-to-one discussion with the chair of the organisation on the role a trustee has played on the board.

1.3 The financial management role of trustee boards

The financial management role of a trustee board is quite unlike that of the board of a commercial entity. Most voluntary organisations are financially accountable to a far greater number of stake-holders, because they are funded by a combination of tax concessions and money from the general public, local government and charitable trusts.

The goal of maximising shareholder value – which can be measured objectively – is not relevant to voluntary organisations. Instead, the whole trustee board (not just the treasurer) must demonstrate value for money and effectiveness, which by their nature are more subjective criteria.

This section of the guide examines the three main financial management functions of the board: financial monitoring; financial procedures; and financial management. In doing so, it examines typical weaknesses and introduces various techniques that will be studied in more detail in later sections.

Also included at Appendix B is a checklist for identifying the financial governance issues that may affect a voluntary organisation. It helps to emphasise the fact that financial management is the responsibility of the whole trustee board.

Financial monitoring
In practice, the financial monitoring carried out by boards may be typified by the following activities and motivations:

- The comparison of budgets for income and expenditure with actual results.
- The consideration of projected sources and levels of income and expenditure.
- The need to report to funders.
- The lack of any value added, instead seen as a compliance function.
- Information which is too detailed and conforming to accounting regulations.
- Totally reactive responses conditioned by when information is presented.

Ideally, however, financial monitoring should be characterised by:

- The use of key financial ratio analysis (which can, for example, highlight financial stability).
- The inclusion of financial performance information against predetermined financial policies (for example, income reserves).

- A committee that is adequately empowered in its role by proper induction, has an understanding of cost structures and understands its relationship with management.
- The provision of information that is understandable, timely and accurate.

Financial procedures

These procedures are designed to ensure the propriety and efficiency of the organisation's activities. They typically include policies for the proper accounting, control and protection of the income, expenditure and assets of the organisation.

By means of delegation the board must ensure that financial procedures appropriate to the size and complexity of the organisation exist. This could be achieved by compiling and distributing a financial procedures manual, and/or by responding to reports on areas of weakness by external auditors. Page 37 gives a typical financial procedures manual for a membership organisation; however, this will need to be tailored to the needs and structure of individual organisations.

The external auditor may discover weaknesses in the internal control procedures that will affect the accounts. The auditor should report these weaknesses to the trustees.

The principal purposes of this report to management are:

- To enable the auditor to comment on the accounting records, systems and controls he or she has examined during the course of the audit: for example, weaknesses in credit control, the reconciliation of ledgers and the maintenance of grant approvals.
- To provide management and trustees with financial statistics that can be used to judge the performance of a charity: for example, the number of weeks' expenditure in reserves, or total staff costs expressed as a ratio of total resources expended.
- To communicate any matter that might affect future audits: for example, new accounting standards.
- To recommend what changes need to be made to systems in situations where there are no other compensatory controls.

The auditor must ensure that the recommended changes have in fact been made.

Financial management procedures

These procedures cover a wider area of decision-making than the purely financial ones: they are the procedures that help management to decide overall strategy and make the best use of resources. Examples might include the decision to outsource an area of operations – catering or payroll, perhaps. Too often, however, the board lacks the expertise to carry out these procedures, or is reluctant to 'step on the chief executive's toes'.

As a result, financial management is often seen as a luxury, since the funding does not allow for it. If done at all, it tends to be restricted to budget construction, with little or no consideration of resource inputs, outputs and outcomes.

This guide will enable more informed decision-making by management and a greater financial management role for trustee boards.

The financial team and the role of the treasurer

The financial management team for a voluntary organisation might comprise the honorary treasurer, a chief finance officer, internal audit function (for the larger charity), external auditors/accountants, investment advisers and bankers. Each is a specialist function in its own right, and together they can do much to ensure that the organisation is managed efficiently and effectively.

In 2003 a group of honorary treasurers began meeting at the Cass Business School as part of an initiative by the Centre for Charity Effectiveness based at the Business School. In 2005 assisted by business school charity students, they produced a definitive guide on the treasurer's role in a charity. This is to be published by NCVO early in 2006. A synopsis of a job description and person specification for a typical treasurer's post has been provided in appendix D.

In conclusion

This chapter has examined how the governance debate is forcing through changes that will help voluntary organisations to clarify relationships between the executive management and the non-executive trustee board, and to establish codes of conduct that are value based.

The importance of having the 'right' trustees is increasingly evident as more emphasis is being placed on the proper induction, training and assessment of trustee boards. All this strengthens the role of trustee boards, enabling them to contribute in a way which adds value to the aims of the organisation. What remains is to provide trustee boards with the financial management skills that will allow them to examine objectively, and perhaps critically, the issues presented to them by management. Armed with these techniques, trustee boards can help to ensure that charitable objectives are met in a way that is demonstrably efficient and effective in the eyes of all key stakeholders.

> The importance of having the 'right' trustees is increasingly evident.

Checklist – what have we learnt?

Questions: answers are in the text or referenced in the chapter. Have a go before looking at them.

1. How is Value for Money defined?
2. What should a quality voluntary organisation be able to demonstrate?
3. What are the two principal financial differences between a commercial organisation and a voluntary organisation?
4. What are the ideal financial monitoring characteristics of a voluntary board?
5. List five key controls that should be contained within a financial procedures manual?

Action points for your organisation

'Audit' your organisation by checking to see if you have:

✓ A clear procedure for the election, times served and retirement of board members.
✓ Undertaken an assessment of the requirements and type of skills you wish for the management committee.
✓ A procedure to record conflicts of interest that may arise for board members.
✓ Undertaken regular self-assessment of the organisation: is it carrying out its mission effectively; appraised the chief executive's performance; reviewed the boards performance – its strengths and weaknesses.
✓ Timely and effective management information to assist with control.
✓ A financial procedures manual. Does it have clear rules on the authorisation of expenditure, cheque signing authority etc.
✓ A board which is pro-active in financial management with a plan for longer-term objectives?
✓ A job description for the honorary treasurer or terms of reference for the finance committee.
✓ An annual 'management letter' from the external auditors.

1.4 Case studies and exercises

Managing conflicts of interest

From time to time every board faces a period of conflict. Sometimes these conflicts are between individual board members, sometimes between factions within the board, and sometimes between the board and the staff. The first thing to note is that conflict is not inherently bad; some tension can be productive. Indeed, many community organisations function as a forum in which conflict can be resolved.

But there is a difference between healthy conflict, where differences of opinion are expressed and debated, and unhealthy conflict, which simply hinders the organisation from fulfilling its mission.

These case studies illustrate the different kinds of conflict that may arise and the lessons that can be learned from them.

1. Conflicts between the board and staff

A chief executive of a thriving community centre had been in post for many years.

Case study
She had extensive management experience and had recently taken a higher degree in management. The trustees, by contrast, were largely unwaged local people, including a large proportion of young mothers and retired people. Few had much experience of modern management, and the chief executive consequently held them in contempt. In her eyes, they did not 'add value'; for their part, they found the endless papers the chief executive presented on topics such as performance indicators, strategic planning, benchmarking, quality standards and appraisal systems almost incomprehensible. The trustees' solution was to recruit an able chair who was familiar with the current management and governance agenda and could consequently begin to wrest control of the organisation back from the chief executive.

The lessons
The management committee and the chief executive must work together, if not in partnership then at least in a mutually beneficial way. Each must respect the role of the other – which means that the chief executive must respect the governance role of the trustees. Even though they may not have the professional and business skills a manager needs, they are still the custodians of the charity. It is easy enough for a high-powered chief executive to marginalise a management committee of ordinary people. But a skilful chief executive draws on the skills the management committee does possess, and empowers them to do better by providing sympathetic trustee development programmes, encouraging trustees to seek outside professional advice,

and presenting information clearly and concisely, if necessary through presentations and question and answer sessions. By contrast, a marginalised trustee board may feel they have no alternative but to recruit a chair tough enough to take back control of the organisation from a domineering chief executive.

Case study

The newly-recruited chief executive of a small counselling organisation had previously been a senior manager in a large statutory agency. He had been accustomed to regular structured supervision, to the informal support provided by colleagues, and to calling in experts from elsewhere in the agency to help with difficult cases. He soon began to feel isolated in his new post, and blamed the trustees for failing to provide adequate support.

The lessons

The chief executive is at the top of the management ladder, no matter how small the organisation. The role therefore calls for leadership and an acceptance that the line management provided in a large bureaucracy is neither appropriate nor possible.

Trying to force the trustees (or the chair) to take on a line management role will overburden them – it is, after all, an unpaid, part-time job – and could generate yet more conflict: the chairs of small voluntary organisations are not necessarily familiar with the concept of supervision as practised in large statutory agencies.

The chief executive can reasonably expect the trustees to set out the strategy and direction of the organisation in policies and plans. The chair and chief executive should aim to develop a good working relationship; in practice that will mean contact at least once a week, probably by phone or fax.

Chief executives who feel they need more support than the trustees can give should explore other avenues, such as peer networks and action learning sets. Part of their new leadership role is to show initiative!

2. Conflict with an individual board member

Case study
A new trustee who had previously been a volunteer has been upsetting people by coming into the office unannounced, bossing staff around, countermanding the director's orders, demanding confidential information and generally meddling in day-to-day affairs.

The lessons
This is a classic example of someone who is confused about which hat they are wearing. Organise a development session for the board and do the 'hats' exercise.
Remind them that trustees must act jointly; they have no power individually except that which is specifically given to them by the board.

3. Conflicts between competing factions

Case study
A prominent member (and disgruntled ex-employee) of a community project recruited family, friends and supporters to stand at the next AGM in an attempt to stage a coup. The coup was only 50 per cent successful, leaving the trustee board evenly split. Most of the following year was spent in stalemate, as each half manoeuvred to get a majority at meetings. Each side tried to gain support by spreading disinformation about the other. As a result, morale among staff and users collapsed, and the planning for the project did not get done, thus jeopardising funding.

The lessons
The values of the organisation need some attention; an attempted coup usually involves subterfuge and is therefore contrary to the principle of openness – as is spreading rumour and disinformation. The leader of the coup is unlikely to be acting from selfless motives, and thus sets a poor example of leadership. The trustee board must act jointly, reasonably and in the best interests of the organisation and its beneficiaries. The welfare of the organisation comes first; trustees who act contrary to its best interests are in breach of trust.
Trustees and potential trustees should be asked to fill in a statement of interests that lists any family, business and political relationships they have with staff and other actual

or potential trustees. This statement will help to avoid conflicts of interest that may bring the organisation into disrepute, and should enable members to recognise when apparently unrelated individuals standing for election form a faction.

4. Conflicts with founders

Case study

The founder of a prominent charity effectively runs the organisation by chairing the executive committee which takes all the important decisions. Few people know the precise remit of this committee; it was entered in the minute book, but no one is quite sure where. The remit apparently contains the phrase 'an open door to trustees who wish to attend' – although none of the trustees feels obliged to attend, or feel particularly welcome when they do attend. Consequently the founder, as chair of the committee, is the only trustee to attend regularly; the chief executive and the senior manager are also present. The chair was selected by the founder, and is a busy person who was given to understand that the role was almost that of a president who merely chaired the once or twice yearly trustee board meetings and the AGM. The other trustees chosen were similarly busy people who understood their role to be largely figureheads.

The lessons

Such situations are difficult to tackle. The chief executive could put an update session on the agenda of the next trustee board meeting or AGM, during which trustees could be sensitively but firmly reminded that they have a duty to be active, and that they must act jointly, reasonably and in accordance with the constitution.

A governance audit would reveal the true remit of the executive committee and the lack of involvement of the other trustees; it would also provide a timely opportunity to examine the values of the organisation.

General principles

Ensure that new trustees and staff are properly selected and adequately inducted.

Make sure that the boundaries between different roles are clearly defined and clearly understood by everyone.

Put the interests of the organisation first. Staff, volunteers and trustees work together to help the organisation fulfil its mission; the only justification for prolonging conflict is where the long-term benefits will outweigh the short-term disruption.

Consider the values that inform your organisation. Trustees and staff may have competing or incompatible values.

Consider Nolan's Seven Principles of Public Life:

- Selflessness
- Openness
- Integrity
- Honesty
- Objectivity
- Leadership
- Accountability

Case study excercises

These next two exercises can be used by trustees as part of a management development programme for example in a role play.

---

1. Founder Issues

'Mind Craft' trust was founded five years ago by a senior art therapist – John Thurstrom – who was concerned that the artistic output of people who had mental health problems was not being displayed in commercial art galleries. John, himself an artist, set up the charity to be a 'clearing house' and advocate between artists who had mental health problems and the commercial art galleries which sell their work. John formed a committee of trustees, made up of direct friends and their friends, which included prominent

---

artists who did not have mental health problems, a leading gallery owner and respective partners in top firms of accountants and solicitors. John was the chair of the trust, which had no paid staff.

John continued to work as an art therapist but after two years explained to his fellow trustees that the charity was not going to get anywhere unless there was some full-time staff. John was due for a year-long paid sabbatical – to write a book – and proposed to his fellow trustees that he would also spend more time on developing the trust. During the year John's energy and enthusiasm transformed the trust, which obtained some contracts with commercial art galleries, receiving a commission of 25 per cent on the sale of each picture as a fee. It also received a substantial donation from a wealthy individual and a grant from a trust. At the end of the first year the trust's income was £250,000 with some five staff in London (in John's house) and a network of volunteer agents/staff spread throughout the country.

John proposed to his fellow trustees that he should continue working for the trust and had arranged a further 12 month sabbatical – unpaid – from his employers. The trustees agreed that he should continue in this role and remain as 'executive chairman'. The solicitor trustee advised that she would write to the Charity Commission telling them of this decision and seeking their approval as John would be paid.

The trust continued to grow, doubling its income by the end of the year. John then proposed to the trustees that he should step down and the trust should appoint a chief executive. After all he said 'I still have my book to write!' A chief executive was subsequently appointed who in-turn appointed new staff and a new London head office was acquired. Six months into the job at a meeting of the trustees, the chief executive explained that the organisation's business plan – which had been drawn up by John – was totally unrealistic. Growth of income to a million pounds was unsustainable as it was based upon verbal, unconfirmed promises and expectations. Staff and volunteers were exhausted and some artists were complaining about the 25 per cent commission the trust took. One artist had contacted the Guardian who had sent a reporter round and said that commercial agents' normal fees were 10 per cent. John replied that the very nature of a voluntary organisation was to be pioneering and adventurous otherwise it would never succeed. Secondly, the higher commission fee was based on promoting the trust and its vision. The chief executive's view was that it would have been a good idea to tell the artists.

Vision was fine but business sense also had to be applied.

Following the meeting the chief executive submitted his resignation with 'immediate effect'. The trustees met and John explained that he had negotiated a further leave of absence and would again 'manage the organisation' until the current problems were resolved.

Questions

1. What are your observations on the governance of the organisation?
2. What different actions could the trustees have taken?
3. What actions should the trustees take now?

2. The treasurer's role?

People concerned with the use of chemicals in food production had founded the Association for Agricultural Advancement in the early twentieth century. The Association had grown to over 10,000 members by the middle of the 1970s but membership had since declined to 7,000 members by the beginning of the year 2000. The trustees of the association met six times a year and consisted of 45 members who were elected from a variety of different professional interests. For much of the twentieth century the association's income had come from membership fees and examination fees from its qualification in nutritional management. In 1998 the association found that its qualification had been superseded by university qualifications and that income from registration and examination fees which had once been 70 per cent of the income was now closer to 40 per cent, some £400,000 in 2000 and still declining at the rate of 10 per cent per year. The association produced a quarterly journal and held lectures for its members whose fees had not increased since 1989 – in part to stem the loss in membership. This had only been partially successful as membership continued to decline by 250 per year. Fees are £85 per annum. However, the annual expenditure exceeded the annual income and the substantial reserves the association had built up in earlier years of £700,000, were being drawn down quite quickly. Some good news and potential for the association was the interest in organic food. Two of the trustees were experts in this area and they had proposed a new qualification.

The trustees had appointed a new chief executive and director of finance in 2000. To support them and to 'manage the crisis' a new committee structure had been agreed at the Annual General Meeting which had abolished all the former committees and replaced them with a smaller executive committee which met monthly. The full trustee meeting was to be half-yearly. The new honorary treasurer, chair and deputy chair formed the executive with the chief executive and finance director. The new executive set about their role with enthusiasm, particularly the honorary treasurer who regularly visited the organisation. With the finance director they reviewed financial procedures and introduced cost cutting measures. Over half the staff in the education department that administered the qualification had been made redundant at a one off cost of £150,000 leaving an ongoing annual expenditure for the year 2000 of £1.2 million.

At the next trustee meeting, the member who edited the journal complained that writers for the journal who received a fee of £50 per annum had either not been paid or found that tax had been deducted. She explained that her job was becoming impossible as people were upset by such 'shabby treatment' and were refusing to write for the journal. One member pointed out that the journal was now the only 'benefit' members received. A former chairman now retired who came down from Scotland to the meetings in London claimed that his expenses had not been paid because his tea receipt for 95p had not been attached. Three months later he was still waiting for payment despite sending it back saying that the society could have the 95p. He went on to say that the fare was in excess of £100, which he had personally incurred, and that as a pensioner this was money he could ill afford.

The honorary treasurer replied that the association was in financial crisis and that all expenditure had to be monitored. He personally checked all expense claims. The writers for the journal had not been paid, as they had not sent in proper invoices or a letter from their tax offices which confirmed that they were self-employed for tax purposes. He had taken advice from the auditors on freelance staff and they had advised him that tax had to be deducted.

One member explained that he had not realised how desperate the situation had become. They asked how long the association had to survive and were they protected from personal liability if the organisation was to become insolvent. Another member said the treasurer deserved everyone's support for his hard work. One of the experts in organic food asked if there had been any progress made on the new qualification. Heated discussions followed before the questions of "How long have we got? What plans were there to get us out of this problem?" were put to the chair. As the chair turned to the chief executive the treasurer interjected 'I am working on these figures at the moment and it would be inappropriate to answer this question until the executive committee had discussed them.'

Questions

1. Estimate the current financial situation of the Association and how long it has got before reserves are exhausted (assuming cost inflation of 3 per cent per annum on expenditure, but no increase in exam fees or membership subscriptions).
2. Is the treasurer correct in his advice on the payment to the writers?
3. Is the treasurer's conduct and current role appropriate?
4. Critically evaluate the current management of the organisation and make suggestions as to how they could improve it.

Answers to case studies

These draft answers are designed as discussion points. As with all case studies there is no definitive answer. However, from the financial management and governance perspective they illustrate points of best practice.

Case Study 1

1. There is potential confusion between John's role as chair, founder and employee. The trustees sought Charity Commission permission for his paid role. If they agree to his again taking over they will have to do so again unless the constitution had been changed.
2. Founders who then become chief executives and back to chairs have a potential conflict with a new chief executive. The other trustees could have appointed a different chair to John to avoid such conflicts.
3. Imposing a business plan as ambitious as this one on a new chief executive by the chair would inevitably lead to conflict. The trustees should have recognised that a potential conflict would arise. They should have provided a mechanism to review the business plan that would have depersonalised the

review. The honorary treasurer for example could have chaired and presented the revised business plan.

4. The organisation's vision has clearly not been communicated and the organisation's accountability to its beneficiaries is confused. While corruption is probably not an issue the potential for exploiting the users is real. Equally, poor communication could lead to embarrassing publicity. Has the charity made clear in its literature and contracts with artists that it charges a higher commission? Why does it charge that amount and has it got the commitment of its supporters to this policy?

5. John is clearly highly committed to the organisation but now needs to take a step back. The trustees if they agree to John's offer of managing the organisation again need to have a clear exit route for John and a succession plan.

Case Study 5.2

1. The Association has an annual income this year of:

Fees £85 x 7000	£595,000
Exams	£400,000
Total income	£995,000
Expenditure	£1,200,000
Redundancy	£150,000
Deficit	£355,000
Reserves	£700,000
Balance on reserves	£345,000

Next Year

Fees £85 x 6750	£573,750
Exams £400,000 less 10%	£360,000
Total income	£933,750
Expenditure (3% inflation increase)	£1,236,000
Forecast deficit	£302,250
Reserves brought forward	£345,000
Balance on reserve	£42,750

The society has just over two years of reserves without changing its expenditure pattern or allowing for interest on its balances.

2. Yes. Unless there is clear evidence that the writers are self-employed or they have signed the appropriate declaration form, tax should be deducted. However, if tax is to be deducted this should be communicated to the writers before they carry out any work.

3. The treasurer has become confused and is acting more like a financial controller than the honorary treasurer. What is the job of the finance director? The honorary treasurer has become too involved in day to day matters instead of taking a strategic vision and facilitation role.

4. The organisation has clearly not thought through its governance. Petty disputes i.e. withholding payment while sorting out 95 pence. The trustees only meeting half yearly will lead to divisions and hostility at a time when it should be pulling together. Not giving or having the financial information to hand and sharing it, given the nature of charity trusteeship as a joint liability is counterproductive. The executive are not different to their fellow trustees. While 45 trustees making decisions is too many, changing suddenly to three trustees has gone to the other extreme and communication is clearly breaking down.

The association has adopted a 'knee jerk' reaction to its problem and turned it into a crisis. It needs to take a strategic view of its future. It has some time and opportunities to develop a new income stream. By making the staff redundant it has lost the capacity to take advantage of this opportunity.

Sample skills audit questionnaire

Name: Date:

1. What kind of expertise do you consider you bring to the Board?

Administration	Information Technology
Campaigning	Legal
Change Management/Restructuring	Management/Management Systems
Consultancy	Marketing
Customer care development	Media/PR
Disability	Networks/Alliances
Equal Opportunities	Policy Implementation
Financial Fundraising General Governance	Research
	Risk Management
History of the Sector Human Resources/Training	Strategic Planning and Training

Comments:

2. What other experience or skills do you feel you offer?
3. Are there any particular areas of X charity work in which you would like to be involved?

Thank you

Financial governance framework

1. Does your charity have a clearly defined organisational structure, and has this been effectively communicated throughout the charity?
2. Does it incorporate all levels within the charity, not just senior management?
3. Do you know what the greatest threats, both internal and external, to your charity are?
4. Has any kind of risk analysis or risk awareness programme been conducted within the charity?
5. Does the charity have a planning cycle that fits with its overall objectives?

6. Does that planning cycle require departments or functions to evaluate the previous year's performance against plans?

7. Are explanations provided where planned objectives have not been met?

8. Do employees understand the significance of controls and what they are designed to ensure?

9. Do written procedures exist for all key areas of the charity's business?

10. Aside from internal audit, are the results of any other independent, objective reviews disseminated throughout the charity?

11. Are the trustees assured of the effectiveness of any controls, plans or procedures in place? If so, how?

12. Is there a process for reporting discrepancies to the trustees? If so, what form does it take?

YES / NO

Suggested contents of a financial procedures manual

Trustees' financial responsibilities
- The executive committee.
- The annual plan.
- Approval of the budget.
- Reserves policy.
- Conflicts of interest.
- Staff financial responsibilities.
- Controls on income.
- Grants.
- Legacies.
- Publication sales.
- Decentralised sales invoicing.
- Credit control.
- Bad debts.

Controls on expenditure
- Estimates and tendering.
- Purchase orders and invoices.
- Bank mandates and cheque signatories.
- Credit cards.
- Petty cash.

Controls on the financial assets
- Reconciling cash book to bank.

- Reconciling purchase ledger.
- Reconciling sales ledger.
- Reconciling stock accounts.
- Reconciling publications stock.
- VAT.
- Inland Revenue.
- Reconciling payroll control.
- Treasury management.
- Investment portfolio.

Exercising budgetary control
- Virement.

Controls on human resources
- Staff complement.
- Staff salaries.
- Staff regrading.
- Extra responsibility allowance.
- Starters and leavers.
- Contracts of employment.
- Travel and subsistence.
- The Probity Book.
- Season ticket loans.

Controls on physical assets
- Computer equipment.
- Computer software and data.

Job description for treasurer

This specimen job description and person specification for a treasurer can be adapted to meet an organisation's particular needs. It is also advisable to provide job descriptions for trustees and honorary officers. In addition to clarifying roles, these descriptions are useful for people thinking about becoming trustees or honorary officers, and for those who are considering nominating others. Comprehensive advice prepared by the Honorary Treasurer's Forum has been published by NCVO. Go to www.ncvo-vol.org.uk

Job title: Treasurer of [name of organisation]

The role of a treasurer is to maintain an overview of the organisation's affairs to ensure that it is financially viable and that proper financial records and procedures are maintained. The responsi-bilities of the treasurer will include:

- Overseeing, approving and presenting budgets, accounts and financial statements.
- Making sure that the financial resources of the organisation meet its present and future needs.
- Ensuring that the charity has an appropriate reserves policy.
- Preparing and presenting financial reports to the board.
- Ensuring that appropriate accounting procedures and controls are in place.
- Liaising with any paid staff and volunteers about financial matters.
- Advising on the financial implications of the organisation's strategic plans.
- Ensuring that the charity has an appropriate investment policy.
- Ensuring that there is no conflict between any investment held and the aims and objects of the charity.
- Monitoring the organisation's investment activity and ensuring its consistency with the organisation's policies and legal responsibilities.
- Ensuring that the accounts are prepared and disclosed in the form required by funders and the relevant statutory bodies: for example, the Charity Commission and/or the Registrar of Companies.
- If an audit is required, ensuring that the accounts are audited in the manner required, and any recommendations of the auditors implemented.
- Keeping the board informed about its financial duties and responsibilities.
- Contributing to the fundraising strategy of the organisation.
- Making a formal presentation of the accounts at the annual general meeting and drawing attention to important points in a coherent and comprehensible way.
- Sitting on appraisal, recruitment and disciplinary panels as required.

Person specification

In addition to the qualities needed by all trustees, the treasurer should ideally also possess the following:

- Financial qualifications and experience.
- Some experience of charity finance, fundraising and pension schemes.
- The skills to analyse proposals and examine their financial consequences.
- A readiness to make unpopular recommendations to the board.
- A willingness to be available to staff for advice and enquiries on an ad hoc basis.

2 Financing the mission

2.1. Defining your mission

All voluntary organisations must first define precisely why they exist and how they plan to fulfil their mission. Only when this has been done can discussions on preparing a budget begin.

This chapter begins by examining the conflict that often exists between those responsible for carrying out the charitable mission and those responsible for ensuring the financial stability of the organisation. It then introduces techniques to improve strategic planning.

Voluntary organisations usually exist because they have a mission: to cure the sick, to advance a profession, to discover new technologies, to educate the public.

Meeting financial goals is essential to fulfilling this mission, but is not the top priority. Managers must ask a 'chicken and egg' question: which comes first, the programmes to fulfil the mission, or the income (earned and voluntary) to finance the programmes? It is important to recognise that aspirations and financial resources are related, and that it is management's task to coordinate the two.

The planning process for voluntary organisations is complex, as they must not only accomplish their mission but also meet their financial goals. An organisation's mission and its financial goals can also be viewed as parallel objectives that complement each other. Certainly, vigorous demand for the services of an organisation is an indication of success. But if financial management is neglected, it will not be long before the whole organisation begins to run on a deficit budget. Once in this situation, the organisation

An organisation's mission and its financial goals can also be viewed as parallel objectives that complement each other.

will find it hard to secure extra funding. Similarly, the provision of services for which there is no need – irrespective of the level of finance – will not enable the organisation to accomplish its mission – and can conversly, result in 'mission drift'.

2.2 The necessity of planning

Voluntary organisations need to plan effectively. For too many organisations, however, this process merely consists of adding a percentage to last year's budgets – which can only be valid in a world where nothing ever changes. For most voluntary organisations, moreover, planning is usually short-term, typically in one to three year cycles, corresponding to funding. This planning also tends to happen in a vacuum, cut off from what is happening in the outside world.

The short-term nature of most funding and the uncertainty caused by constant change are often given as reasons for not planning. But they are very good reasons why voluntary organisations should plan, and in a robust way at that.

Although it is beyond the scope of this guide to give detailed guidelines on strategic planning (comprehensive signposting is given at the end of this book), this chapter will provide a general outline that sets the context for the later sections on financial planning.

For any organisation, planning is a continuous process which seeks, in essence, to describe what the organisation aims to achieve; where it currently stands in relation to those aims; what future actions will be required to achieve those aims; and how the organisation will know when it has achieved them.

2.3 The language of planning

The mission
This is a brief statement of an organisation's purpose and values; it is the reason why it exists. The mission says little about what an organisation will do, or how or when it will do it. Missions should be a long-term statement of intent deriving from the vision that originally inspired the organisation.

Missions should be a long-term statement of intent deriving from the vision that originally inspired the organisation.

Example 1 The Toxoplasmosis Trust: *Our vision is to reduce substantially the incidence and effect of toxoplasmosis (an infection harmful to the unborn child) and ultimately to eradicate congenital toxoplasmosis in the UK.*

Example 2 The Weston Spirit: *The Weston Spirit works in the inner city areas of Britain offering young people, who may be experiencing feelings of isolation and hopelessness, a real alternative to problems such as unemployment, drug use, alcohol misuse, homelessness and abuse.*

Strategic goals

These set out the direction of the organisation; they are a statement of its priorities in the medium-to-long-term. Everything the organisation does should be related back to a strategic goal.

Example 1: The Toxoplasmosis Trust

- To raise awareness of toxoplasmosis.
- To support people affected by toxoplasmosis.
- To campaign to raise the profile of toxoplasmosis amongst government, health carers and the public.
- To ensure better prevention and management of toxoplasmosis.

Example 2: The Weston Spirit

- Have a presence in each major city in the UK.
- Influence policy formulation by and within major organisations and institutions affecting young people.
- Network with other organisations providing high quality youth work.
- Increase our annual membership numbers.

The operational objectives

These are detailed, costed and timed plans of what the organisation will do to meet each strategic goal. They set out a work plan for the organisation, typically over a 12-month period.

Example 1: The Toxoplasmosis Trust

- Organise four pilot study days on toxoplasmosis for midwives around the country.
- Develop a midwives' education pack.
- Send out a toxoplasmosis newsletter to local and hospital laboratories.
- Develop a new fact sheet for parents of children with retinochoroiditis.

2.4 The process of planning

What is, or will be, our strategic position?

To answer this question, a voluntary organisation must gather information. It needs to identify the factors that will influence its results, both in terms of outputs and outcomes. Analysing the external environment is important because opportunities may be missed and threats overlooked until too late.

Despite its importance, this analysis of the external environment tends in practice to be constrained by two factors:

- In many voluntary organisations, urgent immediate demands such as meeting income targets and controlling expenditure leave little time for important, but longer-term, strategic planning analysis.
- Too little is known about how complex external factors affect voluntary organisations.

The effects of these constraints are decreasing, however, as more and more 'professionals' take part in the governance and management of voluntary organisations.

External review

In response to the second constraint, NCVO's Third Sector Foresight project and UK Voluntary Sector Almanac publications, seek to understand these external factors and how they impact on the sector (see further reading and resources).

Here are some brief examples of how external factors can affect voluntary organisations:

- *Economy.* Economic growth, or lack of it, affects the disposable income of individuals and donor companies. In times of uncertainty donors may be less willing to commit to regular donations.
- *Government.* The voluntary sector, particularly social welfare organisations, will be considerably affected if more community care services are transferred to the independent sector.
- *Society.* There is evidence of a shift of public confidence away from traditional institutions, such as political parties, and towards more voluntary forms of association.
- *Technology.* The increasing flexibility of people's work patterns will affect their ability to volunteer their time.

In short, analysing the external environment in which a voluntary organisation works should make it possible to identify opportunities or threats. For example, levels of economic activity, together with society's attitudes towards volunteering, may affect the organisation's income and other resources, and thus its ability to deliver the desired level of services.

Internal review

As mentioned earlier, an internal review should also be carried out as part of the information-gathering process. The aim of this review is to identify weaknesses that must be addressed and strengths that are not being exploited. A list of the areas that should be covered in a review is given below, followed by a description of the tools that can be used to conduct the review.

Leadership:

- Trustee board characteristics and balance
- Trustee board focus: core activities and other decision-making systems
- Skills experience and balance
- Management training

Culture:
- Power groupings
- Power sources: authority, control over resources, ability
- Social norms
- Attitudes

Structure:

- Reporting lines
- Level of integration
- Resources balance
- Information systems

Functional analysis:

- Programme services
- Community development
- Information, training and education
- Fundraising
- Finance and administration

Control systems:

- Planning systems
- Budget systems
- Performance appraisal
- Internal audit (where appropriate)

Tools to use for internal review
Management audit. This sets out to assess the effectiveness of the trustee board, management team and organisational structure in achieving charitable objectives. It will, therefore, be looking at leadership, culture and structure to identify existing and potential weaknesses and recommend ways to rectify them.

Ratio analysis. Key ratios – such as liquidity, fundraising performance, cost ratios and trading profitability (for trading groups) – can, when analysed over time and compared with those of other voluntary organisations offering comparable services, provide a valuable indication of trends and highlight key relationships.

Contribution analysis. This identifies the absolute or percentage amount that a particular programme contributes to the general overheads (after deducting direct programme costs from any earned or unearned income for that programme). The aim is to ensure that each programme makes a contribution to these overheads.

Ratios and contribution are explored in more depth in Chapter 5 (see page 155).

The position audit
Combining the results of the review of the external environment with those of the internal review and comparing them with the organisation's strategic goals, makes it possible to carry out a 'position audit'. This shows:

- where the organisation currently stands in relation to its goals, by identifying what opportunities or threats exist externally;
- what internal strengths need to be exploited;
- what internal weaknesses need to be addressed.

The above assessment will help to identify the strategic choices open to the organisation. These may include the following:

- Should the organisation grow, stay the same, reduce its size – or is a recovery programme necessary?

- Should the organisation remain within its existing market, expand into different geographical locations or enter entirely new markets?
- Does the organisation need to modify the services it provides or develop new ones, or can it maintain the existing portfolio of services?
- Should the organisation become a more specialist, or more general, provider of services?

Choosing a course of action

Once the choices available to the organisation have been identified, there will have to be an evaluation, since it is unlikely that all options will be feasible with the available resources. The choices could be evaluated in terms of their acceptability, suitability and feasibility:

- The criterion for **acceptability** would be whether the chosen strategy fits in well with existing resources, competencies and culture.
- The criterion for **suitability** would be whether the chosen strategy maximises the strengths or reduces the weaknesses of the organisation, and whether it seizes the opportunities or averts the threats offered by the external environment.

Testing for **feasibility** requires the following questions to be asked:

- Is the leadership suitable?
- Is the culture capable?
- Is the organisational structure appropriate?
- Are the functional policies appropriate?
- Are the resources available?
- Is this strategy an improvement on not changing at all?
- Are there procedures for implementation and monitoring?

Each chosen strategy needs to satisfy all these points. If it fails on any, the organisation must assess whether remedial action is possible.

Preparing day-to-day plans

Once the organisation's strategic goals have been identified, they must be translated into day-to-day activities. The Toxoplasmosis Trust, for example, identifies its strategic goals as:

- To raise awareness of toxoplasmosis.
- To support people affected by toxoplasmosis.

Once the organisation's strategic goals have been identified, they must be translated into day-to-day activities.

- To campaign to raise the profile of toxoplasmosis amongst government, health carers and the public.
- To ensure better prevention and management of toxoplasmosis.

Based on these four goals, a set of **operational objectives, or action plans**, has been formulated:

- Organising four pilot study days on toxoplasmosis for midwives around the country.
- Developing a midwives' education pack.
- Sending out a toxoplasmosis newsletter to local and hospital laboratories.
- Developing a new fact sheet for parents of children with retinochoroiditis.

For each of these operational objectives, a detailed plan needs to be drafted. These plan should ideally be SMART, that is:

Specific (detailed),
Measurable (both financially and otherwise),
Attainable,
Realistic and
Timed.

For example, the objective 'developing a midwives' education pack' might be broken down further into the following tasks:

- Identify major issues, medical and otherwise, of which midwives need to be aware.
- Identify main contributors to educational pack.
- Prepare draft, check accuracy of content and design.
- Conduct a limited testing with readers'/users' panel.
- Print.
- Market and promote pack to midwives through hospitals.

The persons responsible for each of these tasks, and the time allotted, should be identified, to provide a basis for performance appraisal.

2.5 Programme resource assessment

At the beginning of this chapter, it was emphasised that mission-orientated goals and financial goals are interdependent; and later, when discussing choice of strategies, it was stated that one of the three main criteria is acceptability in terms of fit (with existing strategies), resources (both financial and otherwise), competence (ability and skills) and culture (leadership style). Any changes that give a new strategic direction to charitable programmes require a parallel adjustment to the financial resources devoted to that programme. This section will look at the financial adjustments needed when expansion (or contraction) of services is planned.

Figure 2.1 shows the kind of connections that should be made between mission orientated goals and financial goals.

Figure 2.1

Goal to accomplish mission	Financial resource
Feed more children to relieve the suffering of the poor	Get donations of food from supermarkets
Double the congregation to spread the church's spiritual message	Market the church through weekly gospel programmes on the public radio
Publish more training manuals to better educate our league members	Recruit skilled writers to update and expand manuals

It may be useful here to consider a situation where a voluntary organisation is faced with the need to reduce expenditure. The finance committee might prepare a list of possible solutions, with committee members marking each solution as V for viable or U for unacceptable, as shown in figure 2.2.

Figure 2.2

Rating	V or U
Research public perception of accomplishments; interview recipients of services to evaluate their needs and ideas	
Establish a development officer to increase contributor base	
Raise membership rates, service fees, publication prices	
Charge for services now offered for free	
Eliminate programmes or downsize staff	
Merge with or take-over another organisation	
Sell off under-utilised assets	
Improve marketing, publish magazine, sponsor public events	
Reallocate resources to realign strengths and weaknesses	
Establish new measurement systems to evaluate performance	

2.6 Organisation resource analysis

Another part of the planning process is a critical look at the organisation's wider financial situation, which provides an opportunity to evaluate its long-term financial stability. The key ratio and financial indicators from the annual financial statements (which are discussed in Chapter Five, see page 155) can be used for this.

Depending on the results of this analysis, the voluntary organisation might adopt certain steps to improve its financial situation. An example is given in the form of a model balance sheet of a church in figure 2.3. At first sight, the church's financial situation may seem healthy. It has £108,510 of unrestricted net assets on its balance sheet, total assets of £390,000 and only £281,490 of debt. This indicates that the church has accumulated assets well in excess of the money it owes.

Figure 2.3 Holy Spirit Church Summary Balance Sheet

	£		£
Building	250,000	Long term debt	200,000
Equipment and furnishing	120,000	Current liabilities	81,490
Current (liquid) assets	20,000		
Total assets	390,000	Total liabilities	281,490
Net assets	108,510	Unrestricted Funds	108,510

However, a closer examination of the balance sheet reveals that the church does not have the money to pay the bills that will soon fall due. Compare the **liquid** assets of £20,000 – that is, the assets currently available to pay bills – with the current liabilities of £81,490. In other words, the debts becoming due in the next year amount to four times the current assets.

The first glance at the bottom line of a financial statement can also be misleading. The church's unrestricted net assets of more than £100,000 might seem reasonable for an organisation of its size. But it is noticeable that the fund balance consists of non-cash assets: that is, the church's equipment and buildings. Because these assets are used every day, they cannot be sold to pay bills. In this condition, the church is vulnerable: a delay of a few weeks in funding can cause havoc, as creditors become increasingly demanding, pay cheques bounce and overdue taxes begin to cause embarrassment.

Once the church's management recognise the financial problem, however, they can devise solutions. Over the next two or three years the church might focus on financial goals A, B, C and D in figure 2.4. To enable these goals to be realised, the church must also take steps to balance its mission and financial goals.

The church would have to introduce formal financial planning. First, it would prepare a budget for the coming year, following the guidelines in Chapter Three (see page 67).

Next, it would convert the budget into a monthly cash flow projection. The church's financial managers would review the accounting systems to ensure that accurate and up to date information is available to assess the financial position at any give time. Lastly, the church might consider using ratio analysis (see Chapter Five, page 155) to improve its current funding position.

Figure 2.3 Holy Spirit Church Summary Balance Sheet

Priority Level 1–10		Macro Resource Goal
	A	Establish working capital base
	B	Maintain three (or more) months operating cash balance (improve cash flow)
	C	Retire debt or reduce accounts payable
	D	Seek endowment funding to provide income to offset annual fluctuations in grant funding.
	E	Buy or build permanent facilities
	F	Establish branches
	G	Conduct marketing campaign
	H	Raise salaries or increase personnel
	I	Improve employee benefits – e.g. pensions
	J	Hire Chief Financial Officer to improve financial reporting, planning and management

In conclusion

Voluntary organisations should be clear as to why they exist and how they will fulfil their mission. A voluntary organisation's mission and its financial goals are complementary to each other, not in competition. Planning is an essential tool in understanding and delivering the mission. Internal and environmental analysis are important techniques in understanding the strategic role of the organisation.

Internal and environmental analysis are important techniques in understanding the strategic role of the organisation.

Checklist – what have we learnt?

Questions: Answers are in the text but have a go before checking them.

1. Draw the financial planning cycle.
2. What are the stages of planning?
3. Outline the four aspects of understanding a strategic position.
4. In evaluating an organisation what are the factors that need to be examined?
5. What additional questions need to be asked of a chosen strategy?
6. Describe the proposed planning quality principles for a voluntary organisation.

Action points for your organisation

Audit your organisation by checking to see if it has:

✓ A mission statement that is relevant and understood throughout the organisation and by its stakeholders.
✓ A strategic plan, with goals and objectives.
✓ A planning process that corresponds to the quality framework.
✓ Action plans with clear responsibilities.
✓ Performance measurement linked to the action plans.
✓ A management committee, which undertakes regular performance and organisational resource assessment.

Case studies and exercises

1. Language line
This case study demonstrates the usefulness of an environmental analysis.

Background
Language Line was set up in January 1990 to provide a telephone interpreting service in seven minority ethnic languages. Remarkably, as director Marc Kiddle observed, 'although similar services were long established in Australia, the United States and Holland, this was the first telephone interpreting service in Britain. It was, then, truly innovative.' At the outset, however, Language Line did not know of the existence of any similar services and so had nowhere to turn for advice or experience.

The initial objective was to offer the service to health organisations in the Tower Hamlets area of London, with plans to extend the scheme to other users and areas. The project received initial support for a pilot from a government task force, British Telecom and a charitable trust. The pilot was judged a success, and in early 1991 it was decided to conduct research to establish whether the project could find alternative sources of income when the initial grants ended. An analysis of how interested potential users might be was therefore needed.

Types of information

Five main types of information should be collected as part of an environmental analysis:

1. Information about the needs and opinions of current and potential users of the services of your organisation. The views of past users of the service will also be valuable in assessing your strengths and weaknesses.
2. Information on important trends and influences in the organisation's environment.
3. The criteria used by grant makers and other funders in deciding whether to support funding applications.
4. Existing patterns of service in areas of activity you wish to become involved in.
5. The activities of organisations with similar services to those of your own.

The director of Language Line and its five permanent interpreters knew that there had been a steady increase in demand from existing users. They believed, from discussions with local officials, that the separation of purchaser and provider roles resulting from reforms of the Health Service was leading to a new emphasis on access to services for minority language speakers. They also knew that there were other concentrations of minority language speakers who made demands on the statutory services – such as the police force and Health Service – that might also become users.

In other areas, however, staff were largely in the dark. Until 1991 the service had been provided free: would new customers be willing to pay for the service?

What were the decision making procedures? Staff were unaware of any direct competitors and did not know how successful their limited public relations activity had been in creating awareness of Language Line.

On the basis of this assessment of the information gaps, the project decided that it needed to acquire information on the following:

- Existing provision of interpreting services for minority language speakers (if any) by potential purchasers.
- Plans of potential purchasers for improvements in interpreting services.
- The decision making procedures of potential new users.
- The awareness potential users had of Language Line and their interest in its services.

The information collection methods used can also vary according to whether the environmental analysis is external or internal (see figure 2.5).

Figure 2.5

Internal sources	External – Secondary	External – Primary
Analysis and discussion	Publications	User surveys
Information on service usage	Material from other	Discussion or focus groups
Published information	organisations, e.g. annual reports	Visits to other organisations
Contacts and networking	Library searches	Exhibitions

Specifically, in the case of Language Line:

- **External.** Review of census data to pinpoint geographical areas with highest concentration of minority language speakers.
- **Internal.** Telephone questionnaire to local authorities, health authorities and police stations in the target area.

Interpreting and presenting the information

In presenting the findings of your environmental analysis, you need to:

- Demonstrate a clear understanding of the needs and expectations of different groups of current and potential users of your organisation's services.
- Identify the opportunities for, and threats to, your organisation as a result of developments in its environment.

- Summarise the management actions you intend to take to maximise the opportunities, and minimise the threats, you have identified.

2. Understanding business language

This exercise de-jargons business terms.

Happy Homes has two properties, which provide short-term residential accommodation for disabled people in the Bristol city area thereby allowing those who care for them to have a holiday. The finance director says "We plan to raise more money to allow us to build more homes – we expect to borrow at a good rate – which will enable us to give more people who look after their relatives a break. After all, we've promised our supporters a 10 per cent increase in places available and we do not want to break our word."

Identify the organisational, business and functional strategies in the above quotation.

Suggested answer

The organisational objective is to expand its service to support people who care for others. The organisational strategy is the decision that this will be achieved by building new homes rather than say diversifying into day support. The business strategy suggests that this be best achieved by building new properties rather than extending current properties. The operational strategy involves the decision to invest in new properties (the service function) which is to be financed by loan finance (the finance function) rather than seeking funds from government or the public.

3. Understanding business planning

You have recently been appointed as the finance and administration director of an ethnic minority national membership based organisation which coordinates local groups. The organisation has an income from various sources of £1.2million. The chief executive has been asked by the management committee to organise its first business planning exercise following a critical report on the organisation by a major funder. They ask for your help. Prepare a briefing note for the chief executive and the three other senior managers outlining the topics which should be covered in the business planning process and advising them on who should be included in the business planning team.

Answer

The note to the chief executive should cover:

1. The reason or rationale for having a business plan. For example: to set down effective criteria for improving the organisation's performance through a process of planning and evaluation.
2. The objectives of a plan.
3. The main components of a business plan, normally:
   a) The organisation's mission, including the extent to which the organisation's values have changed over time and how this should be reflected in what the organisation does?
   b) Internal and external appraisal.
   c) Environmental assumptions.
   d) Clear objectives, ideally quantified.
   e) Strategy (including marketing).
   f) Budgets.
   g) Performance measures to demonstrate efficiency and effectiveness of the organisation.
   h) Feedback system.
4. The staff involvement in the process.

All the organisation's senior mangers and the management committee should be involved in the business planning process.

All the organisation's senior mangers and the management committee should be involved in the business planning process. Not just simply to approve it, but also to own the strategy. While the senior managers will develop the business plan, everyone in the organisation will be involved and therefore will know what is expected of them. This will mean that a hierarchy of objectives and delegated responsibilities from the management committee to operational staff will exist. A failure to involve operational staff and management committee members will result in confusion and a loss of direction.

4. Appraising the external environment

The Emergency Support Service (ESS) is now faced with a changing environment. ESS was founded in 1974 following local government reorganisation to provide volunteers for social services. In the past ESS was funded entirely by national government on a grants basis. The grant was increased in line with inflation every year.

The last government believed a central incremental grant encouraged inefficiency. The government introduced a tapering reduction in grant of £1million per year (the ESS budget was then £6million) and required ESS to instead tender to individual local authorities for its services on a contract basis. Local authority contracts are increasingly being awarded to local voluntary organisations, particularly in Scotland and Wales, or other national charity competitors for example the Women's Royal Voluntary Service and the British Red Cross in England who undercut ESS prices. In addition ESS is faced with a general freeze on government spending in accordance with the new government's commitment to keep within borrowing limits and the previous government's expenditure plans. ESS has a budgeted contingency reserve of one year's current expenditure and has a remaining 20-year lease on its London headquarters.

Appraise the situation of the ESS and recommend appropriate strategies to deal with its problems.

Answer
1. Situation Appraisal
ESS is not in a good position. It has seen its reliable source of income disappear and is now exposed to new and growing competition in a static market. ESS has moved from having one 'customer' central government, to having some 400 new customers throughout the country. Viewed as a 'London English' organisation, it is unlikely to have developed regional structures, marketing skills or commercial acumen. It probably lacks a proper costing system.

2. A strategic plan would have to take the following factors into account:
   a) The competitive environment is hostile with a static market and geographical problems; there are new competitors and barriers of entry for new competitors have been abolished. It is not all bad news however, as ESS is now free to consider tendering to health authorities.
   b) The political environment is unlikely to restore the ESS central grant. Government spending plans indicate that there will be an increase in public sector spending – particularly in the health sector – but not at present. It is not feasible for ESS with limited reserves and assets to undertake a sort of holding operation in the expectation that funding and new markets will increase.
   c) The economic environment predicts low levels of inflation, except in London where ESS is based and here wage inflation has outstripped national levels reflecting the higher cost of living. Low levels of inflation also indicate that contract funds are unlikely to increase. Local and health authorities will seek to maximize the lowest economic cost. For the

voluntary sector economy the increase in funding to the sector has come from government or trading activities. Donations from the public and business have been static. ESS has no expertise in raising funds from the general public or corporations.

d) The competitive environment is not likely to diminish, with national and local competitors. ESS has major problems with its geographical position in dealing with the devolving of power to Scotland and Wales.

3. The organisation structure and culture of the ESS.

a) ESS had been reliant on just one source of finance in a very cosy relationship. This has not prepared it for the rigours of the new contract environment. ESS probably has few marketing skills as it has never had to tender for contracts. Trustees would have been appointed for their 'name' and prestige in government or the voluntary sector. As the organisation has never really had a marketing objective, it does not have the experience in its paid staff or trustees to re-orientate itself. At the same time, it still does have contact with government and a tapering arrangement which might enable it to 'buy' more time to equip itself with those skills.

b) It is possible that the services provided by ESS were organised according to central government specifications. Local government is free to decide on its own service provision and may not have the same priorities. Having been a monopoly supplier with a distinct culture of one type of service delivery this may not be relevant for all local authorities.

c) The one grant a year has meant that the accounting system has not previously priced contracts. It could be that the organisation has no real idea of how much a particular service costs and what should be the contribution to organisational overheads. Losing contracts on price to other national competitors would indicate that there is something wrong with the way ESS prices. On the other hand it may be that other competitors are larger and so benefit from economies of scale; or that ESS is inefficient and lacks proper project management skills.

4. Strategic options available to ESS.

a) Expand into the health service market. This may not be easy as ESS has no relationships or background with health authorities. Existing service suppliers will be hostile to ESS.

b) Develop new services. This is easier said than done as ESS has been a single service organisation. Does it have the skills to develop new services and are these services which local and health authorities would need?

c) ESS could develop a more aggressive pricing policy. It still has a government grant covering some core costs.

d) Change the accounting system for more accurate and relevant cost information.

e) ESS could make itself more efficient by rationalisation.

f) A long-term strategic option would be to assess the need for volunteers, particularly in caring for people who wish to stay in their own home rather than go into residential care. ESS could set itself up as a specialist operator in keeping people at home and charge wealthier people a fee.

g) The competitive static market, with increasing costs, might lead to ESS considering sharing its resources with other voluntary organisations. Alternatively it may have skills in training and supporting volunteers that it could provide to smaller voluntary organisations. ESS could set up joint ventures with other voluntary organisations.

If ESS, having reviewed its options, fails to come up with a viable plan, or the plans it develops requires resources which the organisation does not have, then it should in the interests of all its stakeholders consider merging with another voluntary organisation. This would preserve jobs and the commitment and skills of volunteers

5. Fundraising appraisal

This exercise looks at using appraisal techniques to evaluate fundraising.

Veterans Benovlent Fund (VBF) is a national charity established to help veterans of all ranks from the armed forces and merchant navy suffering illness and disability as a result of active service.

For some men and women their involvement in actions throughout the world can result in psychiatric conditions, post-traumatic stress and physical disability requiring long term support. Drug and alcohol problems have also become greater over the last 20 years. The VBF has a national network of welfare officers as well as residential and therapy centres to ensure that the best care and support possible is available.

The residential centres provide a safe environment for those needing specialist help, together with remedial and therapeutic treatment in the therapy centres. Welfare officers support those people wishing to remain within their own homes and communities.

The VBF participates in lobbying government to improve the support services provided to these men and women, particularly in mental health provision and pensions. The Fund also works with other agencies to provide study teams looking into specialist areas of care or mental health issues.

Clients are referred from agencies, such as the War Pensions Welfare Service, The Regimental Associations, the Royal British Legion, the NHS and Social Services. The age range of the current veterans being supported by VBF is from early 20s to 70s.

Current position

Legislation introduced the need to refurbish the residential accommodation and for one of the three residential centres this has now been completed. The remaining two centres now need refurbishment and it is hoped to commence the work once funds have been secured.

Recently, there has been a fundamental change in the method of support, moving from long-term admissions to an increasing number of clients requiring short-term respite admissions thus allowing them to remain in their own homes and communities.

This significant change, and the increasing demand for support for those with anger, self-esteem, drug and alcohol related problems within the therapy centres, has demanded additional resources. One of the therapy centres has been upgraded and the others must follow if the support demand is to be met, including the urgent need for additional staff.

Welfare officers and their teams around the country are the first port of call for clients and their families, the referring agencies, and the carers. These welfare teams have now reached the point where there is an urgent need for additional staff to ensure the clients and their families can cope with the difficulties caused by the traumas, illness and disabilities.

The income of VBF has remained level over the past three years but must now increase in order to provide the resources needed for refurbishment of the residential accommodation, the therapy centres and additional staff. It does, however, own all the properties and has six months expenditure in reserve.

The new director of fundraising and PR has been informed that the funds received from one of the three service charities (service charity 3) will cease to support the Fund next year, while the other two have given notice that they will need to reduce their donations by 10 per cent (1) and 5 per cent (2) respectively.

The social services have stated that the contribution per residential client will remain at the current level for the next two years and the health authority have indicated that there could be an increase per client in the coming year.

As for many benevolent funds, legacy income has been a mainstay for the VBF but it has seen a substantial drop in the current year. Donations from individuals represent only about 3 per cent of the total voluntary income.

Events have provided an increase in income from the previous year but this has been due to the fact that there was a major overseas trek which may not be repeated in the coming year. Christmas card sales increased in the last year increasing net contribution by 10 per cent on the previous year.

There has been some success in attracting media interest in the work of the Fund and it is hoped that this will have the two-fold effect of increasing income and lobbying power. The trustees have expressed the hope that the PR activity will increase in the coming year.

The chief executive and the trustees are aware that in order to satisfy the resources required by the Fund, there is an urgent need to review the fundraising and have begun to look at the income and expenditure for the year to December 2004. The breakdown is attached.

Veterans Benovlent Fund

The income and expenditure for year to December 2004

Breakdown of income of the fundraising department for year to December 2004			
	Unrestricted	Restricted	Total
	£'000s	£'000s	£'000s
Voluntary income			
Individual	78		78
Trusts	650	143	793
Events	80		80
Legacies	660	222	882
Christmas Cards & Goods	7		7
Service charity 1	250		250
Service charity 2	175		175
Service charity 3	200		200
Statutory income			
Social services	908		908
Health authority	1816		1816
Total fundraising income	4,824	365	5,189
Investment Income			
Investments	211		211
Net gains on Disposal of Assets	3		3
Total VBF Income	5,038	365	5,403

Breakdown of expenditure for the VBF for year to December 2004

	Staff costs	Other direct costs	Other allocated costs	Total
	£'000s	£'000s	£'000s	£'000s
Fundraising	227	332	23	582
Residential treatment and care	2,820	634	230	3,684
Welfare services	790	97	141	1.028
Management and administration	152	14		166
Refurbishment and repairs		186		186
Total VBF Expenditure	3,989	1,263	394	5,646

Exercise 5 questions:

Veterans Benevolent Fund
The chief executive and the trustees have asked you, as the new director of fundraising and PR, as a matter of urgency to assess the effectiveness of the fundraising programme and how to increase the income to allow the requirements of the Fund to be met.

   1a. Analyse the current income and provide an assessment of the areas of weakness and major threat-making recommendations to minimise the effects of these.

   1b. Explain the actions you would propose to develop a strategy to increase the income to meet the future needs and development plans of the VBF.

Suggested answers
   1a. The weaknesses and the major threats
   • Individual donations – only 3 per cent of the total. Research into donor profile would give an indication of strength or weakness of the donor base in terms of sustainability. Could look at potential donor areas in terms of service personnel and families. Direct mail campaign needs to be researched to increase this area of funding.
   • Legacies – drop this year could indicate a trend. Ageing population, economic climate, work patterns, all could affect the future of legacy gifts. House prices are increasing, but often needed for the care and support of elderly. The trend of skipping inheritance – to grandchildren and great grandchildren. Using the house to supplement income. Look into the legacy campaign if there is one and the message.
   • Trusts – second largest contributor to the voluntary income – change in guidelines could substantially affect the unrestricted income. Need to develop the relationships with the major trusts.
   • Service charities – affected by the economic climate and therefore may be experiencing drop in their income – therefore grants will be limited. Discussion with the charities would elicit their reasons for the withdrawal of funds.
   • No corporate donations – this is a major weakness with no indication of whether there have been any attempts to fundraise in this area. It would be wise to

look at the industries where there is a real synergy.

- Statutory income – social services and health authority funds – could be fees or contract work – changes in policy within the areas could be responsible for the reduction or level playing of the income. Vulnerable to the changes in legislation and direction so need to have other resources available to meet the potential deficit.
- Lottery – there appears to have been no attempt to raise money from this source. The Big Lottery Fund might well be a source particularly where dealing with the community – needs to be investigated.
- Community fundraising – look at the activities within the areas of the welfare officers in order to maximise the publicity about the cause and the work undertaken by VBF – look into some of the events and activities in the local communities to provide support if appropriate.
- Trading – Christmas cards and goods probably take up too much time – limit this to just Christmas cards – perhaps sending them out to a wider network as the donors increase.
- Events – the trek was successful – the reason for not doing it again is the over stretched market – is this really the case? – research. Could the service personnel be encouraged to undertake more – local to the areas of support.

1b. Fundraising strategy should be part of the whole overall strategy and not set apart. It is essential that there are good lines of communication between all departments to ensure that the fundraising has a clear perspective on what is needed, not only for the coming year but within the years of the overall strategy. It is also important that the targets set for the fundraising are not expenditure driven but rather a carefully executed budget process. This will allow the fundraising strategy to build on past relationships and meet the needs of the organisation as a whole for the coming year and for the next three years. The strategy should include the following:

- Capital campaign for the refurbishment of the residential and therapy centres – small but could be regional.
- After researching the legacy breakdown – develop a modern legacy campaign.

- Continue with the trust fundraising – developing relationships with warm trusts and at the same time research new potential donors – not a scattergun approach.
- Service charities – meet to discuss the relationship and the potential action for the future. The outcome will dictate how to proceed to ensure that the targets are met.
- Research into potential corporate donors – looking at industries with a synergy with the organisation.
- Develop a campaign to attract new individual donors. The organisation would lend itself to direct mail, but research into the possibility of contacting serving personnel initially in order to increase the income. At the same time research the possibility of a donor recruitment campaign.
- Working with the service delivery departments – look at the statutory funding in order to establish where there could be deficits in the future and plan for replacement resources.
- Research the potential for a Lottery application.
- Research the potential of a major events programme involving serving personnel and families of those receiving support.
- Develop a media campaign which would raise the profile of the organisation.
- Community fundraising – local events to help with the refurbishment.

3 Budgeting

3.1 Budget planning

After the organisation has examined its priorities and refined its mission in accordance with the financial resources available, the budget can be prepared. The budget is a tool for allocating resources and implementing strategic plans. It charts a way of allocating and maximising the use of resources and, ideally, identifies financial problems that could arise in the coming year. The budget provides indicators for evaluating employee performance and gives the staff goals to reach and steps to achieve them.

The budget is a tool for allocating resources and implementing strategic plans.

The scope and size of the voluntary organisation's programmes and asset base will dictate the complexity of its budgets.

As a financial measure of the voluntary organisation's goals, a budget compiles programmes planned for the coming year in some detail based upon certain assumptions: for example, how many students the voluntary organisation expects to enrol; how much it plans to spend on saving which endangered species; the amount of money it plans to raise; or the number of new fee-paying members that will join. It is, in effect, the financial representation of the organisation's plans.

It is important to distinguish between the portion of the budget that can be readily calculated and that which has to be estimated. The budget planner needs both scepticism and optimism. The process necessarily involves uncertainty; decisions are made about a future that the organisation cannot control. Should the financial planner assume that existing programmes will continue? Which (if any) programmes are essential? Before developing the budget, the planners must make the specific policy decisions outlined below.

Balancing

As a first step the organisation must decide whether the budget is to be balanced i.e. with income matching expenditure. An organisation that needs to build up working capital might want to project a budget imbalance of revenue over expenses (a surplus). Alternatively, a deficit budget may be acceptable if it arises from investment in future restructuring, for example. However, the organisation will in most cases cease to be viable if there are recurring operating deficits. One exception may be where a policy decision has been made to rely on income from investments, for example, to finance deficits incurred on charitable programmes. (Obviously the question of the level of organisation reserves required to fulfil the plan must also be addressed at this stage.)

An effective budget also balances programme priorities: the organisation's capabilities and resources are allocated to impact on the maximum number of beneficiaries.

There might be other, more detailed parameters affecting the budget, particularly when budgeting and forecasting is devolved to individual programme or project managers. For example:

- No additional posts unless fully funded (e.g. by external project funding).
- 2.5 per cent growth in non-salaried expenditure, to account for inflation.
- Any new programmes must be fully funded (both in terms of direct and indirect costs).

Timing

Budgets (and the plans from which they are created) must be completed by a deadline that allows ample time for planning in advance of the period to which the budget applies. The lead time required for grant requests and multi-year projects also make it imperative that the budget process is properly timed. Realistic target dates for the completion of planning should be established for all involved to follow.

Evolution

A budget is not a static document, but needs to be updated in accordance with new situations, and to reflect new information as it becomes available.

Many voluntary organisations continue to compare current financial information with the originally approved budget, and provide footnotes explaining the circumstances that have caused the results to be better or worse than originally expected. The original budget will continue to provide valuable information for trustees, but would be ineffective for monitoring purposes. It is therefore good practice to review budgets on a monthly basis, and reforecast when necessary.

Ownership and accountability

A budget developed, monitored and revised in the accounts office is of little value to the programme staff. The people expected to accomplish the programmes, and the financial goals expressed in the budget, must be actively involved in the budgeting process. Unless the people who actually carry out the activities actively participate, a budget's usefulness is diminished and it is far less likely to be met.

Zero basis versus incremental budgeting

Those responsible for budgeting may adopt either a zero-based system or an incremental methodology for preparing the budget for the coming year.

In **zero-based budgeting** the financial planners start from a zero base, assuming that no programme is necessary and no money need be spent. To be accepted, the programmes will have to be proven worthwhile, as well as financially sound, after an evaluation of all elements of revenue and spending. Each programme is examined in order to justify its existence, and is compared to alternative programmes. Priorities are established and each cost centre is challenged to prove its necessity. This can make programme managers feel threatened, so budget setters should exercise sensitivity when using the zero-based method.

An **incremental budget**, on the other hand, treats existing programmes and departments as already approved, subject only to increases or decreases in the financial resources allocated. The organisation's historical costs are the base from which budget planning starts. The focus of the budgeting process is on the changes anticipated from last year's figures; the planning process has already been completed and the programme priorities established. But there are dangers in using last year's figures. Basing the budget on these figures can, if not properly challenged, introduce an element of 'creeping' costs year-on-year. For example, each year the organisation may take 'last year plus 5 per cent' as its figure and fail to query the basis for the decision. In this way, an arbitrary decision in a given year can continue unchallenged for a decade. Also, basing the budget on the actual results can encourage the practice of spending up to the budget in the last few months, to prevent future cuts. Despite these dangers, incremental budgeting is often less time-consuming than the zero-based method, and is also felt to be less threatening to programme managers.

Types of budget

Before the budget process begins, the organisation should decide which type of budget is best suited to its planning and monitoring needs. The basic budget is a comprehensive look at the entire organisation's projections of income or financial support and its expected expenditures. An endless number of supplementary budgets can be created to meet specific planning and assessment needs. The options might include at least the following:

- Annual, quarterly and/or monthly projections of income and expenditure for the entire organisation, as well as for each of its departments and branches.
- Receipts and payments budget.
- Revenue projections by type, such as contributors or student tuition.
- Individual project, department, branch or other cost centre projections.
- Service delivery costs by patient, by student, by member or other client.
- Capital additions (buildings or equipment acquisition).
- Investment income (and/or total return).
- Cash flow (short-and long-term).
- Fundraising event revenue and expenses.
- Retail shop sales.
- Personnel projections.

Advantages and disadvantages

In addition to its value in allocating resources and implementing strategic plans, the budget can produce a wide range of other beneficial results. Programme personnel directly involved in carrying out activities can use it to measure their accomplishments numerically and to respond to unexpected changes. Management can use it to evaluate staff performance. But like any tool, the budget can produce good or bad results, depending on the skill and diligence with which it is used.

The chief advantages of effective budgeting include:

- A thoroughly planned and implemented budget increases the likelihood of a voluntary organisation being financially successful.
- A budget translates abstract goals into determinable bites: it sets performance goals.
- The planning and preparation of a budget forces the organisation to look at itself, set priorities and narrow its choices.

- A budget facilitates coordination and cooperation between the various programmes and financial departments.
- Periodic comparisons between the budget and actual financial performance can signal trouble and allow time for an appropriate response.
- A budget measures how far financial performance meets an organisation's expectations.

For a budget to be effective, it is important that the possible disadvantages are considered and addressed. These may include:

- The presence of controls may stifle creativity.
- Because there are so many unknowns at the time when the budget is prepared, the natural tendency is to emphasise cost control.
- A budget based on historical information alone cannot always keep up with a rapidly-changing environment.
- Non-financial staff do not often participate in the budgeting process, resulting in operational blueprints that have been approved without the input of programme staff (who should be involved where possible).
- A budget is not always easy to implement and may not always be accepted as useful by the management staff.

For a budget to be effective, it is important that the possible disadvantages are considered and addressed.

Who participates in budgeting?

A budget cannot guarantee its own success: it is no substitute for responsible management. Almost everyone involved with a voluntary organisation may appropriately participate in planning its budget: at the very least, the top administrators, programme heads and board members or trustees. A budget should be a compilation of information from all the senior programme and administrative personnel, who have in turn taken account of contributions from the people with whom they work. No one person should be responsible for preparing the budget, although the organisation's accounts department should compile and monitor it.

How far down the organisational ladder the leaders solicit contributions will depend on the organisation's circumstances, structure and resources, but the further the better in ensuring accuracy of information and a true sense of ownership.

The ideal budget is highly participatory, involving input from all the programme staff and volunteers who work to accomplish the organisation's goals.

There will also be a broad range of interested stakeholders, including funders and supporters. Outside funders can sometimes exert considerable influence on the budget: they may want to know if the organisation plans to provide services that are already provided by another organisation in the community; they may try to influence grant recipients to conduct programmes that accomplish the funder's goals.

A budget imposed from the top down, dampens the enthusiasm of staff and can hamper the realisation of the organisation's goals. During the budget process, there will naturally be compromise and trade-off. If staff participate from the outset, they may be more willing to accept alterations not initiated by them. It may also make them more understanding about changes, including budget cuts that affect them personally. The participation of the board, officers, staff and volunteers in the process of setting goals enhances the organisation's chances of achieving those goals. Preparing the budget should motivate personnel and inspire the organisation's performance.

Scheduling the budget process

Ideally, budgeting is a continuous process that repeats itself cyclically and is based on the organisation's long-range plan. This requires sufficient time for the budget plans to be fully developed.

Preparation of the budget should ideally begin six months before the beginning of the period to which the budget applies: for example, an organisation whose financial year ends on 31 March should start preparing the budget for the next financial year by September of the current financial year. This allows enough time to gather reliable forecasting information and to go through an orderly approval process.

The steps to follow include:

Figure 3.2

Step 1. Set goals	Perform strategic planning
Step 2. Establish objectives	Identify programmes and activities to accomplish goals
Step 3. Design programmes	Describe method of actualising the goals
Step 4. Budget preparation and approval	Quantify revenue and expenditures based upon forecasts and programme services accomplishments
Step 5. Monitor progress	Compile reports comparing budget to actual

Use of budgets

Budgets can be used for a variety of purposes, but this guide focuses on how they can form part of funding applications, project appraisal and project monitoring.

> Ideally, budgeting is a continuous process that repeats itself cyclically.
>
> Preparation of the budget should ideally begin six months before the beginning of the period to which the budget applies.

When budgets are used as part of funding applications, their format and construction will be guided by the funder's requirements. Typically, a funder will require costs to be split between capital and revenue items, and where applicable, over the term of the project life (maximum three years). There are likely to be restrictions on the percentage (if any) of apportioned overheads that will be funded.

Changing budgets mid-year

No budget, no matter how carefully prepared, ever comes to pass in its original form. Some voluntary organisations may find a 'living' budget, that regularly changes throughout the year as circumstances change, to be preferable to a fixed and unchanging budget, as long as the 'bottom line' remains the same.

The reasons which could require the budget to change are endless. Budgets often prove inaccurate for reasons of inadequate information or circumstances beyond the organisation's control – an grant renewal is unexpectedly cut back or denied; a major funder defaults on a pledge; a natural disaster compounds the demand for aid to the public; a member of staff leaves, causing disruption.

The issue when unforeseen changes occur is whether the approved budget should be altered or updated to reflect the changing conditions. Alternatively, the monthly management reports can use footnotes to explain significant variances from the approved budget. The attributes of a 'living' or constantly changing budget are compared to a static budget below:

A good solution can be to update the budget on a regular basis (allowing a flexible budget) but to return a separate column showing original forecasts. This can be very helpful in organisational learning and in preparing plans for the following year.

Static Budget	Living or Flexible Budget
Compares dreams at a point in time to reality of current situation	Presents realistic statistics in view of changing circumstances or conditions
No time spent on revisions	Requires continual updating – time intensive
Can waste funds on programme to be discontinued or found to be ineffective	Constant maximisation of resources
Allows unreasonable expectations	Positive context for accomplishment

3.2 Preparing forecasts

Voluntary organisations face particular problems in forecasting their income flow, particularly those supported by contributions and grants. Voluntary donations depend upon the giver's support for the organisation's mission, but the public's concern about a particular social problem – AIDS, for example – may wane. Other intangible factors, such as changes in legislation, can compound the difficulty of making projections.

A service-providing voluntary organisation, such as a school or a professional association, may have a slightly easier task in forecasting future income. People will pay for services if they feel that they are useful. As long as the services are of high quality and meet the needs of users, the organisation can reasonably assume that they will continue to pay for them.

The forecaster first studies current income and spending and asks if they can be sustained at present levels:

- If unusual events have occurred in the past year or two, are they likely to recur?
- Otherwise, is it reasonable to expect an increase in revenue?
- What increase does the organisation expect as the result of an action taken in the past, such as last year's setting up of a development department?
- What increases in revenue might result if some new marketing scheme is added to the expense side of the budget?

Donations and membership

Forecasting the income from voluntary contributions and membership fees becomes easier as an organisation matures. In these circumstances, the best guide to predicting the future is the organisation's own history, and in particular, tables showing several years of revenue. Some voluntary organisations enjoy considerable goodwill generated during years of operation, but new or young organisations may need to be more cautious about forecasting the success of their development plans. However, even for mature organisations, changes in the external environment can have a considerable impact on membership and donations.

Using information about donors generated internally (for example, their age, frequency of giving, average amount of gift) in conjunction with an examination of significant trends in the voluntary sector economy, can greatly enhance the reliability of forecasts.

According to NCVO's Voluntary Sector Almanac (see further reading, page 307), the main factors affecting this type of income are:

- Voluntary income is often described as 'free' income, as it is not tied to a particular outcome; increasingly, however,

Forecasting the income from voluntary contributions and membership fees becomes easier as an organisation matures.

donors seem more inclined to give if there is a specific project.

- Organisations that appeal to the philanthropic motives of individuals are heavily dependent on the trust that has been developed.
- Public confidence in all types of public institutions continues to decline, which is likely to affect levels of giving.
- There is increasing competition, not only among voluntary organisations, but with other types of activity, for the disposable income of individuals.
- Generally, the voluntary sector is experiencing a decline in charitable giving, particularly organisations with an annual income of £1-10 million.

Figure 3.3 shows the main characteristics of voluntary income in a SWOT analysis.

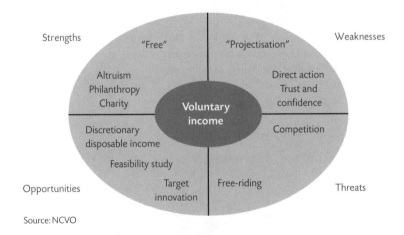

Source: NCVO

Earned income

Service delivery fees

The age of an organisation is also significant when forecasting revenue. A mature organisation will know the average number of student places, research reports or other services delivered in the past few years. The needs of these services, and any policy decisions about their delivery, will already have been reviewed as part of the strategic planning process. The financial planner's job may simply be to express these strategic goals in a financial format: for example, the number of people to be served and the expected price. In some cases, however, this price may not reflect the full cost of the service; a subsidy may have to come from voluntary income and/or investment income.

The age of an organisation is also significant when forecasting revenue.

Grants and contracts

Predicting whether grants from local authorities, charitable trusts and business sponsors will be renewed is full of uncertainty. Have the local authority's funding priorities changed? Has the value of the charitable trust's assets fallen, reducing the amount available for grants?

Corporate sponsorship is usually tied to the sponsor's profit level – which is usually unknown at budget preparation time. Furthermore, the funding of research often has to be based upon incomplete data, which makes prediction equally impossible.

If an organisation's operating overheads, or administrative costs, are paid for out of grants, very cautious forecasting is needed. Think about the consequences when the grant that funds half the executive director's salary is not renewed! If there is a good possibility of grants not being renewed, a flexible or evolving budget (as discussed in the previous section) may be sensible; the budget should also specify alternative courses of action.

Conditions of employment for staff members funded by a grant (and the corresponding expenses budget) should recognise the possibility that the funds may cease.

A SWOT analysis showing the main characteristics of earned income is given in Figure 3.4.

Figure 3.4 SWOT analysis – earned income

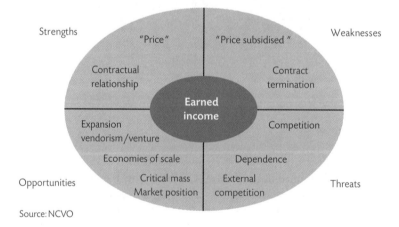

Source: NCVO

Some points to bear in mind when developing an earned income stream include:

- If an organisation enters into a variety of service contracts, there is a risk that it might lose sight of its mission and become financially dependent on contracts.

- Contracts for services – such as providing health care – often lead to significant growth in infrastructure.
- Loss of a contract can have a devastating effect on service delivery organisations, as they typically employ a large number of staff.
- There is considerable competition in certain areas of earned income activities, such as health care, particularly when for-profit companies are also providing the same services.

Investment income

The caution required when forecasting investment income depends upon what proportion of its income the organisation expects to derive from investments; for many voluntary groups, this will be modest. But for an endowed grant-making trust, all of whose income comes from investment, this forecast is vital in establishing funding levels for the coming year.

Forecasting becomes particularly difficult for organisations with long term investment funds. If the funds are administered by a professional investment manager, he or she should provide projections of investment income. However, despite several short-term 'corrections' in recent years, and at the time of writing, current falls in equity portfolio values, the underlying long-term trend for funds has been steady growth.

A SWOT analysis showing the main characteristics of investment income is given in Figure 3.5.

If the funds are administered by a professional investment manager, he or she should provide projections of investment income.

Figure 3.5 SWOT analysis – investment income

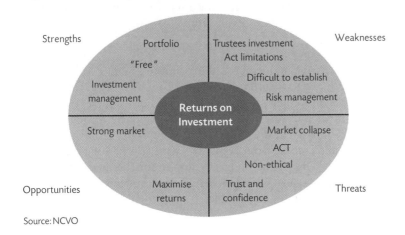

Source: NCVO

Expenses

Most voluntary organisations can predict their expenditure with some certainty, as they have more control over expenditure than income: for example, the cost of salaries and the lease/mortgage on premises will be relatively stable. Historical expenses are, therefore, the basis for the expenditure budget, subject to adjustments for inflation: for example, last year's figures plus three per cent.

One major challenge in forecasting costs is to identify those that are unpredictable: for example, a disaster relief agency may know how much it costs to clothe and house flood victims, but it cannot know when the storms will occur. Again, historical records may be useful.

Demand for an organisation's services is often difficult to predict, so it is essential to acknowledge this uncertainty and submit a flexible budget. The prudent budget planner uses the best possible information to hand, but submits forecasts that are subject to change. Another option is to distinguish clearly between costs that are controllable and those that are uncontrollable.

If expected costs are too high, the financial planner must consider cheaper alternatives. For example, a voluntary organisation may need skilled people to supervise a specialised project, but the salary such people would expect might skew the organisation's overall pay scale. In such a situation, the organisation has several options:

- Outsource the job to another organisation.
- Hire skilled people on a part-time, or hourly basis, to run the project and train in-house staff.
- Eliminate the project, reduce its size or run it jointly with another voluntary organisation.

Phasing the budget

When preparing an income and expenditure budget for a project, it is important to identify when in a 12-month period the income and expenditure items are likely to arise. For example, costs such as insurance and rates are not incurred regularly throughout the period. Similarly, grants might be paid quarterly in advance or in arrears, and income from events will arise just before an event.

This phasing of the budget is important, because without it, useful comparisons between actual and budgeted income and expenditure will not be possible.

Statistical operational data

A voluntary organisation must regularly gather statistics and information relevant to the budgeting and planning process. Each organisation needs a method of measuring its own effectiveness: are its goals being met? What are the results of its efforts? Successes and failures, weaknesses and strengths, should be regularly evaluated and the results used as a basis for making decisions. The sophistication and scope of the self-assessment process will vary according to the organisation, but to be effective not only the performance of the organisation itself but also that of staff, volunteers, managers and trustees should be measured.

3.3 Structuring the budget

A voluntary organisation should have a structure that will ensure the efficient fulfilment of its strategic aims: in practice, this means setting up departments, or appointing project managers, with the responsibility for providing products or services. In most voluntary organisations, budgetary control and budget reports reflect the hierarchy of the organisation. The reporting – from the project manager responsible for delivering services to the board of trustees responsible for the financial health of the whole organisation – will be less detailed the higher up the organisation it goes.

Model budgets and budget monitoring

At board of trustees level, the concern will be to ensure that the organisation meets its financial goals: for example, to achieve a balanced budget of income and expenditure to the end of the year, or to plan for a surplus. A further concern will be to ensure that the organisation has sufficient incoming cash resources to meet its obligations as they fall due.

The income and expenditure budget shown in figure 3.6 will have the totals for rows A to D and a balance shown in row E. Staff costs have been separately disclosed because for many voluntary organisations they represent up to 60 per cent of total expenditure and thus warrant careful monitoring. Total running costs (C) will include both direct costs of projects and an element of organisation-wide costs.

The budgeted surplus or deficit should correspond to the target identified at the initial planning stages.

The headings for each of the columns can be explained as follows:

- Full year budget (1). This represents the original budget or plan, which the organisation's staff and management would have started to compile some six months before the start of the year, and which was approved by the board approximately two months before the start of the year.

Figure 3 Total income and expenditure budget for Environ Alliance Trust

SEPTEMBER 19X9

DESCRIPTION	FULL YEAR BUDGET (1)	This month ACTUAL (2)	This month BUDGET (3)	VARIANCE (4) (3) – (2)	Year to date ACTUAL (5)	Year to date BUDGET (6)	VARIANCE (7) (6) – (5)	Last FORECAST (8)	This FORECAST (9)	VARIANCE to last F/C (10) (8) – (9)	VARIANCE to budget (11) (1)–(9)
TOTAL INCOME (A)	547,270	31,331	27,418	3,913	188,761	234,130	(45,369)	519,838	511,777	(8061)	(35,493)
TOTAL STAFF COSTS (B)	267,493	21,047	21,828	781	111,966	110,775	(1,191)	269,498	271,264	(1,766)	(3,771)
TOTAL RUNNING COSTS (C)	267,493	8,581	16,995	8,414	65,835	100,820	34,985	231,741	226,258	5,483	30,397
TOTAL EXPENDITURE (D) (B) + (C)	524,148	29,628	38,823	9,195	177,801	211,595	33,794	501,239	497,522	3,717	26,626
SURPLUS/(DEFICIT) (E) (A) – (D)	23,122	1,703	(11,405)	13,108	10,960	22,535	(11,575)	18,599	14,255	(4,344)	(8,867)

- This month actual (2), this month budget (3), variance (4): these columns taken together represent the difference from the original budget or plan for the current month as identified by the variance column. This set of figures allows for the examination of current month activities in income and expenditure terms.
- Year to date actual (5), year to date budget (6), variance (7). Taken together, these columns represent the accumulated difference from the original plan or budget, as identified by the variance column. They enable the examination of six-month figures for income and expenditure, and therefore serve as a guide to the feasibility of the year-end financial goals.
- Last forecast (8), this forecast (9), variance to last forecast (10). These columns allow amendments to be made to the original budget, to reflect changing circumstances since it was approved. The variance to budget (11) column enables the effect of changing assumptions on the original plan or budget to be monitored.

The six-month income and expenditure budget for the Environ Alliance Trust (figure 3.6) delivers key messages that should concern the trustee board:

- The original budget planned for a surplus of £23,122 (column 1) to be taken to reserves. At the end of the six-month period the organisation is forecast to make a reduced surplus of £14,255 (column 9).
- The reduction occurs because the current forecast for total income to the end of the year is £511,777, compared with the original budget of £547,270.
- In response to the revised income forecast, the organisation has been cutting non-salary costs, as is evident in the reduction of the running costs budget from the original £256,655 to £226,258.
- The trustee board should examine the possibility that income will further decline and the effect this might have on the work programme of the charity.
- The trustee board should investigate the reasons why income has declined. Have earned income targets been met? Has a grant application fallen through?

Cash flow forcasts
The cash flow forecast is a crucial document for trustees. Any organisation which runs out of cash will collapse, no matter how

worthy its objectives. The cash flow forecast, or cash budget, is primarily used to ensure that the organisation has sufficient incoming resources to meet its obligations as they fall due. The example presented in figure 3.7 is a six-month forecast with the accumulated results to August rolled up into the first column, and a separate column for September. The cash flow forecast is produced by reference to the income and expenditure budgets, which serve as a basis for adjusting the individual entries to reflect amounts accrued or prepaid for each month. For example, since membership subscriptions are invoiced on a monthly basis, the amounts shown in the income and expenditure account will reflect the total invoiced for membership in a particular month. However, the amount shown in the cash flow statement reflects the actual receipt of cash credited to the bank for membership subscriptions in the month. Management will know from previous experience what proportion of subscriptions invoiced in any month will be paid in the following and subsequent months. The six-month cash flow forecast for the Environ Alliance Trust delivers certain key messages that should concern the trustee board:

- From month to month there is a net cash outflow from the organisation averaging £5,000, which is currently being met from the accumulated balance at the bank.
- Although this net cash outflow may be sustainable in the short-term, the trustee board must consider whether additional finance should be sought or must examine the feasibility of reducing the cash outflow by making additional savings.
- The 'project charges' row in both the cash inflow and cash outflow sections recognises that projects which cannot be directly attributed should be charged for general overheads. Since these charges are internal movements of cash, there is no impact on the cash flow of the voluntary organisation.
- It is important to appreciate that the cash flow statement will be different from the income and expenditure figures. The cash flow statement represents movements in cash held at the bank, whilst the income and expenditure statements reflect amounts which are due to the organisation (income) and amounts payable by the organisation (expenditure).
- The cash flow statement will also need to include the effects of value added tax (VAT). This may result in a cash outflow (representing payments to Customs) or a cash inflow (representing a refund from Customs). The impact of VAT on the organisation will depend upon its business activities (see Chapter 8, page 253).

The cash flow forecast is produced by reference to the income and expenditure budgets.

Figure 3.7 Environ Alliance Trust cash flow forecast 19x9

	Year to August	September	October	November	December	January	February	March	Total
	actuals	actuals	budget	budget	budget	budget	budget	budget	budget
Receipts									
Membership subscriptions	34,560	10,588	12,500	12,500	12,500	12,500	12,500	12,500	120,148
Grant income	30,000	2,500	0	0	2,500	0	0	2,500	37,500
Publications	11,024	1,051	920	920	1,990	2,500	920	1,070	20,395
Conferences	13,762	936	1,188	1,938	1,988	1,838	1,738	1,988	25,376
Fees and other income	55,316	14,675	3,500	5,000	5,000	5,000	5,000	5,000	98,491
Project charges	0	0	0	0	0	0	0	0	0
Cash inflow	144,662	29,750	18,108	20,358	23,978	21,838	20,158	23,058	301,910
Payments									
Staff costs	92,250	17,235	17,218	17,237	17,237	17,166	17,166	17,167	212,676
Premises costs	6,669	1,350	1,500	1,205	1,205	1,205	1,305	1,305	15,744
Publication costs	4,877	1,565	1,220	3,000	1,000	1,000	1,000	2,000	15,662
Conference costs	6,358	1,458	1,500	2,500	2,500	2,000	1,500	1,500	19,316
Other running costs	32,974	6,859	5,000	5,000	5,000	5,000	5,000	5,000	69,833
Project charges	0	0	0	0	0	0	0	0	0
Cash outflow	143,128	28,467	26,438	28,942	26,942	26,371	25,971	26,972	333,231
Net cash inflow/(outflow)	1,534	1,283	(8,330)	(8,584)	(2,964)	(4,533)	(5,813)	(3,914)	(31,321)
Bank balances at beginning of period	42,344	43,878	45,161	36,831	28,247	25,283	20,750	14,937	42,344
Bank balances at end of period	43,878	45,161	36,831	28,247	25,283	20,750	14,937	11,023	11,023

The trustee board should ask the following key questions of management:

- If income projections decline further, what effect will this have on the organisation's ability to carry on with its projects?
- Are there any contingency plans to safeguard projects? (For example, borrowing or bridging-type loans).
- Is it feasible to launch an immediate fundraising appeal?

To answer the above questions, the trustee board may need to be supplied with more detailed budget sheets on which each department's income and expenditure will be monitored.

As mentioned above, the trustee board may wish to seek further explanations of the income and expenditure position of Environ Alliance Trust, and for this purpose should be provided with the detailed departmental breakdown (figure 3.8). This report would be provided as a matter of course to the director and departmental managers.

The format of the report remains the same, making it easier to prepare. The main highlights from this report are:

- The chief executive's office, research and policy and services departments currently run on a deficit budget, being financed through membership subscriptions (see column 1, row D). This may be based on management's policy of allowing members' subscriptions to pay for policy and research activity and members' services. However, as is evident from the detailed report, such an arrangement requires careful cost management, as it may not be possible to pass on increasing costs to members through increased subscriptions.
- The income from the research and services department is significantly below that budgeted at the end of six months. The variances in column 7 under year to date income clearly show this. There may be many reasons for this decline in income: for example, the original budget was not phased for income and therefore meaningless variances are being generated; income generation activities have not been undertaken; or loss of funding has resulted in the shortfall.
- It is important to recognise that, when profiling the budget, the budget holder will need to consider the timing of when income and expenditure may arise within the year. Although it is reasonable to assume that certain expenses, such as rent, are incurred evenly over 12 months, this is not always the

case: for other items, the budget holder will need to consider when in the year a particular activity will give rise to income being earned or expenditure incurred. In the absence of such profiling, large variances can occur, rendering the budget practically useless as a management tool.

- In response to the identified shortfall in income, Environ has made significant savings in the running costs of both the research and services departments, as demonstrated by the variances identified in column 7 under running costs (row C).

- As a result of the identified shortfall in income, Environ has decided to reforecast its total income, as is shown by the latest forecast figures for income, column 9. Column 11 reveals the total effect of these revisions on the original budget: total income is now forecast at £511,777, compared with the original budget of £547,270, a variance of £35,493.

- Because of the revised total income figures, Environ had decided to defer or cancel programmes and expenditure in the research and services departments.

Figure 3.8 Detailed departmental breakdown, Environ Alliance Trust

DESCRIPTION	FULL YEAR BUDGET (1)	This month ACTUAL (2)	This month BUDGET (3)	VARIANCE (4) (3) – (2)	Year to date ACTUAL (5)	Year to date BUDGET (6)	VARIANCE (7) (6) – (5)	Last FORECAST (8)	This FORECAST (9)	VARIANCE to last F/C (10) (8) – (9)	VARIANCE to budget (11) (1) – (9)
INCOME											
Chief Executive	100	0	83	(83)	210	415	(205)	100	100	0	0
Research and Policy	101,050	3,668	5,391	(1,723)	25,948	46,677	(20,729) (2)	97,655	93,912	(3,743)	(7,138)
Services Development	129,690	1,685	4,556	(2,871)	18,206	41,638	(23,432) (2)	104,783	99,785	(4,998)	(29,905)
Membership	120,000	11,998	8,698	3,300	60,209	57,730	2,479	121,000	121,000	0	1,000
Non Team	196,430	13,980	8,690	5,290	84,188	87,670	(3,482)	196,300	196,980	680	550
TOTAL INCOME (A)	547,270	31,331	27,418	3,913	188,761	234,130	(45,369)	519,838	511,777	(8,061) (4)	(35,493)
EXPENDITURE											
Chief Executive	45,000	3,700	3,750	50	18,750	18,700	(50)	45,000	45,000	0	0
Research and Policy	72,758	6,239	6,062	(177)	33,405	31,628	(1,777)	77,610	77,011	599	(4,253)
Services Development	122,887	8,915	9,779	864	47,878	49,260	1,382	120,532	121,940	(1,408)	947
Membership	11,173	878	931	53	4,398	4,656	258	10,681	10,638	43	535
Non Team	15,675	1,315	1,306	(9)	7,535	6,531	(1,004)	15,675	16,675	(1,000)	(1,000)
TOTAL STAFF COSTS (B)	267,493	21,047	21,828	781	111,966	110,775	(1,191)	269,498	271,264	(1,766)	(3,771)
Chief Executive	5,930	2,150	494	(1,656)	4,126	2,471	(1,655)	5,930	7,930	(2,000)	(2,000)
Research and Policy	71,991	1,249	5,471	4,222	13,527	29,035	15,508 (3)	67,080	62,731	4,349 (5)	9,260
Services Development	112,051	1,899	5,857	3,958	19,080	42,665	23,585 (3)	91,394	88,060	3,334 (5)	23,991
Membership	36,308	1,252	2,173	921	14,452	13,993	(459)	36,962	37,162	(200)	(854)
Non Team	30,375	2,031	3,000	969	14,650	12,656	(1,994)	30,375	30,375	0	0
TOTAL RUNNING COSTS (C)	256,655	8,581	16,995	8,414	65,835	100,820	34,985	231,741	226,258	5,483	30,397
Chief Executive	(50,830) (1)	(5,850)	(4,161)	(1,689)	(22,666)	(20,756)	(1,910)	(50,830)	(52,830)	(2,000)	(2,000)
Research and Policy	(43,699) (1)	(3,820)	(6,142)	2,322	(20,984)	(13,986)	(6,998)	(47,035)	(45,830)	1,205	(2,131)
Services Development	(105,248) (1)	(9,129)	(11,080)	1,951	(48,752)	(50,287)	1,535	(107,143)	(110,215)	(3,072)	(4,967)
Membership	72,519 (1)	9,868	5,594	4,274	41,359	39,081	2,278	73,357	73,200	(157)	681
Non Team	150,380 (1)	10,634	4,384	6,250	62,003	68,483	(6,480)	150,250	149,930	(320)	(450)
SURPLUS / (DEFICIT) (A) - (B) - (C)	23,122	1,703	(11,405)	13,108	10,960	22,335	(11,575)	18,599	14,255	(4,344)	(8,867)

Budgets and budgetary control

When used properly, budgets can enable effective financial control of a voluntary organisation. Since they often reflect the organisational structure and are typically assigned to departments, projects and individuals, budgets are a way of assigning specific responsibility for the resources that have been allocated according to a plan of activities. It should be possible to trace back each of these activities to the strategic aim it seeks to meet. In this way, the organisation can move from its high level strategic aims to identifying objectives and to drawing up detailed activity plans that have been costed and approved in the form of a budget.

Budgetary control is the practice of holding departments, projects and individuals to account for allocated resources, by comparing actual results for income and expenditure against the costed plan of activities. Budgets and budgetary control can affect the way people behave; many studies have shown that departmental or programme managers seek to safeguard the level of spending allocated to them. Meeting the budget targets often becomes the primary objective for individual employees, a tendency that is reinforced if that individual's performance and reward are determined by whether the targets have been met. Empire building and manipulating the budget in order to meet targets can rapidly become the order of the day. This causes the link between strategic aims and actual activity to become blurred, if not lost, and at worst budgets become used to measure organisational performance; the fulfilment of charitable aims ceases to be the primary measure of performance.

To guard against this loss of direction, the management of voluntary organisations need to monitor and measure their outcomes and the impact they have on society (according to their strategic aims) as well as its financial performance – this is clearly evidenced by the recent move towards 'impact reporting'.

The management committee and board of trustees need to be informed about both the organisation's financial health and its effectiveness in meeting its strategic aims. As mentioned in Chapter 2, programme aims and financial goals are interdependent, and success in one cannot be achieved at the expense of the other.

To be able to provide this more balanced reporting, the voluntary organisation needs to monitor and measure performance over a broader range of criteria than simply the financial.

3.4 Communicating financial information

The responsibility for compiling financial reports often falls on the finance officer or finance department, who are charged with maintaining financial data and manipulating it in a variety of ways to produce reports. These reports set out to inform a wide range of stakeholders, including project managers, the organisation's management and trustee board, funders and regulatory bodies. The design and content of these reports should be determined by the needs of the audience; it is not enough to blindly follow a predetermined template. The internal audience would usually be presented with management accounts consisting of income and expenditure and cash flow reports, whereas for external audiences – such as funders and the Charity Commission – the form and content will often be prescribed beforehand.

For many people in voluntary organisations, 'management accounts' mean reams of paper covered in numbers that are produced by the accounts department and ignored by everyone else. Management accounts are, however, vital for running an organisation effectively – so what should be done to make them more accessible?

The information provided must be relevant

Management accounts must contain the financial information that the reader actually needs to plan and control the financial resources for which he or she is accountable. The finance officer who is preparing the management accounts must, therefore, be aware of the issues that affect the organisation in general and the reader in particular.

Understanding the organisation's cash flow may be much more important than income and expenditure. How often are balance sheets used, and have restricted funds been used according to the donor's wishes?

The information must be up to date

There is a trade-off between accuracy and speed: the more accurate the information, the longer it will take to produce. Management needs to understand the organisation well enough to determine at what point accuracy ceases to affect the decision being made.

The information must be accurate

Inaccurate information is worse than no information at all. Accuracy here means not only eliminating data handling

Inaccurate information is worse than no information at all.

errors – miscodings, wrong entries, incorrect totals or transfers of figures – but also ensuring that nothing is omitted.

The accounts must be intelligible

However timely and accurate the accounts may be, they are of no use if they do not inform the reader. Management accounts frequently contain too many numbers presented in a discouraging format. The finance officer must be clear about who the audience is and what information they need to make the decisions expected of them.

The accounts must be available

Users should have access to management accounts at the times when they need them. This is unlikely to coincide with predetermined deadlines for monthly reporting. For many organisations, however, this flexibility may be impossible, particularly if the accounts are held on a manual system. But it should remain an objective for organisations with computer accounting systems to allow non-accounting staff 'read only' access to information.

The accounts must descibe what is actually going on

What do readers understand 'actual' to mean? Expenditure and payments are not the same thing, but do they realise that? What the user of management accounts sees in the 'actuals' column will depend on the method of accounting for transactions that is adopted. If users are not clear about which transactions are included, they can seriously misinterpret the true financial position.

Using a cash accounting policy, an amount will appear in the actuals column only once a payment has been made: for example, once a cheque has been written. This might be some time after the legal liability has been incurred and well after a commitment has been made to spend the funds. If management accounts only reflect the commitment once the liability has been met, the risk of overstating 'free' funds is considerable.

A first step in rectifying the above position is to move to an accruals accounting policy, by accruing liabilities when they are incurred rather than recognising them only when they are met. This means, for example, charging invoice values as expenditure and coding payments to creditor balances.

Figures are useless in isolation. To make sense of them, a user needs to compare them with suitable other comparators. Some useful comparisons of results might be:

- The five most successful UK charity results, suitably adjusted.
- Your best ever performance.
- Any commercial organisations listed as an example of best practice in the DTI Inside UK Enterprise scheme.
- Your closest competitor.
- Your equivalent organisation overseas.

Who owns the management accounts?

Because budgets are produced by the accounts department, that department is often seen as owning them. Users need to feel that they are the owners of management accounts rather than merely passive recipients. This question of ownership can be resolved by addressing the following issues:

Involvement. The more the user can influence the management accounts, the more likely they are to value them as a decision-making aid. This does, however, require the user to have commitment and the relevant skills. Involvement is more likely when:

- Operating or programme staff (those involved in spending the money) prepare the budgets.
- Programme staff have a detailed understanding of the organisation's priorities.
- Programme staff contribute to the design of reports, albeit within the statutory framework.
- The inputting of data – such as invoice details – is performed by programme staff instead of accounts clerks.
- Users are able to get reports whenever they need them.

Organisations
should
recognise that
information is a
resource which
should be
made freely
available to all
staff.

Transparency. Organisations should recognise that information is a resource which should be made freely available to all staff (but without compromising privacy). In this way, both good and bad news can be communicated.

Accountability. Those who make decisions about the use of the charity's financial resources should be held accountable for those decisions. Accountability can be achieved by requiring the users of management accounts to:

- Prepare budgets using a zero-based approach, where the user has to justify the resources needed.
- Explain variances that arise, so that problem areas are identified and action taken.

- Reforecast year-end results as the year progresses, so that programme staff are encouraged to think about whether they are on track.
- Revise budgets if the resource requirement for the programmes has changed.

Trust. Users of management accounts should feel that they are trusted to manage the resources for which they are accountable. This can be difficult, as it requires the accounts department to strike a balance between wise stewardship of the charity's financial resources and obtrusive policing. In practice, trust means:

- Examining the levels of authority that users exercise, and perhaps increasing them in order to give the users the discretion to spend resources.
- Managing expectations by stressing that the budget is a plan based on assumptions that may not hold true – it is not to be used for disciplinary purposes.

3.5 Budgets and IT solutions

For years voluntary organisations of all sizes have used spreadsheet applications to prepare management accounts. It is no surprise, therefore, that Excel is the tool most commonly used by accountants. Information technology (IT) is used to produce budgets because of its speed and convenience, but a successful budgeting system is a lot more than just a spreadsheet. This section gives guidelines on how to organise, design and implement budgetary control using spreadsheet applications. They will help organisations to use information technology solutions that genuinely assist management rather than hinder it. Larger organisations should be aware that there comes a point when a spreadsheet solution is outgrown and they should look to the myriad of specific budgeting and planning tools that are on the market.

Pre-planning
A budgetary control system has a number of different elements that will vary from organisation to organisation. A straightforward system might be for departmental/project budgets consolidated to an organisational level, with the ability to track these against actuals month, for the year-to-date, and for the same period last year. For anything other than the simplest application, there are key stages to developing a spreadsheet model that should be followed:

System design

Before entering data into the spreadsheet, think carefully about the design of the system. Talk to the people who might need to extract information from the system when it is complete. It can be difficult to change the format of a spreadsheet-based budget after it has been created. At this stage, the level of detail required should be decided and the best design of the system indentified to achieve this. Users should be familiar with some of the more advance features of a spreadsheet including multi-dimensional capabilities and macros. If in-house skills do not exist in this area users should consider some training.

Thought should be given to any interfaces required to external systems such as the accounting application itself. Do you, for example, want to import data into the spreadsheet from the finance package – or vice versa? If individuals are completing their own departmental budget, can you give them their own forms to complete which you can automatically consolidate into the system?

Model specification

Next, it is usually worth laying out the more detailed system specification. Look at what information will be kept on which sheets, what data will be stored in separate files, use of tables etc. Thought should be given to any security requirements to ensure sensitive data such as salaries are not accessible by unauthorised users.

System backups should also be checked to make sure there is a resilient fallback for the work you are doing.

If you have several people working on the application make sure they all have the appropriate version of the spreadsheet you are using.

Documentation

Thought should be given to the amount of documentation you wish to prepare on the system. Make sure there is sufficient material so that if the designer of the system is away someone else can understand how it is put together. Make sure you provide documentation for users to help them use the application.

Spreadsheet development

This is the point at which the actual building of the system begins. Too many people ignore the preceding stages and jump straight into spreadsheet development. This usually results in needlessly complex models that take longer than necessary to develop, based on assumptions that were not part of the original brief.

Testing

Even after thorough planning and careful spreadsheet development, it is a good idea to test all components of a system. This can be done by entering several sets of data and checking the logic; historical data with known results is useful for this purpose.

Implementation

The effort required for implementation will vary according to the complexity of the system, the number of people who will use it and whether training or ongoing support will be needed.

3.6 Computerising the accounts

Most voluntary organisations of any size have, or are considering, computerising their accounts. The benefits are typically saving staff time, obtaining more detailed or more accurate information, and producing reports and answering queries more quickly.

It is usually clear when an accounting system is failing to meet the needs of an organisation, or when the resources it is consuming seem out of proportion to the results. In some cases, improving the existing manual system may be all that is needed. However, every organisation is different; here are some suggested criteria that you might consider when deciding whether to computerise:

- Is your annual income or expenditure more than £100,000?
- Do you have several different projects that need separate accounting?
- Do you handle a large number of similar transactions?

If the organisation is small, with a simple financial structure, it should be possible to design an effective manual system for the main accounting records.

However, within such a manual system there may be areas of work involving a large number of repetitive transactions – such as subscriptions – that lend themselves to computer assistance.

When to start?

A potentially good time to change systems is at the end of the financial year. Unfortunately, this means that the busy period, when annual accounts are being prepared, will coincide with any teething troubles in the computer system – although potential problems can be minimized by careful planning and preparation.

Planning should begin well in advance: for a smallish organisation typically three to six months before the start of the changeover. These early discussions should include a review of the

A potentially good time to change systems is at the end of the financial year.

additional resources needed to install the new system: for example, will it be necessary to bring in outside expertise and/or temporary assistance? Are there any sources of funding, or free expertise or assistance, for this investment? At this early stage it can be useful to visit similar voluntary organisations in order to learn from their experiences.

What to avoid

Here are some guidelines on what not to do:

- Using 'informal' systems – those that allow entries to be changed at a later stage without a clear record being kept of the amendment.
- Expecting staff without adequate training, supervision or control to enter complex data reliably.
- Becoming over-sophisticated – for example, by trying to provide excessively detailed analysis or automating procedures better left manual.
- Allowing one enthusiastic employee or volunteer to set up a system that only he or she can understand.

Which package?

It is often the case that a package that lends itself to a project-based system would be most useful, as that reflects the structure (and funding pattern) of many voluntary organisations.

There is a trade-off in choice of package between cost, ease of use and the range and sophistication of features that are offered. Make sure you evaluate any proposed solution to make sure it meets your needs. Talk to other charities similar to you and see what they use to get an idea of what might work for you. Choose a supplier with care – ideally based on good references from your contacts. Try and see if you can pilot the product before you buy it, to make sure it meets your key requirements. Talk to your accountants to get their views on the proposed solution.

How to set up?

In the computer package, income and expenditure headings will be represented by codes (a chart of accounts) that will enable you to analyse income and expenditure.

This needs careful thought, as no two charts of accounts will be the same, but a few general tips may help:

- Work backwards from the reports you want to produce to determine the most convenient structure and sequence of accounts.
- Use different levels of analysis as appropriate, perhaps using

a separate code for each individual's training costs, but one code for, say, postage.

- Leave generous gaps between codes to allow for new developments.

Who needs training?

Almost everyone in the organisation, and perhaps a few people outside, should be made aware of the new system. Those with the main training needs will be the people who prepare information for inputting – for example, whoever looks after the petty cash – or who receive output information: for example, the members of the committee who read the final reports.

Checklist – what have we learnt?

Answer the following questions before checking with the answers in the text.

1. List the key decisions that have to take place in budget planning.
2. Describe the differences between a fixed and flexible budget.
3. What is the purpose of preparing a cash budget.
4. How does variance analysis work.
5. List the key action points when planning to computerise the accounts.

Action points for your organisation

Audit your organisation to see if it has:

- ✓ A budget manual.
- ✓ A cash budget.
- ✓ A flexible budgeting system, particularly for budgetary control reports.
- ✓ Appropriate forecasting techniques.
- ✓ An IT strategy.

Giltim Union – A comprehensive examination of a budgeting system

This case study provides a comprehensive examination of a budgeting system.

Specifically, it allows the reader to:

- Evaluate the Giltim budget reporting system in terms of design, speed, frequency, clarity, and overall effectiveness for region, division and head office.
- Criticise the design of the report.
- Establish how well the budget system motivates regional secretaries to achieve union objectives.
- Consider how senior management could make the system more effective.

Top management approach to reporting

The general secretary and controller of Giltim insisted upon a rapid and efficient system of reporting monthly operations. They believe in up-to-date reports to enable timely action by head office, division and regional secretaries. However, they believe that regional secretaries should not wait until the month-end to deal with critical problems, but should deal with them on a daily basis.

Regional reports were reviewed on an 'exception' basis, comparing actual performance against budget. This was felt to be good for morale, and regional secretaries were expected to explain over-spending but not under-spending.

Monthly flash reports

On the third business day after the month end, each region faxed key figures for income, gross surplus and net surplus to division and head office, together with the variances from budget. A summary of these figures was studied the next day by senior management, which was concerned about critical variances.

Monthly detailed reports

On the eighth working day the regional operating summary and supporting reports were due at divisional head office. These were consolidated to show the results by region and division, then distributed the next day to senior management.

In addition, at the beginning of each month regional secretaries were expected to submit current reforecasts of anticipated performance for the month and year-end. Such re-forecasts enabled head office to shape financial plans and to get regional secretaries to look at their programmes on a yearly as well as a day-to-day basis.

Dealing with regional problems

When a potential problem became apparent, daily reports on it were required for the division and head office. A specialist team was sometimes sent to the region concerned to make recommendations. It was up to the regional secretary to accept or reject these; but it was generally expected that they would accept such 'advice' gracefully.

Income decline

If a decline in income became evident early in the year, and the regional secretary could convince senior management that the change was permanent, the regional budget could be revised to reflect the new circumstances. But if income fell below the predicted level towards the year end, no revision was allowed.

Regional secretaries were expected to go back over the budget with their staff to see where cost reductions could be made that would do the least harm. Specifically, they were expected to consider what could be either eliminated or postponed until next year.

Branch and region coordination

Whenever problems arose between regions and branches, local managers were expected to solve the problems themselves. Members' needs always came first.

However, if the local programme involved a major regional expense out of line with the budget, this was decided upon by division or head office.

Motivation of regional secretaries

Regional secretaries – and indeed, all of their staff – were motivated to meet surplus targets through promotion and pressures from division and head office. In addition, each month the regions were ranked competitively for recruitment efficiency, and the results were published widely throughout the union. Inter-region competitions, with prizes, were also conducted for special cost reduction programmes, improvements in methods etc. Regions were encouraged to stress quality and delivery to meet competitive pressures. All regional workers knew that, to survive in the competitive market, Giltim had to produce high-quality services in time and at reasonable cost.

Conclusions

Regional secretaries and other staff were not particularly happy under the system, but they worked hard to achieve targets and were generally successful, despite changes in the market conditions.

Schedule of monthly regional report:

- *Regional operating summary.* Income, costs, other income and expense. Actual against budget for the month and year to date. Percentage analysis on sales and assets employed.
- *Income analysis.* Income by membership bands. Actual, budget and variance analysis for the month and year to date.
- *Regional variance.* Cost of material, labour and variable expense. Actual budget and variance analysis.
- *Recruitment and sales.*
- *Regional fixed expense.* Regional expense other than variable and special expense. Actual, budget and variance analysis.
- *Special costs and surplus.* Special items under the control of the regional secretary, including sale of scrap, methods improvement, standard revisions, cost reduction programmes etc. Actual, budget and variance analysis.
- *Regional investment.* Stock, capital projects, debtors included in computation of assets employed by the region. Actual, budget, variance and ageing analysis.

Evaluation of reporting system

Design. Reports include actual and target data. Head office requires re-forecasting of activity that deviates from budget. Highlight on excess spending over budget, but no importance attached to under-spending. Concentrates on problem areas with special reports. Report sample is badly designed.

- *Speed*. Flash reporting in three days and full reporting to head office in eight days provides timely data for management. Probably achieved by cut-off of activities before the month end and efficient data processing.
- *Frequency*. Excellent: monthly data on regular operations, weekly or daily for critical problems.
- *Clarity*. Poor layout and lack of graphical presentation.
- *Effectiveness*. Highly effective for head office control of activity against budget. Provides control data to focus manager on target achievement and critical problems. Probably over-emphasises short-term meeting of the budget at the expense of long-term performance.

Performance of region and design of report

Figure 3.9 Giltim Union, No.1 Region Operating Statement, March

	This month Actual £	Last month Budget £	This month Actual £	Last year Actual £
Recruitment Income	170,168	294,325	162,271	289,979
Other Income	47,132	16,000	37,420	13,111
Total Income	217,300	310,325	199,691	303,090
Variable Costs	142,217	187,500	137,821	192,175
Gross Margin	75,083	122,825	61,870	110,915
Fixed Costs	41,211	36,400	38,174	41,118
Operating Income	33,872	86,425	23,696	69,798
Operating Income as % of gross income	15.59%	27.85%	11.87%	23.03%
Special costs (surplus):				
Method Improvements	−17,426	−21,300	−28,322	−12,174
Standard revisions	24,174	9,400	7,416	6,811
Price variances	−12,111	−6,000	3,567	4,667
Miscellaneous	−8,126	−6,000	−30,100	−22,179
TOTAL	−13,490	−23,900	−47,438	−22,875
Region surplus	47,362	110,325	71,134	92,672
Assets employed	1,816,411	1,874,426	1,742,112	1,052,112
% Return	2.61%	5.89%	4.08%	8.81%

Source: School of Social Entrepreneurs

It was difficult to evaluate the performance of Region No 1 from this report (figure 3.9) as 'year to date' figures were not provided. However, evaluation of March's performance raised many questions that need investigation and must be answered before meaningful conclusion and effective action can be taken:

- Recruitment income is seriously below target: is this a national trend or a regional failure?
- Variable cost of recruitment and sales controlled: is this due to office efficiency?
- Fixed costs seriously above target: why?
- Operating income well below target both in amount and percentage: is this due to failure of income?
- Special costs and surpluses generally consistent with targets, but why did regional secretary fail to cut costs to make up for the lack of activity?
- Region income well below target and return on assets employed unacceptable.

The following improvements are suggested in the design of the report:

- Eliminate 'previous month' and 'last year' columns, since the budget is the real target.
- Show only actual data for the month and the year to date with variance from the budget (not the budget itself).
- Eliminate all data below £1,000 to reduce the digits to significant items only; reports should not be too dense with figures.
- Design each report page as a complete entity supported by detail on subsequent sheets.
- Design report with graphics sections to emphasise signals.

Motivation of managers

1. System provides highly centralised control by head office and is probably defensive.
2. Extensive interaction in setting the targets probably conditions managers to accept them. Personal contact with head office staff and visit by controller most helpful.
3. Unreasonable to expect regional secretaries to meet surplus budget if recruitment falls off, but quite possible for them to feel bound to do so and to believe that they can and do achieve budget!
4. Regional secretaries probably under-spend on maintenance, research, training etc. in the early months of the year until income levels indicate that they can 'afford' to spend up to the budget cost levels.

5. Regional secretaries motivated to achieve target by:
   - Budget preparation process.
   - Senior management interest in and follow-up of reporting.
   - Salaries and bonuses.
   - Competition between regions.
   - Staff assistance and daily reports on critical problems.
   - Requirements to continually re-forecast any expected performance below target.
   - Budget effect on personal promotion in the Union.
6. Tendency to achieve short-term targets with some loss of long-term potential. However, this loss may not be significant.
7. Long-term planning retained by head office and divisional management (the latter is fairly powerless). Little motivation to think beyond current year at region level. Poor development of regional secretary's potential.
8. Fairly dynamic environment created by the constructive friction between region, head office and division.
9. May achieve a lower level of long-term performance, but all staff are not merely cost orientated but out-turn orientated too.
10. System meets senior management objective of surplus now. Puts surplus responsibility close to operations that achieve surplus. Related to the specific industry sector features of delivery, quality and efficient cost control.

Changes recommended

1. Consider the technical, human and organisational problems that any change would have to overcome. Managers may prefer 'the devil they know', and may therefore be reluctant to accept any new system.
2. Consider all the alternatives and their implications:
   - Make division out-turn orientated: that is, positively seeking opportunities to generate income as a contribution to costs (regions become only cost orientated).
   - All-budget revision when income falls off (managers more motivated to justify revisions than to achieve out-turn budgets).
3. Proposals:
   - Try to assign income and surplus responsibility to one manager in one centre.
   - If this is not possible, introduce some flexibility in

budget revision when income falls off substantially.

- Expand budget system for a three-year horizon. Plan every year for three years ahead. Let the annual budget targets be developed from the first year of plan.
- Include all managers in short- and long-term planning process.
- Introduce a training and development programme for managers to give them an understanding of long-term and short-term planning.
- Discourage the idea that meeting the budget is the same as doing the management job!

Learning points

- Budget reports should be available three to eight days after the month end.
- Achieve fast reporting, day early cut-off and efficient use of IT.
- Design reports for use by managers, not accountants: simple, graphic, exciting.
- Signal the key factors, do not give the complete detail.
- Design reports for local as well as top management.
- Recognise that manager motivation is not automatically achieved by participation, but is a complex phenomenon resulting from the total system.
- Managers may sometimes not be rationally responsible, but may be convinced that they are, and act accordingly. Behaviour is not completely rational in logical or economic terms; emotional needs.
- To modify the budget system and motivate the managers is a complex problem.
- They may not work as effectively under a new and 'better' system.
- Set surplus centres as close to operations (the 'front line') as practicable, to make managers not merely cost orientated but also surplus orientated.
- Head office 'advice' may really be orders.
- Region 'agreement' may really be imposed by head office.
- Technical problems with the budget are fairly easy to solve, but the human problems are not.
- The involvement of senior management in the budget process is vital if it is to motivate managers.
- A three-year horizon involving all managers is more useful than mere budgetary control each year. This

provides the underlying data for the annual and monthly budget targets.
- Design the budget system with reference to senior management objectives, industry sector key factors and the organisational structure of the union.
- Measure the effectiveness of the budget system by what the managers do, not by what they say.
- Review and redesign budget reports periodically to meet changing needs.
- Recognise that reports for head office may not necessarily meet local management needs; thus leading to two (or more) reporting systems, formal and informal.

Giltim Union: Revised Regional Operating Summary – March

	This Month		Year to date	
		(Under)/Over		(Under)/Over
	Actual	Budget	Actual	Budget
	£'000	£'000	£'000	£'000
Recruitment Income	170	(124)	847	(122)
Other Income	47	31	84	56
Total Income	217	(93)	763	(66)
% Gain/ (loss)	-	(30.0%)	-	(7.9%)
Variable costs of recruitment & sales	142	(45)	384	(64)
Gross margin	75	(48)	379	(2)
% Income	34.6%	(5.1%)	49.6%	3.6%
Fixed costs	41	5	211	10
Operating income	34	(53)	168	(12)
% Income	15.7%	(12.4%)	22.0%	
Special costs (surplus)	(13)	(11)	12	11
Regional surplus	47	(64)	156	(1)
% Income	21.7%	(13.8%)	20.4%	
Assets employed	1,816	(58)	1,816	(58)
% Return	2.6%	(3.3%)	8.6%	8.4%

Source: School of Social Entrepreneurs

The budgeting process

This list of key questions should be reviewed by the chief finance officer or other person responsi-ble for organising the budget and compiling the information. It could also be reviewed by the board finance committee to establish whether all the appropriate steps in the process have been taken.

1. *Why is a budget useful?*
   - It outlines in financial terms the goals and policies approved by the board.

- It is a method of monitoring adherence to, and deviations from, plans throughout the year.
- Its preparation causes the organisation to focus on planning, evaluation of programmes, and accomplishment of its mission.

2. *Is the budgeting process properly timed?*
   - Can the proposed staff or project changes realistically be implemented before the financial year end?
   - Is board membership scheduled to change prior to budget approval? (Avoid making a new board responsible for a budget they didn't approve.)
   - If the budget is approved by members, when is the annual meeting?
   - Must major funding requests be submitted in advance of approval of the overall budget? If so, consider the need for a two or three-year plan.

3. *What type of budget is appropriate for this organisation?*
   - Is a zero-based budget needed for critical evaluation of priorities to force a serious cutback in the level of expenses?
   - Are existing programmes examined as closely as proposed projects?
   - Will a functional or line-item budget allow for proper review of programme goals?
   - Is the budget based on existing operations, with incremental increases or decreases for economic conditions?

4. *Who prepares the budget?*
   - Is a budget committee needed?
   - Would a budget committee made up of accounting department staff, board members and outside advisers be effective?
   - If each department does the initial preparation, are standard formats and instructions distributed to ensure consistency?
   - Is the final budget comprehensive, including restricted funds, endowments, capital improvements and all financial aspects?

5. *What are the stages in budget preparation?*
   - Develop goals and objectives for a three to five-year period first (long-range plan, dreams).

- Quantify long-range goals, such as raising an endowment, financing new facilities or increasing staff.
- Evaluate last year's results:
  i. Were objectives achieved?
  ii. If not, were they unreasonable?
  iii. What caused variances? Were mid-year revisions appropriate?
  iv. What changes were indicated by ratio analysis?
- Establish objectives for the coming year.
- Prepare programme justification.
- Prepare estimates of income and expenses of programmes.
- Compile, evaluate and balance the results.
- The budget should be approved first by the staff, then by the board (with intervening stages as the nature of the organisation dictates).
- Amend the budget when the monitoring process shows a need for change.

6. *Evaluate programmes and services rendered*
   - Who are the stakeholders?
   - Is the organisation reaching them?
   - Should promotion be budgeted?
   - Is the cost per person too high?
   - Is a competing organisation providing the same service?

7. *Evaluate the pricing of services*
   - Should changes be made? Price increases or decreases? (NB there are of course more factors to be considered in altering prices than purely cost considerations.)
   - Would audience/membership etc. increase with a decrease in prices, resulting in more revenue?
   - Are funding sources available to cover free or reduced-cost services?

8. *Evaluate fundraising activities*
   - Can board members and other volunteers devote sufficient time to help the organisation reach its fundraising goals? If not, should consultants or new staff be hired?
   - Is an annual special giving campaign necessary in addition to the membership campaign? Would it drain the membership?
   - Can project sponsors or co-sponsors be found?
   - Should a planned giving programme be established?

9. **Evaluate expenses**
   - Could alternative approaches improve efficiency and thus reduce costs?
   - Is the use of volunteers effective?
   - Would 'investing' in a paid development director or volunteer coordinator more than pay for itself?
   - Are computers used effectively?
     i. To save money, are cheaper but time-consuming or inadequate programmes being used?
     ii. Would networking, email or a website pay for themselves through savings in time and mailings?
   - Are fixed and variable costs segregated? If so, are they properly allocated to programmes?
   - Are changes in salary level factored in to benefit costs?

10. **Consider outside forces**
    - Is funding likely to be cut owing to the depressed state of the economy?
    - Has there been a shift in population? Have local major employers closed down? Are standards in the profession changing?
    - Are accreditation or grant requirements changing?

11. **Before final approval, consider these issues**
    - Is there any doubt about the reliability of projections?
    - Do sufficient cash reserves exist to cover shortfalls?
    - Re-evaluate policy goals if cuts have to be made.
    - Could projects be carried out in cooperation with, or by, another organisation?
    - Would charts or graphs illustrate trends and make decisions clearer?

12. **Prepare supplementary budgets to implement the overall budget**
    - Cash flow projections.
    - Investment objectives.
    - Capital expenditure timing.
    - Restricted fund budgets.

13. **Devise a follow-up system for monitoring the budget**
    - Use timely financial reports to compare actual expenses and income with those budgeted.
    - Revise budget to reflect recurring changes during the year. (With acknowledgement to Jody Blazek.)

Exercises

Budgetary control. Fixed v Flexible. A worked example:

A disabled person's charity has a trading subsidiary, which is a wood workshop. The workshop makes children's rocking horses for local authority children and foster homes at a set price. Budgeted results and actual results are shown for May 20X1.

	Budget £	Actual results £	Variance £
Rocking horses made	100	150	50
Income(a)	10,000	15,000	5,000
Expenditure:			
Materials	3,000	4,250	(1,250)
Wages	2,000	2,250	(250)
Maintenance	500	700	(200)
Depreciation	1,000	1,100	(100)
Rent and rates	750	800	(50)
Other costs	1,800	2,500	(700)
Total costs (b)	9,050	11,600	(2550)
Surplus (deficit) a-b	950	3,400	2,450

Notes

1. In this example, the variances are meaningless for the purposes of control. Costs were higher than budget because there were 50 per cent more rocking horses made. The variable costs would be expected to increase above the budgeted costs. There is no information to show whether control action is required for any aspects of income or expenditure.
2. For control purposes, we need to know:
    a) Whether actual costs were higher than they should have been to produce 150 rocking horses.
    b) Whether actual income was satisfactory from the sale of 150 rocking horses.
    c) Whether the number of rocking horses made and supplied has varied from the budget in a good or bad way.

The correct approach to budgetary control is to:
1. identify fixed and variable costs
2. produce a flexible budget.

In our example we have the following estimates of cost behaviour:

a) materials, wages and maintenance costs are variable
b) rent, rates and depreciation are fixed costs
c) other costs consist of fixed costs of £800 plus a variable cost of £10 per rocking horse made and distributed to the local authorities.

The budgetary control (variance) analysis should be:

	Fixed Budget(a)	Flexible Budget(b)	Actual (c)	Variance (b) – (c)
	£	£	£	£
Rocking horses made	100	150	150	
Income	10,000	15,000	15,000	0
Expenditure:				
Variable				
Materials	3,000	4,500	4,250	250
Wages	2,000	3,000	2,250	750
Maintenance	500	750	700	50
Semi-variable costs:				
Other costs	1,800	2,300	2,500	(200)
Fixed costs				
Depreciation	1000	1000	1100	(100)
Rent and rates	750	750	800	(50)
Total costs	9,0501	12,300	11,600	700
Surplus	950	2700	3,400	700

Discussion.

1. In producing and distributing 150 rocking horses, the expected surplus should be the flexible budget surplus of £2,700 rather than the fixed budget surplus of £950. Instead the actual surplus was £3,400, £700 more than expected. The reason for this improvement is that costs are lower than expected as the projected income on 150 horses was exactly as expected.

2. Another reason for the improvement was that the local authorities took all the produced rocking horses. As the cost of producing each unit was less than the price paid by the local authority a surplus (contribution) was made on each rocking horse. What would have happened if the local authority had not taken and paid for the additional rocking horses?

3. Understanding costs and in particular the difference between fixed, variable and semi-variable is vitally important in understanding finance, and in particular budgetary control reports. (Costing is discussed in chapter 5.) Issues requiring further investigation are:

   a) The wages did not rise in exact proportion (controllable variance) and are £750 less.
   b) The other variable cost element (controllable variance) is over by £200.

4. The fixed costs are non-controllable and do not require any more attention from the manager's perspective

---

Exercise 3.1

ASH Hospice has devolved a number of service functions into business units and treats them like separate organisations. One unit is 'Medical and Surgery Supplies' which supplies products to the hospice wards. The unit uses the 'just in time method' so no stocks are held, as deliveries from the local hospital are made each day. The unit pays £20 for each pack of raw materials supplied, which it then assembles.

The unit has a budgetary control system, which is based upon fixed budgets; i.e. no adjustment is made for changes in the volume of supplies required. You have recently been appointed as the finance director. You note that actual monthly output is frequently very different from the budgeted output. You are concerned to find that the hospice management team pays little attention to the variances contained in the monthly budgetary report, as they say 'it is now a separate business' and we are only concerned with the 'bottom line'.

The budgetary control report for May 2000 is set out below. You have identified that those items, which are marked with V, are variable and change directly with output.

You therefore decide to redraft the May 2000 budget report replacing the original fixed budget with a flexible budget. You also compile a report to the management team, which sets out the problems with the original budget format and explains how flexible budgeting could improve the monthly budget report.

Item	Fixed budget		Actual	Variances
	£		£	£
Quantity supplied (packs)	1,000		1,150	150
Revenue	100,000	V	120,750	20,750
Costs:				
Supplies	20,000	V	23,000	(3,000)
Wages and salaries:				
Packing staff	20,000	V	24,150	(4,150)
Maintenance	2,000		1,950	50
Supervision	3,000		2,800	200
Management and administration	4,500		4,650	(150)
Total	29,500		33,550	(4,050)
Packaging function:				
Cleaning equipment	1,000	V	1,035	(35)
Sterilising equipment	500	V	460	40
Bagging equipment	250		275	(25)
Total	1750		1770	(20)
Expenses:				
Production	1,250	V	1,495	(245)
Maintenance	1,500		1,550	(50)
Management and administration	2,300		2,890	(590)
Buildings	850		720	130
Total	5900		6,655	(755)
Depreciation:				
Cleaning equipment	400	V	460	(60)
Sterilising equipment	1,500	V	1,725	(225)
Bagging equipment	2,500		2,500	0
Maintenance equipment	1,300		1,300	0
Office equipment and furniture	950		950	0
Total	6,650		6,935	(285)
Total cost	63,800		71,910	(8,110)
Surplus (deficit)	36,200		48,840	12,640

Answer to Exercise 3.1

Medical Supplies Unit – Revised budget report for month of May 2000

Item	Flexible budget	Actual	Variance
	£	£	£
Quantity supplied (packs)	1,150	1,150	0
Revenue	115,000	120,750	5,750
Variable costs:			
Supplies	23,000	23,000	0
Packing staff	23,000	24,150	(1,150)
Cleaning equipment	1,150	1,035	115
Sterilising equipment	575	460	115
Production	1,438	1,495	(57)
Depreciation:			
Cleaning equipment	460	460	0
Sterilising equipment	1,725	1,725	0
Total variable costs	51,348	52,325	(977)
Contribution	63,652	68,425	4,773
Fixed costs:			
Maintenance salaries	2,000	1,950	50
Supervision salaries	3,000	2,800	200
Management and admin			
Salaries	4,500	4,650	(150)
Bagging equipment	250	275	(25)
Maintenance	1,500	1,550	(50)
Management and administration	2,300	2,890	(590)
Buildings	850	720	130
Depreciation:			
Bagging equipment	2,500	2,500	0
Maintenance equipment	1,300	1,300	0
Office equipment and			
furniture	950	950	0
Total fixed costs	19,150	19,585	(435)
Surplus (deficit)	44,502	48,840	4,338

Memorandum

To: Management Team

From: Finance Director

Date: 8 June 2006

Reference: Monthly Budgetary Control Reports.

Medical and Surgery Supplies budgetary control reports compare the actual revenue and costs with a fixed budget, i.e. a budget which does not take into account the affect that changes in output volume have on costs.

This causes two particular problems:

1. The variances for those costs which are variable, are misleading. For instance, the packing staff wages show an adverse variance of £4,150 for May 2000, but as output was 15 per cent higher than budget there is every likelihood that £3,000 of the variance is simply due to more hours being worked to obtain the higher output.

2. The effect of volume changes on surplus is hidden as variable costs are not grouped together, but are included under their particular expense groupings. This means it is difficult to identify the contribution made, or lost, by increases or decreases in the number of supplies made.

The solution to these two problems is to adopt a marginal costing format and flexible budgeting.

A marginal costing format will group the variable costs together and subtract them from the revenue to obtain the contribution for the month. The fixed costs can then be subtracted from the contribution to obtain the surplus. This approach will clearly identify the costs which can be controlled by the medical supplies manager i.e. the variable costs, such as the packing staff wages and those which cannot be changed in the short-term, i.e. the fixed costs, such as management salaries. This should mean that the manager can concentrate upon the costs they can do something about, rather than being distracted by unavoidable fixed costs.

A flexible budget will adjust the budget for revenue, variable costs and the contribution to take into account the volume of output. As a consequence, the variances which are shown on the budget report will be due to price or efficiency deviations and not caused by volume. This will mean that the manager will be able to concentrate upon dealing with inefficiencies, as the costs of these will be highlighted, instead of being masked by volume changes. For instance, the £3,000 adverse variance for supplies will disappear but there will still be a £1,150 adverse variance on packing staff wages to explain.

Exercise 3.2 – A budgetary control problem

St Wilfreds' provides a night shelter and day advice centre for the homeless people. The budget has been prepared on providing 4,500 free meals every week. Although meals are free, each is recorded with a ticket, taken so the organisation can show how many people they are helping. The budget calculations and budgetary control report for week 17 is being reviewed by the warden and finance officer.

Expenditure	Per Meal	Fixed	Variable	Total	Actual	Variance
Provisions	50p	0	2,250	2250	2200	50
Labour	20p	240	900	1140	1180	(40)
Electricity	4p	0	180	180	175	5
Equipment rental	-	500	0	500	500	0
Maintenance	1p	0	45	45	43	2
Management	-	300	0	300	300	0
		1040	3375	4415	4398	17

The report shows that the organisation is better off by £17. Closer scrutiny of the individual variances shows that labour costs were considerably higher than expected but this has been outweighed by a lower than expected cost for provisions.

As the finance officer re-work the budget and report your findings if only 4,000 meals were consumed that week.

Answer to Exercise 3.2

Expenditure	Per meal	Fixed	Variable	total	actual	Variance
Provisions	50p	0	2000	2000	2200	(200)
Labour	20p	240	800	1040	1180	(140)
Electricity	4p	0	160	160	175	(15)
Equipment rental	-	500	0	500	500	0
Maintenance	1p	0	40	40	43	(3)
Management	-	300	0	300	300	0
		1040	3000	4040	4398	(358)

It now becomes clear that St Wilfreds' is actually £358 worse off than it should be at that level of activity. There are no favourable variances and the cost of provisions is actually £200 higher than it should have been for 4,000 meals. You must compare like with like to show the true performance.

4 Resource management

4.1 Maximising resources

A voluntary organisation's resources, or assets, are best managed from the perspective of a going concern: that is, without assuming any limit on the organisation's existence. Although the finance officer will strive to get the best return on invested assets, he or she must be sure that the organisation has sufficient liquid assets available to finance current operations. The goal, therefore, is to maintain the optimum balance between available assets and invested, or growing, assets. A going concern operates in a financially solvent fashion. Solvency in this context means the ability to pay the organisation's debts in a timely manner or to meet its financial responsibilities.

The goal, therefore, is to maintain the optimum balance between available assets and invested, or growing, assets.

This chapter will consider how a voluntary organisation's resources flow and interact, and examines tools for managing that all-important resource: cash. Issues to consider when accepting and protecting restricted and endowed funds are explored, reserves policy along with formulation and types of borrowing.

For a voluntary organisation to be financially solvent and operate as a going concern, its managers must, after the budgets are developed, focus on two more objectives:

1. Smoothly financing current operations by making the most efficient use of current, or liquid, funds.
2. Maximising available and obtainable resources to enhance return on the resources or capital.

The task of accomplishing these objectives can be called either asset management or resource allocation.

Getting resources

To further examine the resource picture, the organisation's managers must consider the choices available for obtaining those resources. A voluntary organisation's funding comes from one or more of the following sources (or a mix of more than one source):

- General public
- Government
- Business
- Internally generated

There is a wealth of published information and advice about funding and income generation that cannot be summarised here. The intention of this section is to whet the finance officer's appetite by exploring, firstly at a strategic level, ways of maximising the use of resources that might be overlooked, and secondly, at an operational level, policies to maximise the working capital available. For further information please see the resources section at the end of the book.

4.2 Forming alliances

Strategic alliances may be formed for any number of reasons, not always financial.

Alliances between voluntary organisations can take a variety of forms: from networking groups to funding partnerships, from joint ventures on specific projects to full mergers. Mergers will almost certainly require the advice and permission of the Charity Commission; the others are examples of less formal collaboration. This section of the guide will look at both informal partnerships formed with a view to reducing costs, and at full mergers undertaken for more strategic reasons.

Consortium arrangements

Although a merged organisation may have greater purchasing power, and may therefore be able to secure price reductions on items ranging from insurance premiums to photocopying paper, there are other ways of achieving the same objective. For example, a number of organisations, including NCVO, have brokered deals on behalf of the sector with banks, insurance companies and other service providers so that their members can benefit.

Agency arrangements

These may be an option where a charity's operations have a considerable geographical spread, as it may be inefficient to run small and relatively expensive branches, or to have resources tied up, in an area where another charity or commercial operator is already well established. The charity may therefore like to consider appointing a separate organisation as its agent to carry out operations on its behalf.

The terms of such agency arrangements would need to be negotiated, but the commission or fee payable might be more attractive financially than continuing with the current situation.

Joint ventures

These can be established as a matter of contract between the parties, or by establishing a joint venture company in which the respective interests are reflected at board level. Agreements will typically regulate:

- The nature of the venture undertaken jointly.
- The respective contributions of each party.
- The financing of the venture.
- Matters relating to termination.
- Details of activities which can only be undertaken if jointly agreed.

One advantage of joint ventures is that they do not involve the sharing of liability that characterises a 'true' partnership. They can also contain arrangements for their orderly termination, either because a specific project, for which the joint venture was set up, has been accomplished, or in the event of one of the participants breaching its obligations.

Mutual support

These are arrangements where charities can see mutual benefit in collaborating but do not wish to set up a formal joint venture: for example, Age Concern and Help the Aged, charities that both pursue their own separate issues, also collaborate on research into matters of mutual concern.

Collobrative working

NCVO has established a collaborative working unit to support charities wishing to work more closely together but where merger is not appropriate. For more information visit the NCVO website at www.ncvo-vol.org.uk.

4.3 Charity mergers

Mergers are common in the commercial sector but have, until recently, been less so in the voluntary sector. A merger is the joining of two organisations to form one organisation. Reasons for voluntary organisations to merge include:

- Financial reasons.
- Operate more efficiently and provide more effective services.
- Avoid duplication.
- Avoid competition.
- Develop a unified voice.
- Improve image.

The Charity Commission supports charities merging and intends to publish guidance (check Charity Commission website), but it also reviews the register of charities to identify overlap and duplication. Sometimes funders encourage charities to merge, while changes in public support can also encourage charities to merge, as evidenced by the AIDS/HIV charities. Mergers are complex, and voluntary organisation mergers have more than just financial criteria to consider. While missions may seem the same, there can be complex delivery and cultural problems that can lead to mergers being called off, as for example, the homeless charities Shelter and Crisis and the public health charities RSH and RIPH. Moira Gutherie, author of *Mix, Match, Merge* (City University Business School, 2000) identifies the following six steps to merger:

1. Clarify the key issues, desired benefits and likely costs.
2. Initiate checks on partner organisation.
3. Each organisation separately assesses the opportunity presented by combining.
4. Each organisation agrees what needs to be done before combining and a merger steering group works out detailed recommendations on issues which need to be addressed prior to merger.
5. Legal merger takes effect.
6. Post merger integration starts.

David King (Honorary Treasurer of NCVO) was Director of Operations of Cancer Research UK, which to date has been the biggest charity merger. He identifies the following practical issues for a successful merger:

- Planning is the key element in any successful merger, which should include:
  - proper cost benefit analysis
  - proper merger plan before you start
- The vital role of the merger committee:
  - Membership should be limited in number
  - Committee should meet regularly
- All charity's stakeholders (including charity workers, volunteers) should be kept informed
- Merger should rationalise and justify the trustee board membership.

King also points out that charities can underestimate the management time needed for mergers and the costs involved, particularly:

- Consultants professional fees
- Due Diligence review
- Legal advice and additional audit work
- Staff costs and possible redundancy
- Property considerations
- Promotion of new branding

Merger is therefore an option not to be considered lightly. In addition it is not the only possible solution to an overcrowded charity sector. Cooperation and joint ventures should also be considered and can be less painful and cheaper alternatives.

> Merger is therefore an option not to be considered lightly.

4.4 Outsourcing

Although the concept of outsourcing has been around in the commercial sector for decades, it has only recently taken off in the charity sector. Outsourcing is a good way to maximise the use of your limited resources. Many charities are now buying in fully-managed services and processes from third parties as a strategic tool in order to concentrate on their core activities. Not only does this free up their staff's time and energy, but it adds value to the non-core activities, improving the way the charity operates.

The Charity Commission and sector leaders are recommending outsourcing and collaborative working as a significant method of decreasing administrative costs and working more efficiently. Outsourcing can vary from a small organisation outsourcing its entire back office to a larger charity outsourcing a specific process, such as its catering or payroll function.

So what should be outsourced?

- Functions which are common to most organisations irrespective of their individual focus e.g. cleaning services, book-keeping.
- Labour intensive services e.g. book-keeping, direct mailing.
- Areas requiring specialist skills e.g. accountancy, legal, graphic design.
- Fluctuating work patterns e.g. campaign administration, event administration.

One way to understand whether a process, function or department should be outsourced is to look at two aspects:

1. Strategic importance to the charity; and
2. Commonality of area.

If an item is of significant strategic importance and unique to the charity (i.e. its trustees) then it is very unlikely to be outsourced. However, as an area that is low in strategic importance and common or high in volume (i.e. accounts payable) then it is a candidate to be outsourced. The important aspect in this approach is to determine the strategic importance of an area. For example, everyone says that it is strategically important to pay suppliers, but is it? Do trustees really concern themselves about which supplier to use, the terms, how they are paid? When you start to ask these types of questions it is very rare for an accounts payable function to be strategically important to a charity.

The following illustrates a way of plotting the approach. If one draws a diagonal line from the upper left to lower right, anything on the left side could be potentially outsourced.

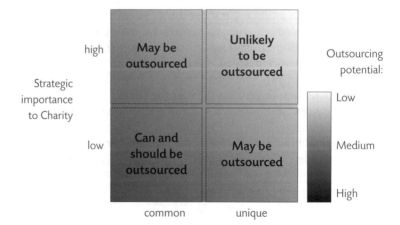

For many organisations, the delivery of its core services is the first priority and what the staff are trained to do. The support functions may be a distraction away from this – a use of resources that does not add value to the charity.

Benefits of outsourcing

According to voluntary organisations, the main benefits of outsourcing are:

- **Quality and experience**
  A specialist provider is likely to be able to provide a better service than if a function was performed in-house by a non-specialist, where it may not be the key task for that staff member.

- **Cost savings**
  If services are being shared with other charities costs will be saved through the more effective use of resources. It is highly likely that outsourcing the function will be cheaper than doing it inhouse. This means that more can be spent on fulfilling the aims of the charity.

- **Flexibility and change management**
  Charities are continuously changing in terms of size and structure. By outsourcing, volumes can fluctuate without causing the charity too much trouble / having to change staff numbers.

- **Time**
  Management's time is often wasted carrying out, or managing, administrative activities. This could be much better spent looking at the more strategic issues and driving the charity forwards.

- **Shared risk**
  Charities will not be tied down to using the same resources and as technology or situations change the charity need not invest heavily.

Though these are the common ones, there are intangible benefits as well which normally lead to enhancing the above tangible benefits.

Problems with outsourcing

Outsourcing has its problems. The most common ones that are experienced or perceived are:

- **Loss of control**
  This is often a perceived disadvantage to outsourcing. However with good contracts and communication processes in place this should not create a problem.

- **Inflexibility**
  Once a function has been outsourced, it may be very difficult/expensive to bring it back inhouse. However, if a watertight contract is put together at the outset and communication lines are good, this situation need not occur.

- **Reduced learning capacity due to a depleted skill base**
  The skill base of the organisation may drop if key functions are removed. This may mean that the organisation becomes more reliant on external providers. On the other hand, why should an organisation invest time and effort learning about new developments that are not core to the organisation? If the outsourcing relationship is set up properly, it is likely that the charity will be kept up to date with relevant skills and developments.

- **Staff morale**
  This is a problem if job losses occur due to outsourcing, or if people are not 'bought into' the idea of outsourcing. Effective communication can often help with this, as can treating an outsourcer as a partner not a supplier.

As with any business decision, it is important to weigh up the pros and the cons in relation to the way your organisation works. Outsourcing should certainly not be a flippant decision as it will affect the way your organisation works. Handled well, it is likely to improve the efficiency and effectiveness of the organisation.

Outsourcing can be an extremely effective tool to both lower costs and gain expertise not owned inhouse.

Successful outsourcing

Outsourcing can be an extremely effective tool to both lower costs and gain expertise not owned inhouse if the relationship is managed correctly.

Outsourcing failures are almost always due to poor planning, unclear expectations and lack of communication. If problems are not alleviated at the beginning of the process, they can be costly in terms of time and money to put right later.

It is essential for charities to assess the situation carefully prior to outsourcing. Charities should ask themselves if they actually do need a different service other than what is currently in place. If they do, they should decide how they will judge the alternatives. If not, they should look at how to improve the existing process.

They should look at internal utilisation of staff and other assets, and assess the impact of each. In assessing the impact, they should not only look at those directly associated with the main-stream task, but also supporting infrastructure and so on, such as office space; transport and expertise. Then they should determine the extent to which these resources are utilised, for example, is the charity's minibus used all of the time. If not, could it be hired out, or could the charity hire a minibus when required. Then deter-mine broad replacement costs and timescales, match these to those of potential suppliers and look for areas where they overlap.

When deciding to outsource, it is important to:

- Have clear objectives, and to ensure that the main parties involved are bought into these objectives.
- Have a clear understanding of the charity's objectives.
- To recognise that cost is only one aspect, and to take into account the effect that outsourcing will have on the charity.
- Clearly understand how the activity is carried out at present, get the relevant people involved, and communicate this to the potential providers.
- Ensure that the service provider:
  - Guarantees to meet specific service levels.
  - Has greater specialist knowledge than it would be possible to develop in-house.
  - Has experience within the sector.
  - Evaluates the service delivery against set objectives.
- Pay particular attention to staff morale and personnel issues.
- Involve senior executives.

If done correctly, outsourcing can deliver long-lasting and contin-uous benefits to a charity. Done poorly, or with misaligned objectives, it becomes a major problem that takes more time, energy and money to sort out.

A detailed checklist of the issues involved in outsourcing is on page 144.

4.5 Cash flow planning

Often the most important resource for a voluntary organisation – apart from its staff and volunteers – is its cash. To maintain solvency, the organisation must have sufficient liquid assets. Certain non-cash assets, such as donations receivable, will eventually become cash and are a part of the liquidity management process.

Such assets are commonly called 'current assets' on a financial statement and are defined as those which will turn into cash within a maximum of 12 months: monthly student tuition fees receivable, bookshop inventory etc.

To maintain solvency, the cash must flow smoothly and be readily available when it is time to pay creditors and salaries.

> To maintain solvency, the cash must flow smoothly and be readily available when it is time to pay creditors and salaries.

Accountants' cash flow statements

It is important to realise that the 'cash flow statement' which accompanies sets of company accounts is not the same as a cash flow forecast. The cash flow forecast is a budget prepared to show anticipated future cash in and cash out; usually on a monthly basis. The cash flow statement is a highly specialised, even arcane, document which reconciles the accruals method of accounting with the cash position, and is normally prepared by professional accountants with the final accounts. Essentially, it is intended to deal with the perennial question of users of accounts: "how come the income statement shows a surplus, but the overdraft has gone up?" It starts with the surplus or deficit shown by the income statement and reconciles the adjustments made by conventional accrual-based accounting, showing how eventually the figures agree with the year's movement in the bank balance.

Cyclical and seasonal fluctuations

The other side of cash flow planning addresses timing cycles and cash flow management generally. For most voluntary organisations, cash inflows and outflows fluctuate throughout the year, for many reasons other than accounting ones. For example:

- Churches typically receive generous donations during the Christmas season and much scantier ones during the summer vacation.
- Schools often require parents to pay a full year's tuition before the school year begins.
- Some membership organisations, such as unions, collect their members' dues once a year.
- Grants may be received quarterly, or contract money quarterly in arrears.

For the many voluntary organisations whose funding arrives at irregular intervals throughout the year, cash flow planning is essential. The fluctuations in cash probably cannot be entirely controlled.

However, it is important to appreciate that the organisation may be insolvent, at least technically, if there is insufficient cash to pay bills when due.

Cash management is about achieving maximum effectiveness of cash receipts and payments, thereby making sure that the money is working for the charity and returning a satisfactory yield, but is still available when needed.

Best practice guidelines suggest that voluntary organisations should:

- Collect money from debtors as quickly as possible, whilst exercising tact.
- Centralise payments, and streamline procedures for different functional areas, such as accounts payable and payroll, by using (for example) BACS payment methods.
- Develop close partnerships with customers and suppliers to negotiate mutually beneficial payment policies.
- Consolidate banking relationships by choosing banks that can offer customised cash management services: for example, handling appeal monies.
- Develop accurate cash flow forecasting techniques and models that are linked to budgets and strategic plans.
- Conduct regular cash management reviews to check controls and ensure appropriate use of current technology: for example, telephone/Internet banking;
- Ensure that investing, borrowing, payment and other financial transactions are properly authorised.

Much of the above may be self-evident, but it is surprising how often voluntary organisations ignore the fundamentals of good cash flow management.

Designing cash budgets

Once the annual operating and capital budgets are authorised, they can be converted into a cash budget to verify the availability of resources; in other words, to see if the organisation can finance the plan. The cash budget is prepared on a monthly basis to pinpoint possible cash shortfalls. The task is to summarise the projected sources and uses of cash for the coming year, according to the actual months of receipt and payment.

Especially close attention is needed if cash flows fluctuate widely, or if months of deficit funding are expected.

To do so, first estimate when collections of year-end receivables will occur. Next, calculate the normal time lag, if any, between the invoicing or billing for services or pledges (the point at which income is recognised in the accounts under the accrual system) and the actual arrival of the money in the bank.

Record the expected inflows of cash from revenue-producing activity on a monthly basis.

Correspondingly, chart the expected cash payments according to when the actual payment is to be made. The prediction should be based on past experience and an element of educated guess-work. Expected capital expenditures, sale of assets, borrowing, debt repayment and other financing transactions are then recorded by month.

In the light of any deficits revealed by the cash flow budget, consider whether there is a need to borrow or to redesign the entire budget. Monitoring the cash budget is a continuous process. Especially close attention is needed if cash flows fluctuate widely, or if months of deficit funding are expected. Although it is possible to perform this task monthly by hand, cash flow budgets produced on computer spreadsheets save countless calculations.

The model cash flow statements for a professional business association providing services to both corporate and individual members is shown as figures 4.1 and 4.2.

The first version of the cash flow produced a substantial deficit in the month of August.

The management of the professional business association has then reworked the cash flow to eliminate the deficit balance in August. This has been achieved by rescheduling the timing of membership fees, receipts from information services and publication sales. On the payments side, payments for marketing have been delayed till later in the year and payments for information services spread more evenly throughout the year. By this process, it has been possible to eliminate the deficit in August while at the same time maintaining both the total receipts and payments for the year the same as before, and presenting a healthier cash flow position.

Beyond cash flow imbalances

Ideally, a voluntary organisation always has cash in reserve for unforeseen circumstances. A new organisation in particular needs to budget for revenue surpluses in its early years until a sufficient level of cash is accumulated. To a young organisation struggling to meet its payroll, building a cash reserve may seem like a luxury it can ill-afford. Nevertheless, the financially prudent organisation

Figure 4.1 Cash flow projection for the year – version 1

	January	February	March	April	May	June	July	August	September	October	November	December	Total
RECEIPTS													
Corporate members fees	10,000	40,000	20,000	30,000	10,000	5,000	3,000	2,000	30,000	40,000	30,000	50,000	270,000
Individual members fees	3,000	10,000	8,000	12,000	6,000	2,000	1,000	800	1,200	5,000	11,000	30,000	90,000
Information services	14,000	14,000	12,000	12,000	12,000	10,000	10,000	8,000	16,000	14,000	14,000	14,000	150,000
Publication sales	20,000	20,000	20,000	20,000	20,000	10,000	10,000	10,000	25,000	25,000	25,000	25,000	230,000
Professional training	8,000	8,000	20,000	8,000	8,000	2,000	2,000	2,000	22,000	8,000	16,000	6,000	110,000
Annual meeting	10,000	5,000	5,000										20,000
Royalty income	0	6,000	0	8,000		20,000			8,000				42,000
Interest income	200	200	200	200	200								1,000
Total receipts	65,200	103,200	85,200	90,200	56,200	49,000	26,000	22,800	102,200	92,000	96,000	125,000	913,000
PAYMENTS													
Salaries & payroll taxes	30,000	30,000	30,000	30,000	30,000	30,000	30,000	30,000	30,000	30,000	30,000	30,000	360,000
Pension benefits	2,500	2,500	2,500	2,500	2,500	2,500	2,500	2,500	2,500	2,500	2,500	2,500	30,000
Professional fees	1,000	1,000	12,000	10,000	1,000	1,000	1,000	1,000	1,000	1,000	1,000	1,000	32,000
Supplies	2,200	2,200	2,200	2,200	2,200	2,200	2,200	2,200	2,200	2,200	2,200	2,200	26,400
Telephone	1,667	1,667	1,667	1,667	1,667	1,666	1,667	1,666	1,667	1,666	1,667	1,666	20,000
Postage & shipping	1,667	1,667	1,667	1,667	1,667	1,666	1,667	1,666	1,667	1,666	1,667	1,666	20,000
Building costs	2,000	2,000	12,000	2,000	2,000	2,000	2,000	2,000	2,000	3,000	4,000	3,000	38,000
Equipment repair & insurance	1,100	1,100	1,100	1,100	1,200	1,200	1,200	1,200	1,200	1,200	1,200	1,200	14,000
Printing & publications	12,000	8,000	12,000	9,000	12,000	9,000	11,000	9,000	20,000	9,000	10,000	16,000	137,000
Travel	1,000	1,000	6,000	1,000	3,000	3,000	1,000	1,000	3,000	3,000	3,000	4,000	30,000
Meetings & classes	500	500	18,000	500	2,500	500	0	1,000	2,000	2,000	1,500	3,000	32,000
Information services	4,000	15,000	15,000	9,000	5,000	4,000	4,000	4,000	5,000	5,000	5,000	5,000	80,000
Marketing	11,650	11,650										23,300	46,600
Purchase of equipment	10,000										7,400	10,000	27,400
Total Payments	81,284	78,284	114,134	70,634	64,734	58,732	58,234	57,232	72,234	62,232	71,134	104,532	893,400
Excess (deficit) of cash	(16,084)	24,916	(28,934)	19,566	(8,534)	(9,732)	(32,234)	(34,432)	29,966	29,768	24,866	20,468	19,600
Cash at beginning of month	60,000	43,916	68,832	39,898	59,464	50,930	41,198	8,964	(25,468)	4,498	34,266	59,132	60,000
Cash at end of month	43,916	68,832	39,898	59,464	50,930	41,198	8,964	(25,468)	4,498	34,266	59,132	79,600	79,600

Figure 4.2 Cash flow projection for the year – version 2

	January	February	March	April	May	June	July	August	September	October	November	December	Total
RECEIPTS													
Corporate members fees	10,000	40,000	20,000	30,000	10,000	5,000	3,000	17,000	15,000	40,000	30,000	50,000	270,000
Individual members fees	3,000	10,000	8,000	12,000	6,000	2,000	1,000	800	1,200	5,000	11,000	30,000	90,000
Information services	14,000	14,000	12,000	12,000	12,000	10,000	10,000	12,000	12,000	14,000	14,000	14,000	150,000
Publication sales	20,000	20,000	20,000	20,000	20,000	10,000	10,000	20,000	15,000	25,000	25,000	25,000	230,000
Professional training	8,000	8,000	20,000	8,000	8,000	2,000	2,000	2,000	22,000	8,000	16,000	6,000	110,000
Annual meeting	10,000	5,000	5,000										20,000
Royalty income	0	6,000	0	8,000		20,000			8,000				42,000
Interest income	200	200	200	200	200								1,000
Total receipts	65,200	103,200	85,200	90,200	56,200	49,000	26,000	51,800	73,200	92,000	96,000	125,000	913,000
PAYMENTS													
Salaries & payroll taxes	30,000	30,000	30,000	30,000	30,000	30,000	30,000	30,000	30,000	30,000	30,000	30,000	360,000
Pension benefits	2,500	2,500	2,500	2,500	2,500	2,500	2,500	2,500	2,500	2,500	2,500	2,500	30,000
Professional fees	1,000	1,000	12,000	10,000	1,000	1,000	1,000	1,000	1,000	1,000	1,000	1,000	32,000
Supplies	2,200	2,200	2,200	2,200	2,200	2,200	2,200	2,200	2,200	2,200	2,200	2,200	26,400
Telephone	1,667	1,667	1,667	1,667	1,667	1,666	1,667	1,666	1,667	1,666	1,667	1,666	20,000
Postage & shipping	1,667	1,667	1,667	1,667	1,667	1,666	1,667	1,666	1,667	1,666	1,667	1,666	20,000
Building costs	2,000	2,000	12,000	2,000	2,000	2,000	2,000	2,000	2,000	3,000	4,000	3,000	38,000
Equipment repair & insurance	1,100	1,100	1,100	1,100	1,200	1,200	1,200	1,200	1,200	1,200	1,200	1,200	14,000
Printing & publications	12,000	8,000	12,000	9,000	12,000	9,000	11,000	9,000	20,000	9,000	10,000	16,000	137,000
Travel	1,000	1,000	6,000	1,000	3,000	3,000	1,000	1,000	3,000	3,000	3,000	4,000	30,000
Meetings & classes	500	500	18,000	500	2,500	500	0	1,000	2,000	2,000	1,500	3,000	32,000
Information services	4,000	8,000	8,000	8,000	8,000	8,000	8,000	8,000	5,000	5,000	5,000	5,000	80,000
Marketing	10,000	10,000									13,300	13,300	46,600
Purchase of equipment										10,000	7,400	10,000	27,400
Total Payments	69,634	69,634	107,134	69,634	67,734	62,732	62,234	61,232	72,234	72,232	84,434	94,532	893,400
Excess (deficit) of cash	(4,434)	33,566	(21,934)	20,566	(11,534)	(13,732)	(36,234)	(9,432)	966	19,768	11,566	30,468	19,600
Cash at beginning of month	60,000	55,566	89,132	67,198	87,764	76,230	62,498	26,264	16,832	17,798	37,566	49,132	60,000
Cash at end of month	55,566	89,132	67,198	87,764	76,230	62,498	26,264	16,832	17,798	37,566	49,132	79,600	79,600

plans from the very start to build working capital reserves equivalent to several months of operating expenses.

Whenever cash flow budgets indicate excess cash reserves, plans for temporary investment are in order. As much money as possible should be kept in interest-bearing accounts in order to maximise yield. Once cash reserves exceed the current year's need, the opportunity for longer-term investment arises. This task of resource management requires complex decision making; ideally, by a finance committee with the assistance of professional investment managers. Investment policies must weigh the permissible level of risk to the organisation's resources against the expected return.

More money in the bank

The financially astute voluntary organisation will ensure that its cash balances work in its favour by keeping its money for as long as possible.

Whether the organisation is able to earn interest on the money, or to avoid paying interest on funds it must borrow, or on bills it pays late, money in the bank is obviously desirable. A voluntary organisation can also charge interest on late payment and offer discounts for early payments.

The membership renewal system should remind members promptly that it is time to send in their fees or donations.

The submission of quarterly cost reports for grants payable by instalments should never be late. The fundraisers will know the deadlines for submitting grant requests to potential funders well ahead of time. Unfortunately, there are many voluntary organisations with cash flow problems that are slow in sending the renewal notices or grant reports that would provide the funds to pay staff.

On the outgoing side, bills should be paid when the terms for purchase require it and not before. A regular cycle can be established – say the first and 15th day of the month – for bill payments. These set days are made known to the staff and creditors, so that all know when they will receive their money. Such a simple policy can save considerable effort and earn interest by keeping the money in the bank longer.

To borrow or not

When the cash flow budget indicates that a deficit in cash will occur during the year, a voluntary organisation faces a tough decision. Does the organisation attempt to borrow the funds, can it find new funding, or does it reduce projected payments?

The answer will of course depend on several factors. Is the deficit temporary? Will it reverse itself in a few months? For a new organisation, interim borrowing may not be an option. For a mature one that is, for example, expecting to refurbish old buildings, there may be alternatives. The decision must be based on the facts of the case.

Securing a loan requires good planning. When the need for short-term indebtedness is recognised as a part of the budgeting process, solutions can be found. The budget itself probably shows that the situation will reverse itself with money expected to be received later in the year. For an organisation in this situation, preparing a business plan in order to make a formal application to a bank is a useful exercise. If a bank cannot be persuaded to make a loan, the voluntary organisation goes back to the drawing board and revises its budgets and/or finds new funding sources.

A cash deficit created by proposed capital acquisitions may have a simpler solution, as the tangible nature of a capital asset makes it suitable as security for a loan. Therefore, it may be possible, even for a new organisation, to borrow money needed to equip the organisation.

Lenders expect to be able to get their security back if the organisation defaults on payments. However, lenders dislike foreclosing, particularly on a charity, because of the bad publicity they receive; therefore they will not rely solely on the security offered but will look to the longer-term cash flows.

4.6 Prudent investment planning

Once the voluntary organisation accumulates cash assets beyond its operating needs for the coming year, it can begin to develop permanent investment plans. In managing the organisation's investments, the trustees have a duty to maximise the value of the assets and therefore to obtain a good return. However, the trustees should not risk assets by investing in highly speculative ventures; they must balance risk against return.

The trustees must also balance the future needs of the voluntary organisation against current needs, so they should consider whether the maximisation of income for current consumption is in the best interest of future beneficiaries. Trustees need to balance long-term capital growth against short-term income generation. Capital growth should be, at the very least, sufficient for assets to maintain their value compared to inflation.

Investment management is discussed in more detail in Chapter 7. (Also see NCVO's *Good Investment Guide* – more details in further reading and resources, see page 307.)

4.7 Restricted funding

In the recent past, the funding environment of the voluntary sector has changed dramatically. Voluntary organisations are increasingly being funded to deliver specific outputs in return for grant funding, or more formal arrangements under contracts.

As a result, there has been a rapid increase in funding for the delivery of specific charitable programmes and a consequent decline in funding of a more general nature.

Over the last decade a 'contract culture' has grown up. Instead of receiving grants, a growing number of charities are entering into legally-binding agreements (contracts) with public bodies to provide services to the public on behalf of those bodies. A contract will specify the services to be provided by the charity and what the charity is to be paid for providing them. It will also include provisions, in greater or lesser detail, setting out the legal obligations that each of the parties accepts in order to fulfil the purposes of the contract.

On the positive side, a contract can establish a partnership between the charity and the public body and clarify their relationship by specifying in detail what is expected from each party. A contract can also offer a secure source of funding over the period it covers.

On the other hand, some charities feel that entering into contracts with public bodies would lead to the loss of their independence: their freedom to set their own policies and to decide, within the range of their charitable objects, what services to provide.

Charities must ensure that they take all their costs into account when pricing a service to be provided under contract on behalf of a public body. These costs will comprise direct costs, capital costs and indirect costs (or overheads). Chapter 5 (page 155) provides details on how projects should be fully costed and priced to prevent the organisation indirectly funding public services from unrestricted funds.

Restricted funding can be defined as funds which have donor-imposed restrictions or where the voluntary organisation raises funds for a specific appeal. The reasons for the growth in restricted project funding are many, but the general scarcity of funding means that charitable trusts, and other funders, are under increasing pressure to obtain maximum value and impact from the projects they fund. As a result, they are reluctant to provide core funds, for which outputs and impacts are much more difficult to quantify.

Restricted funding can be defined as funds which have donor-imposed restrictions or where the voluntary organisation raises funds for a specific appeal.

Perhaps the most important financial requirement relating to such income is the responsibility to isolate the money. Under trust law, the voluntary organisation owes a fiduciary duty to contributors and grantors to use funds for the purposes for which they are given. Accordingly, before accepting restricted funds, an organisation must have in place a mechanism for tracking the receipt of such funding and the expenditure that can be set off against it. The restrictions imposed can vary in their tightness. A wildlife conservation charity raising funds by mailshot may work under the very broad restriction that the funds collected 'are to help preserve wildlife'. At the other end of the spectrum, the funding could be restricted to saving a particular type of tree in a certain part of Africa because its wood is used for musical instruments and the supply is dwindling.

By accepting restricted funding, the trustees of the voluntary organisation have accepted the responsibility of ensuring that the restrictions are met. It is important that in their fundraising – for example, public appeals – voluntary organisations do not unintentionally create restricted funds by the way in which they advertise.

There are, however, some circumstances when a restriction can be removed or made less stringent: for example, where the objective for which the funds were originally raised is no longer relevant, or where the project has been completed or is deemed impossible to complete. In the first case, it will be necessary to contact the original donors or, if that is no longer possible, to obtain the permission of the Charity Commission.

Exit strategies

Since the majority of funding arrangements are uncertain and are limited to a three-year period at most, the voluntary organisation must ensure, well before the funding comes to an end, that it has strategies to cover the next phase.

If the project is to be continued, this next phase will usually involve finding other sources of income, either from another funder or by income generation. If the original objectives have been met, the closure of the project may involve financial liabilities for staff redundancy.

4.8 Endowments

There are two types of endowment fund:

1. Permanent endowment funds are donations that have been given to the voluntary organisation to be held as capital, with no power to convert the funds to income. These may be cash or other assets.
2. Expendable endowment funds are donations that have been given to a voluntary organisation to be held as capital, but where the trustees do have a discretionary power to use the funds as income.

An endowment gift is usually invested to produce income to fund a specific project – such as scholarships – or unspecified operational costs. Although endowment funding is a highly desirable resource, the terms of the endowment must be thoroughly discussed with the donors before the gift is accepted.

When is an organisation ready to seek endowments? Potential endowment funders must perceive it as sufficiently permanent or stable to survive for a long time; it is for this reason that universities, hospitals, and churches have traditionally attracted such funding.

The other important issue is the terms governing the voluntary organisation's use of the gift. If these are to meet the organisation's needs, the following must be agreed upon:

An endowment gift is usually invested to produce income to fund a specific project

- **Life span of endowment.** For how many years must the endowment remain restricted? Can the funds be used for another purpose in times of crisis? If so, what type of crisis? What happens to the endowment funds should the organisation cease to exist, or the charitable objective be met?
- **Definition of income.** Are realised gains treated as current income? Is the endowment principal – defined as its original sum – certain, or is it the original plus all appreciations less declines in underlying value?
- **Nature of investment.** Do the endowment creators wish the assets originally given to be retained? Can they be sold? Must they be sold in a particular fashion, or offered for sale to particular persons first? If sold for cash, is there a restraint on the way in which the cash can be reinvested?

It should be clear by now that endowment funding needs to be carefully considered, as it brings many onerous responsibilities.

4.9 Charity reserves

Charity reserves have been a controversial issue for some time. The media has criticised many large national charities for apparently accumulating large reserves while at the same time conducting additional fundraising appeals. Furthermore, many funders automatically look at the fund balances shown in annual accounts when deciding whether to approve applications for funding.

It is generally assumed that voluntary organisations should not hold on to charitable funds for long periods of time, since the organisation was granted those funds to provide services. This may well be true, but it is also necessary to consider the question of reserves from the point of view of resource management. From this point of view, the existence of reserves is a sign of good financial management. This view is reinforced by the Charity Commission Research Study on Charity Reserves, which also found that the majority of charities were under-reserved.

Any organisation requires a minimum level of reserves to fund working capital requirements, and/or contingencies identified at the planning stage as being necessary to safeguard the continuing activities of the organisation.

The existence of reserves is a sign of good financial management.

What are charity reserves?

The Charity Commission in its publication CC19 defines reserves as 'income that becomes available to the charity and is to be expended at the trustees' discretion in furtherance of any of the charity's objectives (sometimes referred to as 'general purpose' income), but which is not yet spent, committed or designated (i.e. is 'free')'. This excludes the following (as defined by CC19):

- Permanent endowment.
- Expendable endowment.
- Restricted funds.
- Designated funds.
- Income funds that could only be realised by disposing of fixed assets held for charity use.

The Charity Commission now takes the view that voluntary organisations should 'explain and justify' the level of reserves they hold. In order to meet this requirement, even the smallest of organisations that aspire to financial security must have a reserves policy.

Reserves policy

The policy should cover:

- The reasons why the charity needs reserves.
- The level (or range) of reserves the trustees believe the charity needs.
- What steps the charity is going to take to establish or maintain the reserves at the agreed level (or range).
- Arrangements for monitoring and reviewing the policy.

The essential steps in developing a reserves policy are as follows:

1. Review existing funds.
2. Analyse income streams.
3. Analyse expenditure and cash flows.
4. Analyse the need for reserves.
5. Calculate the reserves level.
6. Formulate reserves policy.
7. Presentation of reserves policy.

Assessment of reserve needs

The charity's reserves policy should be based on:

- Its forecast for levels of income in future years, taking into account the reliability of each source of income and the prospects for opening up new sources.
- Its forecast for expenditure in future years on the basis of planned activity.
- Its analysis of any future needs, opportunities, contingencies or risks, the effects of which are not likely to be able to be met out of income if and when they arise.
- Its assessment, on the best evidence available, of the likelihood of each of those needs etc. arising and the potential consequences for the charity of not being able to meet them.

Checklist – what have we learnt?

Answer the following questions before checking with the answers in the text:

1. Describe the various alliances voluntary organisation can form.
2. How is cash flow planning different from a cash budget?

3. What are the aims of a cash flow statement?
4. With good financial planning what will a voluntary organisation understand?
5. Describe the various reserves a charity can hold.

Action points for your organisation

Review your organisation to see if it:

✓ Has arrangements with other organisations.
✓ Outsources any activities.
✓ Prepares forecast cash flow statements.
✓ Has a financial plan, which shows how cash balances are created or what it does with excess cash, balances.
✓ Has recently reviewed its investment manager.
✓ Has an accounting system that can track restricted funds.
✓ Has fundraisers who are aware on how to word appeals so that they do not create restricted funds.
✓ Has a policy on how to apportion overhead costs and obtain full cost recovery.
✓ Has a reserves policy.

Case studies

1. The Women's Centre

This case study looks at the challenges faced by a voluntary organisation that has just lost its funding. It examines how the organisation can exploit its resources to ensure survival; the issues discussed are not exclusively financial ones.

The case study examines the following areas:

• Initial reaction.
• Longer-term response.
• The impact on the organisation.
• Determining factors.
• Lessons.
• Conclusions.

The Women's Centre was set up in an outer London borough by a group formed in 1993. Working as a collective, the centre provided a women-only space; ran activities such as health groups, support groups and adult education; provided drop-in and advice sessions; and campaigned on women's issues locally. In a borough that rejected the idea of a women's centre, they turned to a London-wide funding body for capital and revenue funding. This enabled them to open the centre three weeks before the funding body was abolished, funding was lost and the staff made redundant.

Applications for replacement funding to the local borough and the London Boroughs Grant Scheme were unsuccessful. By this time the centre was running on an entirely voluntary basis – the running costs were covered by the residue of the grant funding – but was exploring other sources of funding.

Initial reactions to loss of funding

Inevitably, the reactions of paid staff and the management committee differed from unpaid collective members: the livelihood of paid staff was under threat, whereas unpaid members often had other things to move on to.

For many voluntary organisations – and the Women's Centre is no exception – funding is a form of recognition; and so, when that funding was taken away, so was the recognition.

However, the fact that the centre had opened its building just before the loss of funding, seems to have lightened some of the gloom.

Longer-term responses

Although the loss of funding was in some sense an ending for the Women's Centre, the opening of its new building marked an important beginning. This gave the women considerable energy to face the future.

Although uncertainty about future funding made it difficult to plan, the clear priority was to get the new building used. It was therefore decided to staff the centre with a rota of volunteers, holding self-financing Workers' Education Association classes and renting out space to other organisations (such as the local Legal Resource Centre) for specific sessions.

Before the funding was cut, the Centre had invested in some useful equipment, including a camera, video equipment and a minibus; the minibus brought in some income from hire fees. It was also agreed to encourage the women using the centre to make a contribution by standing order and paying subscriptions for newsletters.

The collective also changed its method of operation. In the absence of a central decision-making body, and because of the difficulty of finding new women to join the group, the responsibility for specific tasks (such as newsletter production, dealing with correspondence, minibus bookings or garden maintenance) was taken on by volunteers identified from the mailing list.

The impact on the organisation

Loss of funding can have wide-ranging effects; at a personal level on individuals, and at an operational level on the work programme. It was a particularly difficult time for paid staff, who went through long periods of uncertainty and then, in some cases, had to face redundancy and unemployment.

Staff and others felt that the withdrawal of funding showed that their work was not valued. As a result, the centre lost some of its most active members, and the increase in workload and responsibilities this brought for the remaining members led to exhaustion. This temporary crisis was overcome by changes in the organisation's structure and the allocation of work.

It was not long before conflict broke out between management and staff about who held the power in the organisation. This power struggle was not new. In the past it had been papered over or ignored, but now, as the threat to the organisation and fears about its future raised the stress level, it came to seem more important.

At the operational level, the loss of funding caused the Centre to restrict the work it did; as is usual in these situations, outreach and development were the main casualties.

In addition to the effects of losing its paid staff, the Centre's ability to carry out its work was seriously hindered by the amount of time that had to be spent in fundraising, filling in grant appli-cations and lobbying potential funders.

One positive result was that members felt that the loss of paid staff had strengthened the collective. The disagreements between paid workers and members were now behind them; members had to have a genuine commitment to working for the Centre if they wanted it to survive. They had learned to cut out unnecessary areas of work and concentrate on the essential. The women felt more motivated because they felt that they had something to contribute.

Determining factors
The Centre was seen as the example of an ideology that was represented nowhere else in the area; this further increased its determination to survive.

Some lessons
Having one main funder. This made them feel insecure and severely limited their options. However, having more than one funder was considered to be too time-consuming; also, the interests of funders might have conflicted, causing problems for the organisation.

Ways of working. There had been a lack of urgency in what was done before funding was lost: applications should have been made sooner and there should have been more planning.

Dependence on paid workers. This had caused problems when funding ran out. The paid staff who left had a lot of valuable information in their heads, but they had not been properly debriefed; as a result, unpaid members lost the benefit of that information.

Some conclusions
The Women's Centre managed to survive, but not without difficulty. It achieved this by exploiting a number of assets:

- A clear and adaptable organisational structure.
- A supportive governing body.
- Clear aims and priorities.
- A long existence.
- Strength of members' commitment.
- Contacts and support within the community.
- Economic resources (such as skills, premises, equipment).
- Political resources (the support of powerful people and organisations).
- An understanding of the situation in which it found itself.
- An awareness of the options open to it.

Many of these assets are a source of competitive advantage, arising either from the voluntary organisation's internal strengths or its position within the sector (see Chapter 2, page 41).

One of the Women's Centre's strengths had been its ability to adapt to its new situation and develop a more appropriate structure. It managed to persuade a large number of women to work at the centre on a voluntary basis, perhaps because it is focused on its aims. It had strong links with the community and important material resources (including the building and the minibus); these tangible assets used to generate income. On the other hand, as a radical women's organisation it lacked political resources, and its limited knowledge of the situation it found itself in meant that its choices were restricted.
(With acknowledgement to Centre for Voluntary Organisation, LSE.)

2. BCD

This case study examines the familiar situation where a voluntary organisation has obtained funding for a project from a variety of sources, but the total funds are still insufficient. The organisation turned to commercial lenders for the remainder, but without success. Finally, the organisation approached the Local Investment Fund (LIF), a charity in its own right.
LIF provides:

- Loans to community enterprises that are unable to obtain all the funds they need from a bank.
- Help to community groups that are meeting local need by providing goods, services and jobs, and are aiming to be self-sufficient.
- Funding exclusively to non-profit organisations.
- Loans from £25,000 to £250,000 at near commercial rates.
- Loans that are only part of the total amount needed.

The case study provides a valuable insight into how a project is assessed and some of the concerns of a lender when evaluating a project for funding.

Background

BCD was set up in 1979 to alleviate poverty and advance education by supporting workers' cooperatives and small starter businesses, and by providing training courses for cooperatives and minority ethnic and other disadvantaged

groups. It is a company limited by guarantee, and
controlled by a voluntary management committee elected
annually by the membership, which is composed of representatives of the cooperative movement, the local
community and tenants. Any surplus goes to the improvement of BCD services and resources.

BCD's flagship project was the short-life rehabilitation
of over 10,000 square feet of retail and office space in Acer
Street, leased from the London Borough of Conifer.

BCD has a record of success in enabling women,
minority ethnic groups and refugees to gain a foothold in
the market, and in providing suitable facilities for small
voluntary sector and community groups. Its training
courses are targeted on existing co-operative businesses,
refugees and local people in need of business skills.

Working closely with other local agencies, BCD is now
taking advantage of the myriad opportunities brought
about through City Challenge, the European Regional
Development Fund (ERDF), the Single Regeneration
Budget and the local authority.

BCD's plans for rehabilitating Acer Street involved the
retention of existing businesses in the area, and the
opening of many new units for community business start-
ups and youth enterprise activity. These units will be let to
community organisations on flexible terms that take
account of the fact that many such groups do not have a
track record.

These measures are enabling BCD to bring about an
integrated range of new openings, and a coherent infrastructure in which Conifer's community-based business
and voluntary sector is set to flourish.

The funding proposition

The overall costs of the Acer Street refurbishment and lease
purchase are estimated at £837,500.

The project is being supported by ERDF (£212,500) and
City Challenge Gap Funding (£350,000). Commercial
finance of £175,000 is required in the development phase,
with a further £100,000 needed to purchase a 99-year
lease from the London Borough of Conifer at the end of
the refurbishment period. A total of £275,000 therefore
remains to be financed.

In 1995 BCD approached the Local Investment Fund
(LIF) for a £275,000 loan as part of the package of finance
required for the refurbishment of Acer Street.

The project met the criteria set by LIF for such projects; what remained to be decided was the amount of finance LIF would provide. Among the documents submitted to LIF was a rent budget, reproduced as Figure 4.3.

Project viability

LIF was particularly concerned about the assumption underlying the level of voids and common areas (that is, the periods between lettings and the common areas which are not lettable), which was that they would reduce from 70 per cent to 35 per cent in the year 1997 and then to 20 per cent for the remainder of the projection. These targets would have to be met if the loan repayments were not to become a drain on the organisation.

Strengths
- BCD Limited appears to be a well managed and efficiently run organisation.
- The loan will be fully secured in the event of the failure of BCD.
- The proposal meets LIF criteria in supporting regeneration of impoverished communities through providing economic opportunity.
- The project has the support of local agencies including the Government Office (ERDF/SRB) and City Challenge.
- The project professionals are experienced, with good track records.

Weaknesses
- The project must build occupancy levels quickly to 80 per cent and then maintain them in order to meet projected loan payments.
- This project, taken together with other development projects in the pipeline may exceed staff capacity.

Conclusion

The LIF Council of Management agreed finance of £175,000 for BCD. Although this means that £100,000 remains to be financed, the organisation was able to secure this from the proceeds of an option to sale on another property within their portfolio.

(With acknowledgement to LIF)

Figure 4.3 BCD Acer Street post development rent budget

Year	1996	1997	1998	1999	2000	2001	2002	2003	2004	2005	2006	2007	2008	2009	2010
% voids	70	35	20	20	20	20	20	20	20	20	20	20	20	20	20
Sub rent rise 20% every five years						20%					20%				
Head rent review & costs rise 20% every five years						20%					20%				
Rent Receivable	79,738	79,738	79,738	79,738	79,738	91,698	91,698	91,698	91,698	91,698	105,453	105,453	105,453	105,453	105,453
Less: Voids and areas	55,817	27,908	15,948	15,948	15,948	18,340	18,340	18,340	18,340	18,340	21,091	21,091	21,091	21,091	21,091
Total rental income	23,921	51,830	63,790	63,790	63,790	73,358	73,358	73,358	73,358	73,358	84,362	84,362	84,362	84,362	84,362
Head lease rent	6,000	0	0	0	0	0	0	0	0	0	0	0	0	0	0
Repair/ maintenance	0	1,000	4,000	4,000	4,000	4,800	4,800	4,800	4,800	4,800	5,760	5,760	5,760	5,760	5,760
Advertising	1,000	1,000	1,000	1,000	1,000	1,200	1,200	1,200	1,200	1,200	1,440	1,440	1,440	1,440	1,440
Legal/ technical	2,000	1,000	1,000	1,000	1,000	1,200	1,200	1,200	1,200	1,200	1,440	1,440	1,440	1,440	1,440
Staff costs	12,000	12,000	12,000	12,000	12,000	14,400	14,400	14,400	14,400	14,400	17,280	17,280	17,280	17,280	17,280
Establishment, admin & overheads	2,000	4,500	4,500	4,500	4,500	5,400	5,400	5,400	5,400	5,400	6,480	6,480	6,480	6,480	6,480
Rates liability	0	2,000	3,190	3,190	3,190	3,827	3,827	3,827	3,827	3,827	4,593	4,593	4,593	4,593	4,593
Total expenditure	23,000	21,500	25,690	25,690	25,690	30,827	30,827	30,827	30,827	30,827	36,993	36,993	36,993	36,993	36,993
Net Income	921	30,330	38,100	38,100	38,100	42,531	42,531	42,531	42,531	42,531	47,369	47,369	47,369	47,369	47,369
£275,000 repayment	450	33,000	33,000	33,000	33,000	33,000	33,000	33,000	33,000	33,000	33,000	33,000	33,000	33,000	33,000
Balance carried forward	0	471	-2,199	2,902	8,002	13,102	22,634	32,165	41,697	51,228	60,759	75,129	89,498	103,868	118,237
Balance	471	-2,199	2,902	8,002	13,102	22,634	32,165	41,697	51,228	60,759	75,129	89,498	103,868	118,237	132,606

Outsourcing

Objectives
There should be:

- Clear objectives, the implications of which have been thought through.
- A recognition that cost is only one aspect.
- A commitment on the part of the organisation to manage the relationship.
- Reliance on the contract as a manual, rather than as a set of legal rights and obligations.
- A focus on people, those whose work is to be outsourced, and their importance to the organisation.
- Clarity about what services are required and how they are currently being provided.

The supplier
The prospective supplier should offer:

- Specialist assistance: the supplier should have an excellent track record for the services being outsourced, so the organisation can obtain greater specialist input than it is able to develop in-house.
- Economies of scale: since the supplier is performing a similar function for other organisations.
- Access to technology: the supplier has a better opportunity to be at the forefront of developments.
- Cost savings.
- Shared risks: suppliers are better equipped to handle many types of risks, such as those related to volume.
- The chance to free up management to concentrate on the organisation's core services.

The contract
This should offer:

- Terms for checking the supplier's performance.
- Flexibility to implement contract variations.
- Terms dealing with charges and compensation.
- Flexibility for new services and projects.
- Terms for developing existing services.
- The means of resolving day-to-day operational problems.

Test Exercises

Illustrative Exercise 4.1 – work through the following

The new honorary treasurer of Age Concern Winton is reviewing the management accounts prior to the management committee meeting with the finance officer.

Age Concern Winton (ACW) provides the following services:

- A drop-in day centre, offering various leisure and educational activities.
- A refreshments and lunchtime meal service.
- A new home visit, service which starts on the first day of the new financial year.

In addition ACW runs two shops selling donated and new 'fair goods'. It receives income from various financial services (insurance) as well as the occasional legacy.

ACW has a director who is supported by the following staff:

- An activities coordinator.
- A home visits coordinator.
- A catering manager and supervisor.
- Two shop managers.
- A finance officer.
- A secretary/administrator.

ACW is based in its own building, which was donated to it five years ago. A local estate agent has estimated the building would be worth £150,000 and derives an annual rent of £10,000 per annum.

The building is divided into 40 per cent of the space being for the education and leisure activities, 40 per cent for meals and 20 per cent for offices. The home visits coordinator is based within these offices and takes up 10 per cent of the space.

An annual budget is prepared each year by the finance officer, with assistance from the honorary treasure, from the latest estimates based on last year's financial accounts. These also form the financial reports provided to the trustees and staff. The first draft budget and the finance officer notes are:

ACW *budget for the year*

1. Salaries (inclusive of on costs):

	£	£
Director	28,000	
Finance officer	20,000	
Co-ordinators	40,000	
Canteen manager	16,000	
Catering supervisor	12,000	
Shop managers	22,000	
Secretary	16,000	154,000

2. Overheads

Home visit volunteer exps	6,000	
Shop purchases	18,000	
Shops rent and rates	7,000	
Leisure material	3,000	
Cleaning	4,000	
Audit	3,000	
Food purchases	14,000	
Telephone, post and stationery	7,000	
Shops telephones	3,000	
Insurances	5,000	
Shop insurances	4,000	
Travel	6,000	
Sundries	8,000	
Shop cleaning	2,000	
Capital kitchen equipment	5,000	95,000
Total expenditure		249,000
Income		

Funds brought forward	16,500
Central grant from local authority	80,000
Activities services grant	30,000
Activities services charitable grant	10,000
Home visits contract	20,000
Shop sales	60,000
Catering sales	30,000
Home visits	6,000
Legacy	10,000
Financial services	6,000
	268,500

Surplus of income over expenditure	19,500

Notes to the budget

1. A payrise of 3 per cent for the year has been budgeted. On-costs are 10.5 per cent, with 3 per cent contribution to a personal pension scheme paid gross.

2. Home visits – volunteer expenses are priced at £3 per visit. Local authority contract is based on a per-capita charge of £10 per visit, paid 10 days after receipt of a monthly visit report.

3. The legacy has been confirmed and is due to be paid during the 5th month of the year. It has restrictions, and is to be only spent on the education and activities projects.

4. Catering meals are priced at 75p per meal day-ticket, comprising morning coffee, lunch and afternoon tea. The price is based on what the catering manager, supported by the users catering committee and the local health authority representatives, considers to be an appropriate price and service for old people needing a good meal. There are 160 places per day available.

5. Funds within the charity comprise:
    *   Restricted funds £10,000 for education projects.
    *   General fund £11,500.
    *   Designated fund for kitchen equipment £5,000.
    *   Cash at bank £21,000.
    *   6 per cent capital bond in the local building society, maturing in two years time, purchase value £10,000. The bond pays no income to avoid paying income tax.

6. Grants are paid mid-quarterly.

7. Shop sales are even throughout the year except in months 5 and 12 when they are respectively half and double normal takings, reflecting one shop being closed in month 5 and Christmas in month 12.

8. Purchases are paid monthly in arrears. Current food stocks are valued at £1,200; shop stocks £1,500. New kitchen equipment is to be installed in month 2 and is payable on delivery.

9. Payment for all operational services are paid weekly, except for professional and overhead administrative expenses which are paid quarterly in arrears. There is £5,000 outstanding overhead expenditure at the start of the year.

10. A charitable trust pays a grant of £10,000 for the activity services on the first day after the end of the half-year – in full.

Discussion.

The honorary treasurer is unhappy with the budget, pointing out that activities should be reflected in cost centres and how much each contributes to covering general overheads. Equally, there is no cash flow forecast, can the organisation pay its way for the following year. They are also not happy with the views of the catering manager and believe there should be changes in the planning process in the future for determining the budget for projects/cost centres?

Stage 1 – Prepare a new budget based on cost centres:

Answer to stage 1:

Actual Budget

Cost centres/Projects	Catering	Shops	Activities	Home visits	Total
Sales	30,000	60,000			90,000
Purchases	-14,000	-18,000			-32,000
Gross profit					58,000
Project income			40,000	26,000	66,000
Total income	16,000	42,000	40,000	26,000	124,000
Direct expenditure					
Salaries	28,000	22,000	20,000	20,000	90,000
Rent & rates	4,000	7,000	4,000	200	15,200
Leisure activities			3,000		3,000
Cleaning	1,600		1,600	80	3,280
Shop cleaning		2,000			2,000
Shop telephone		3,000			3,000
Shop insurance		4,000			4,000
Vol. expenses				6,000	6,000
	33,600	38,000	28,600	26,280	126,480
Contribution to					
general overheads	-17,600	4,000	11,400	-280	-2,480
Expenses					-64,000
General staff					-720
Cleaning					-3,000
Audit					-7,000
Tel. post & stationery					-5,000
Insurances					-6,000
Travel					-8,000
Rent & rates					-1,800
Sub total					-95,520
Operating profit (loss)					(-98,000)
Central grant					80,000
Legacy					10,000
Financial service					6,000
Rent in kind income					10,000
					106,000
Surplus on budget					8,000

Stage 2 – prepare a cash flow budget:

Answer to stage 2:

							Cashflow 1
Income	1	2	3	4	5	6	Total
Central Grant from local authority		20,000			20,000		40,000
Activities service grant		7,500			7,500		15,000
Activities service fees							0
Home Visits contracts		1,666	1,666	1,666	1,666	1,666	8,330
Shops sales	4,800	4,800	4,800	4,800	2,400	4,800	26,400
Catering sales	2,500	2,500	2,500	2,500	2,500	2,500	15,000
Home Visits	500	500	500	500	500	500	3,000
Legacy					10,000		10,000
Financial Services	500	500	500	500	500	500	3,000
	8,300	37,466	9,966	9,966	45,066	9,966	120,730
Expenditure							
Salaries	12,833	12,833	12,833	12,833	12,833	12,833	76,998
Shops purchases	1,500	1,500	1,500	1,500	1,500	1,500	9,000
Food purchases	1,200	1,167	1,167	1,167	1,167	1,167	7,035
Operational services	3,000	3,000	3,000	3,000	3,000	3,000	18,000
Professional and admin expenses	5,000				5,500		10,500
Kitchen Equipment		5,000					5,000
	23,533	23,500	18,500	24,000	18,500	18,500	126,533
Cash inflow/outflow	-15,233	13,966	-8,534	-14,034	26,566	-8,534	-5,803
Balance brought forward	21,500	6,267	20,233	11,699	-2,335	24,231	21,500
Balance carried forward	6,267	20,233	11,699	-2,335	24,231	15,697	15,697

Stage 3 discuss findings from new management accounts and cash flow:

Answer to stage 3:

Interpretation of data

- During month 4 the charity is currently scheduled to go into deficit.
- The charity either needs to plan how it is to deal with the situation, i.e. by raising further funds or by entering into negotiations with the bank to arrange a short-term over
- The information received in respect of the shops does not give meaningful information as to whether one of the shops is making losses or not – further work would need to be done on the shops.

Taking into account the views of the catering manager

- At present the people receiving catering meals are being charged 75p for the whole day. This includes morning coffee, lunch and afternoon tea. If coffee and tea were charged separately at 25p per day then this would result in an increased receipt per day of 50p, i.e.
  - Coffee 25p
  - Lunch including tea or coffee 75p
  - Tea 25p
  - Making a total of £1.25
- Current budget is based on:
  - 250 days (i.e.(52*5) – 10 days in respect of Christmas and other holidays)
  - * Total capacity which is perhaps unlikely.
  - More prudent budget is 160 maximum less 25% void = 120
  - £1.25 x 250 days x 120 places = £37,500
- Calculate a new cash flow:

Answer – new cash flow taking into account revised charges.
(see over)

				Cashflow 2			
Income	1	2	3	4	5	6	Total
Central Grant from local authority		20,000			20,000		40,000
Activities service grant		7,500			7,500		15,000
Activities service fees							0
Home Visits contracts		1,666	1,666	1,666	1,666	1,666	8,330
Shops sales	4,800	4,800	4,800	4,800	2,400	4,800	26,400
Catering sales	3,125	3,125	3,125	3,125	3,125	3,125	18,750
Home Visits	500	500	500	500	500	500	3,000
Legacy					10,000		10,000
Financial Services	500	500	500	500	500	500	3,000
	8,925	38,091	10,591	10,591	45,691	10,591	124,480
Expenditure							
Salaries	12,833	12,833	12,833	12,833	12,833	12,833	76,998
Shops purchases	1,500	1,500	1,500	1,500	1,500	1,500	9,000
Food purchases	1,200	1,167	1,167	1,167	1,167	1,167	7,035
Operational services	3,000	3,000	3,000	3,000	3,000	3,000	18,000
Professional and admin expenses	5,000			5,500			10,500
Kitchen Equipment		5,000					5,000
	23,533	23,500	18,500	24,000	18,500	18,500	126,533
Cash inflow/outflow	-14,608	14,591	-7,909	-13,409	27,191	-7,909	-2,053
Balance brought forward	21,500	6,892	21,483	13,574	165	27,356	19,447
Balance carried forward	6,892	21,483	13,574	165	27,356	19,447	17,394
Notes	Reworked for the additional fees re: tea and coffee						

New Cash flow forecast:

  a) Resolves deficit and now moves to surplus.
  b) Resolves cash flow problem - £625 extra per month.

- i.e. £37,500/12=£3,125 per month less £2,500 originally received.

Cash position
In respect of the bond of £10,000, the charity pays no income tax. It may be worth considering redeeming the bond and keeping it as a bank deposit in order to smooth the charity through its cashflow problems.

Use of the cash budget

In month 4 ACW was scheduled to go into deficit, and although plans are implemented to avert this, there is only a surplus of £165. This surplus could easily disappear if something unforeseen happens. The budget could be used to take to the bank manager to discuss an approved overdraft. The bond could be used as security, and approved overdrafts carry lower rates of interest than unapproved ones.

5 Special financial procedures

5.1 Performance monitoring by financial indicators

This chapter expands on the procedures that will prove useful to the financial planner. Using ratio analysis to assess performance sheds a different light on resource flows and allows the evaluation of revenue sources.

Cost accounting allows the voluntary organisation to control and calculate the costs of services and programmes. Money spent is reclassified according to its functional category – for example, counselling, vaccinations and food services – in addition to generic type, such as supplies, salary and rentals.

Ratio analysis permits financial planners to identify trends, recognise strengths and pinpoint weaknesses that may not be readily apparent. As an addition to the financial statements and budgets, ratios provide an alternative view of a voluntary organisation's financial health.

Traditionally, private sector ratio analysis is carried out by looking at three major areas:

1. Profitability
2. Liquidity
3. Efficiency

It is important to remember that each of these areas needs to be compared with another set of figures in order to be meaningful. Most commonly, the comparison is with the organisation's previous year's results, but if there are similar organisations it may be possible to do a comparative analysis.

1. Profitability

Within the voluntary sector, 'profitability' may not be an issue – though if parts of the funds are raised through shops, for example, then for all practical purposes the normal private sector tests would apply. In any case, a wide range of operational indicators can be useful. Comparing the various types of income received over a five-year period can reveal trends that could be meaningful. Knowing how much it costs to serve a user is necessary to evaluate whether the price of services is appropriate. For example, the managers can see which contracts or services have particularly high labour costs per £ of income generated.

2. Liquidity

This relates to the ability to pay debts as they fall due, and is normally assessed by two ratios – the 'current ratio' and the 'acid test'.

The **current ratio** divides the current assets by the current liabilities. (Bear in mind that the word 'current' in accounting terms means payable or receivable within 12 months.) So if the current assets on the balance sheet totalled £40,000 and the current liabilities £20,000, then the current ratio would be 40/20 or 2:1; in other words, there are twice as many current assets as current liabilities. Traditionally, this has been regarded as a 'safe' ratio, but this is due to the nature of commercial trading. A trader first has to sell his stock, which takes time, and then has to collect the money from the debtor, which also takes time. On the other hand, the goods the trader purchased have to be paid for, usually in 30 days. Thus, selling is a two-stage process whereas buying is a one-stage transaction – hence the idea that it is prudent to have twice as many current assets as current liabilities.

This, however, does not really apply to many voluntary organisations, few of whom hold substantial stocks; so 2:1 is perhaps on the generous side. However, it would normally be regarded as risky to drop below a ratio of 1:1 (when curret assets are equal to current liabilities).

The 'acid test' ratio looks at a shorter time-span; it takes into account assets and liabilities due within the next three months at most. Here 1:1 is safe; about 0.8:1 is acceptable.

Figure 5.1 uses ratio analysis to test a voluntary organisation's financial situation; the calculations used are based partly on the financial statements. The implications of the results are discussed.

Figure 5.1: Current ratio: overall financial health

Current Ratio				
	Holy Spirit Church		Ass'n of Managers	
	ratio		ratio	
expendable current assets*	£20,000	1	£220,000	1.9
current liabilities**	£80,000	4	£116,000	1
* expendable cash and assets convertible to cash				
** amounts payable within the next 12 months				

The current ratio compares the organisation's resources available to pay the bills during the coming year. With its 1:4 ratio, the church obviously has a serious problem. With its 1.9:1 ratio, the Association of Non Profit Managers can comfortably pay the bills and have some cash left over. What if the ratio was above 2:1? Too high a ratio sacrifices income for safety.

The difference between current assets and current liabilities is also called working capital. When working capital is adequate, a voluntary organisation may be in a position to make long-term investments, or begin a new project. This formula can also be calculated and compared for restricted and unrestricted fund current ratios.

The **acid test,** or quick ratio test, shown in **figure 5.2**, is used to see if the organisation can pay its bills for this current month or quarter if calculated on a quarterly basis.

Figure 5.2: Acid test ratio

Current Ratio				
	Holy Spirit Church		Ass'n of Managers	
	ratio		ratio	
Cash or assets due in 1 month	£20,000	1	£110,000	1.5
Total expenses in same period	£40,000	2	£74,000	1

Ask the question, 'Is the acid test or quick ratio at least 1:1?' If the ratio is below 1:1, ask, 'Can the organisation survive the month if receipt of funding is delayed?' The church finance committee may wish it had asked these questions sooner as it faces what is now a serious financial situation: debts equalling two times its assets available to pay the debt.

The overall **liquidity ratio,** shown in figure 5.3, measures how long the organisation could survive if it received no new money. The Association of Non Profit Managers has enough money to pay its normal bills for a little more than three months, but the Church has only 1.8 months of money. For an organisation with an endowment or other permanent funds, a similar calculation would be made to compare the permanently restricted, or unexpendable funds, with total annual expenses.

Figure 5.3 Overall liquidity ratio

	Holy Spirit Church	Ass'n of Managers
Expendable fund balances	£20,000	£220,000
Total monthly expenses	£10,833	£67,000
Number of months	1.8	3.3

Holy Spirit Association of NPO Church Managers
Figure 5.4 analyses the percentage of the organisation's support received from members' subscriptions and general donations over a three-year period, to see if this funding has changed significantly. The example shows a seven per cent decline over three years and could indicate a serious problem unless the organisation has deliberately focused on developing other sources.

Figure 5.4 Operational indicators: income source comparison version 1

	Year 1	Year 2	Year 3
Membership dues & donations	£105,000	£100,000	£95,000
Total Income and support	£300,000	£320,000	£340,000
ratio	35%	31.2%	27.9%

Year 1 – Year 2 – Year 3
How does the current year's income portion for a particular income source compare with last year's (see figure 5.5)? Is the change planned or expected? Should the reasons for the change be analysed? Should any action be taken in response to the change?

Figure 5.5 Income source comparison version 2

Association of Non Profit Managers		
	Prior Year	Current Year
	£	£
Corporate members fees	258,000	270,000
Individual members fees	87,800	90,000
Information services	147,000	150,000
Publications sales	215,000	230,000
Professional training	108,000	110,000
Annual meeting	42,000	20,000
Interest income	3,000	1,000
Total income	860,800	871,000

Association of Non Profit Managers

Prior Year – Current Year – ££

The Charity Accounting Statement of Recommended Practice (SORP) requires total expenditure to be classified under the headings: prior year, current year in the annual accounts. It is therefore important to monitor how these figures change. They may serve as some measure of worth for a grant provider, which will be interested to see how much of its money is used directly in charitable service provision. Many grant making bodies shy away from funding groups with apparently high administration expenses. The example in figure 5.6 shows that expenditure on charitable objectives has fallen by 10 per cent over four years, while administration costs have increased from 2.6 to 10 per cent.

Many grant making bodies shy away from funding groups with apparently high administration expenses.

Figure 5.6 Cost ratios

	Year 1	Year 2	Year 3	Year 4
Pounds spent on:	£	£	£	£
Direct char. objectives	280,000	300,000	320,000	304,000
Fundraising & publicity	100,000	110,000	120,000	140,000
Management & admin	10,000	20,000	40,000	50,000
	390,000	430,000	480,000	494,000
Percentage ratio:				
Direct char. objectives	71.8	69.8	66.7	61.5
Fundraising & publicity	25.6	25.6	25.0	28.3
Management & admin	2.6	4.7	8.3	10.1

Figure 5.7 shows how reliant the voluntary organisation is on particular sources of income to fund its total expenditure. In this example, the organisation is heavily dependent on donations and gifts (which may include income from fundraising events and appeals). This source of income has funded just over half the total expenditure in the first year, and is still rising in the second year.

Figure 5.7 Cost ratios

	Prior Year		Current Year	
	£	Ratio	£	Ratio
Donations and gifts	890,677	50%	1,647,832	56%
Legacies	668,278	38%	815,872	27%
Grants received	42,500	2%	134,432	4%
NLCB grants	–	–	159,634	5%
Investment income	48,378	3%	77,605	3%
Other income	116,187	7%	130,486	5%
Profit on disposal of investments	3,929	–	15,532	–
Total income	1,769,949		2,981,393	
Total expenditure	1,676,419		2,366,483	

Other ratios are also useful:

- **Staff cost as a percentage of total expenditure.** This indicates the proportion of the total expenditure that is (at least in the short-term) fixed. Further analysis can distinguish between the staff costs of those who deliver the organisation's mission and those in management and admin-istration.
- **Fundraising costs as a percentage of total expenditure.** This shows the relative efficiency of fundraising appeals and events, at least in financial terms. The recent decline in giving has had the effect of increasing this percentage, as fundraising generally has become more competitive.

3. Efficiency

This relates balance sheet items to income statement items. The two ratios most likely to be relevant to voluntary organisations are the debtor collection period (credit given) and the creditor payment period (credit taken). Ideally, for maximum efficiency, the debtor collection period should be shorter than the creditor payment period.

Service delivery indicators

Non-financial indicators can also be used when planning services, preparing funding applications or bidding for contracts. Here are some examples:

Non-financial indicators can also be used when planning services.

- Number of beneficiaries, overall and for each service.
- Number of staff per beneficiary by service and overall.
- Cost per beneficiary, overall and for each of the main areas of service.
- Number of information requests on a rolling average.
- Number of press mentions on a rolling average.
- Capital cost of buildings per beneficiary and per unit.

5.2 Cost accounting

This section will demonstrate why costs are important in voluntary organisations and look at some techniques for cost management.

The terms 'cost' and 'cost accounting' have many definitions; here are some useful ones:

- **Cost** is 'a measure of the resources used up in obtaining goods and services'; 'the amount of expenditure (actual or notional) incurred on, or attributable to, a specified thing or activity'; 'to ascertain the cost of a specified thing or activity'.
- **Cost accounting** is 'the establishment of budgets, standard costs and actual costs of operations, processes, activities or products; and the analysis of variances, profitability or social use of funds'.

Figure 5.8 includes some of the most fundamental issues that voluntary organisations have to cope with. It is therefore crucially important, in the interests of both internal cost measurement and management and external reporting, that proper techniques exist to address these issues.

In this section, cost accounting techniques will be described under the following headings:

- **Cost ascertainment:** how much does a service, product or activity cost?
- **Planning:** what level of activity and resource allocation can the voluntary organisation undertake?
- **Resource maximisation:** are we making the best use of available resources?

Figure 5.8 Cost accounting

What to charge for services/products?	Establish a pricing structure which covers total costs incurred and so helps ensure future viability of service.
Determine total cost of a project for which funding is sought or contract with local authority.	Help ensure funding for project/grant of contract is based on both a 'competitive price' and covers its costs.
Negotiate charge for internal services / general overheads.	Ensure that core costs of organisation are allocated to projects on a reasonable basis.
Should the voluntary organisation accept the contract price given by a local authority?	The organisation needs to be certain about what are the projects total costs if it is toaccept a contract for services.
Cost control for budget reporting purposes.	Ensure that budget parameters set at planning stage are met, e.g. balanced budget.
Cost management for cost reduction purposes.	Ensure long-term financial viability.
Identify internal strengths & weaknesses.	Exploit cost advantages and/or commit to corrective action.
Maximise resources employed by organisation.	Conduct a strategic review of activities to consider possibility of outsourcing, formulating alliances etc.
Performance evaluation.	Maximise impact on society/ outputs for minimum costs.
Implement fund accounting principles.	Trust law requires a separation of funds provided for specific purposes, and the Charity Accounting SORP requires classification of expenditure according to functional categories.

Cost ascertainment

The question of what a product, service or activity costs is becoming more important for voluntary organisations. Furthermore, as conditions of funding become more stringent, and core funding becomes increasingly difficult to obtain, organisations need to be very clear about costs, not only at the organisational level, but also at project level.

The total cost of a service or product can be broadly divided into:

- *Direct costs*. These are costs incurred as a direct result of carrying out a particular activity. Running educational courses, for example, would involve the cost of trainers, room hire, course materials and probably most of the education officer's time; but if the organisation did not run courses, it could probably avoid these costs.
- *Indirect costs*. These are shared organisational costs which are difficult to apportion to a specific project or activity. Examples include the project manager's time, some administration costs and some premises costs. Organisations are finding it increasingly difficult to obtain funding for indirect costs if these have not been apportioned across other project costs.

In most cases, it is possible to identify accurately the direct costs of a project or service. What is less clear, is how to identify indirect costs and the share of these costs that should be allocated to the end product or service.

The process of sharing out the indirect costs among a number of products or services is called 'overhead absorption' or 'overhead recovery'. It can be a very arbitrary process: for example, how much of the account clerk's salary cost should be allocated to each service or product? It may be easiest to simply divide the total salary cost by the number of projects served, but this may not reflect the true cost of serving a project or product. Later in this chapter we will see how the absorption of overheads can be a more sophisticated operation.

Why absorb overheads?

Overhead absorption is often criticised for its arbitrary nature. So why should the finance officer undertake the task at all? Why not simply concentrate on the direct costs that can be accurately allocated to services and products?

There are two main reasons why it is important to calculate the fully absorbed costs of a product or service:

- **To understand the long-run costs of products and services.** This can be useful in many decisions, including pricing. Some voluntary organisations take the total cost and add a percentage to determine the selling price. This is known as 'cost plus' pricing, but it is not always appropriate in a competitive market: suppliers may have to set prices according to what the customers are prepared to pay, rather than what the supplier would like to charge!

- Under the fund accounting principles specified in the Charity Accounting SORP, most organisations are required to identify separate expenditure on restricted funding projects. This means that they will need to allocate indirect or support costs to services or projects.

At this stage an example may prove helpful. This has been adapted from *The Complete Guide to Business and Strategic Planning for Voluntary Organisations* by Alan Lawrie (see further reading and resources fr details).

The Community Health Project is a voluntary health education project with five main activities:

- Education and training: courses for teachers and health workers.
- Youth project: specific health work with 12–22 year olds.
- Public enquiries: enquiry point for a wide range of public calls.
- Resource centre: producing and disseminating teaching and resource materials.
- Rural project: community health work with isolated communities.

The Current Budget:
The staff costs are analysed as:
The change to a project-based accounting system came about for the following reasons:

- The budget did not show the cost of individual projects.
- Funders and purchasers wanted to become more 'project' based.
- There was an urgent need to cost and price contracts properly.
- It was difficult to raise money for core costs.

The treasurer and manager have reviewed the projects and identified the following cost centres; all future income and expenditure will be allocated to one of them:

- Education.
- Resource centre (including public enquiries).
- Youth work.
- Rural work.

The first task will be to identify and allocate direct costs to each of the above cost centres. The treasurer and manager have together identified the following basis of apportionment. Firstly, for non staff costs:

- Building costs: fixed percentage (based on floor space occupied by each activity).
- Resource materials: actual usage (based on review of last 12 months' invoices).
- Minibus: approximate costs of past usage.
- Telephone and admin: a quarter of all telephone costs (£1,500) and one-tenth of admin costs (£2,000) were estimated to be the direct costs of the resource centre's public information work.

The results of this review are shown in figure 5.9.

Figure 5.9 Direct non-staff costs per cost centre

	Admin	Materials	Minibus	Telephones	Building costs	Total allocation
BUDGET	20,000	3,000	5,000	6,000	20,000	
Cost Centre						
Education		1,500			6,000	7,500
Res. centre	2,000	800		1,500	8,000	12,300
Youth work		500	1,000		4,000	5,500
Rural work		200	3,500		2,000	5,700
Not allocated	18,000	0	500	4,500	0	31,000

The treasurer and manager have now looked at staff costs and have agreed the allocation of time spent by each staff member to the four cost centres.

Figure 5.10 Allocation of staff costs to cost centres

COST CENTRE	Manager	Ed. Officer	Info. Officer	Res. Officer	Clerk	Total allocation
Education	30% i.e. 8,400	70% i.e. 16,100	20% i.e. 4,400		10% i.e. 800	29,700
Resource centre	20% i.e. 5,600	15% i.e. 3,450	60% i.e. 13,200	75% i.e. 14,250	20% i.e. 1,600	38,100
Youth work	5% i.e. 1,400		20% i.e. 4,400	25% i.e. 4,750		10,550
Rural work	5% i.e 1,400	15% i.e. 3,450				4,850
Not allocated indirect cost	40% i.e 11,200				70% i.e. 5,600	16,800
Total	28,000	23,000	22,000	19,000	8,000	

It was also agreed that 40 per cent of the manager's time and 70 per cent of the admin clerk's time could not be allocated to a particular project and would therefore form part of indirect costs.

At this stage, only the direct costs have been allocated to cost centres, and the position so far can be summarised as follows:

Figure 5.11

COST CENTRE	Direct non staff costs	Direct staff costs	TOTAL DIRECT COSTS
Education	7,500	29,700	37,200
Resource centre	12,300	38,100	50,400
Youth work	5,500	10,550	16,050
Rural work	5,700	4,850	10,550
Total	31,000	83,200	114,200

The amounts still to be allocated (indirect costs):

Non staff costs	£23,000	Staff Costs £16,800	Total	£39,800
	(see fig.5.9)			(see fig.5.10)

The remaining £39,800 (£23,000 non-staff costs and £16,800 staff costs) represents the indirect costs of the community health project, and is now allocated to the four cost centres according to the floor space occupied shown in figure 5.12.

Figure 5.12 Allocation of indirect costs

COST CENTRE	% Share	Indirect	Direct costs	TOTAL COST CENTRE
		£	£	£
Education	30	11,940	37,200	49,140
Resource centre	35	13,930	50,400	64,330
Youth work	20	7,960	16,050	24,010
Rural work	15	5,970	10,550	16,520
Total		39,800	114,200	154,000

Having reorganised the information from the income and expenditure budget into a cost centre framework, the treasurer and manager now have a much better idea of the true cost of running the current services. For example, although the trust grant for rural work is £15,000, the total cost of carrying out this work is in fact £16,520, which suggests that it is losing the Community Health Project £1,520 in the current year. The project is now in a much better position to decide whether to continue this work (and subsidise the loss from other income) or to approach the trust for extra funding.

Developing a cost-centred approach can raise a number of other issues:

- Many voluntary organisations are very poor at costing their work: the cost involved in operating and providing good management is often underestimated, not properly identified or even ignored. This attempt to do 'quality' work on the cheap can easily lead to a long-term crisis.
- Many organisations that have adopted a cost-centred approach have found that the true cost of providing a service or activity is greater than the funding being offered. This information enables the organisation's managers to be more assertive when negotiating with funders, or taking the strategic decision to subsidise and/or fundraise to cover the loss.

- Problems may arise when people in one cost centre believe they are more 'profitable' than another centre. Cost accounting and absorption costing are management tools that allow decisions to be made about priorities; they are not concerned with assigning value to an activity. Normally, value will be measured in non-financial terms.

The absorption costing model discussed above is not without its weaknesses, however. Amongst these is the arbitrary way in which indirect overheads are allocated to services or products. With the Community Health Project this was done on a simple percentage basis, and as a result the rural work was seen to be losing the organisation money. However, the results may well have been different had the percentages used to allocated overheads been different – and hence a different decision about continuing with the rural work might possibly have been made.

A further weakness of absorption costing is that it fails to explain to management why costs are incurred. This is because, under most accounting systems, costs are accumulated in the general ledger using a natural classification system of salaries, printing, rents, insurances etc and then reported by the department or project manager responsible. As a result, the project manager lacks any real understanding of the activities or processes that are ultimately responsible for these costs. This means that, whenever cost cutting is needed, management will tend to reduce headcount first, since this is by far the largest cost item. But the work remains untouched, to be shared out between fewer people!

5.3 Ensuring full cost recovery

In order for charities to be sustainable in the long-term, funding must cover both project costs and a fair proportion of overheads. This is what is known as full cost recovery. In 2002 the Government acknowledged the need for full cost recovery in the HM Treasury report, *Role of the Voluntary and Community Sector in Service Delivery, A Cross Cutting Review* (2002).

Secondly, charities need to monitor their overhead costs to consider efficiency over time, and ensure the maximum use of their resources.

Full cost recovery also makes common sense. How can you make rational decisions and future plans without knowing the true cost of a project or service, and how this impacts overheads and free reserves?

How can you make rational decisions and future plans without knowing the true cost of a project or service?

This section introduces the concept of ensuring full cost recovery for funding, and describes some of the issues surrounding this.

Core costs

In order for us to establish what is meant by full cost recovery we must first identify what are the overheads of a charity which cannot be directly attributable to a service or project. These are the core costs of the charity. Core costs also relate to the strategic and governance costs for the organisation.

Core costs are wide ranging and can include the following:

Central functions
- Chief Executive
- Human resources and personnel costs
- Information technology and computer costs
- Finance management
- Other administration and secretarial functions
- Fundraising (for general purposes)

Operational costs
- Equipment – IT, printing etc.
- Premises – rent, mortgage
- Associated premises costs – heat, light
- Telephone, fax, postage
- Travel and subsistence
- Staff recruitment, training and supervision
- Strategic direction

Governance
- Support of the trustee structure

Other
- Training
- Research and development costs
- Monitoring and evaluation
- Quality assurance
- Accountancy and audit

These costs sit throughout the organisation, and removing any of these costs would impair the service and work that the charity provides.

The list of core costs cannot be definitive and is typically different for different charities – this highlights the different types of charities in the sector, and the multitude of ways the sector delivers against charitable aims.

Current practice in funding core costs and overheads

Having established what overhead and core costs are, are these being adequately funded when a funding submission is made?

Unfortunately, in practice general overheads and core costs are not being funded adequately. The fault for this lies with both the funders and funded organisations.

Funded organisations

Funded organisations often do not know what the full costs of activities are and typically have lacked the skill base to complete calculations. Funders may be legitimately concerned at the level of overheads and this may be reinforced by the lack of sophistication and transparency around overhead costs in the charity being funded.

Funded organisations may forget to apportion a true level of overhead to a project and therefore will subsidise this from 'general' reserves – this is ultimately not sustainable in the long term.

Calculations have sometimes been completed many years ago and overhead rates are often used which are inapplicable to the current infrastructure.

Funders

Funders typically have a pot of money to allocate to projects. They may be reluctant to fund overheads, preferring to just provide money for project costs, believing that they can fund a wider number of projects, but neglecting the sustainability of these projects.

Alternatively many funders may add an arbitrary fixed percentage as an overhead charge – such as 10 per cent or 15 per cent – but this figure is often inaccurate and may be well below the actual overhead costs.

Common experience

Experience has shown that by being open and transparent in quantifying overheads and core costs has allowed the funder to develop a real understanding of the true project costs, and so develop a more meaningful working relationship with the charity. This has often led to an increase in funding an appropriate level of overhead costs.

> In practice general overheads and core costs are not being funded adequately.

However, if after having completed calculations in a transparent way funders are still not prepared to fund overheads, you may then ask them which part of the costs they wish to ignore. It may focus attention when a funded organisation says 'of course we can run the project, but with reduced funding we will be unable to make any telephone calls, use any computers or ensure the quality control mechanisms around the project', for example!

Overhead and core cost levels

Having established that a fair proportion of overheads and core costs are, in general, not being funded, is there a standard reasonable rate that could be applied?

All charities are different

All charities have different rates, by the nature of their maturity and by the nature of what they do.

For example, a mature not-for-profit organisation may have a considerably lower level of overheads than a small, growing, regional charity, due to better economies of scale.

Similarly, a charity based around ophthalmic research may have a greater need for use of Braille texts and 'voice-over' software. This may increase overhead costs against similar organisations purely by the nature of what they do.

In conclusion, each charity is individual and will need to engage in active communication with funders to develop an appropriate level of overheads and core cost funding.

There is a perceived wisdom that a low level of overhead costs and core costs is good. If these are too low, then the charity may cut back on vital infrastructure or governance costs at the detriment of quality of service delivery. A key example is that charities can spend too much time chasing funding, and not enough time focusing on future strategy and their core objectives.

> Each charity is individual and will need to engage in active communication with funders to develop an appropriate level of overheads and core cost funding.

Growth and development

In *Who Pays for Core Costs?* (see further reading and resources for details), Julia Unwin examines the issue of funding overheads in detail. She proposes three distinct funding models:

1. Full project funding – in which a reasonable level of overheads and core costs are given to a mature charity in steady state.
2. Development funding – through which infrastructure costs are met for a time in order to give a charity time to grow and develop; and

3. Strategic funding – where a funder recognises the need for a charity to exist as it meets a common strategic need, and funds this over an agreed period.

If a charity is in a growth or development phase, it may be wholly appropriate to provide core cost funding at a higher level than normally expected to help establish the work of the charity and its strategic aims.

Many trust funds and government funders are willing to fund core costs separately from project costs and as a distinct class of funding.

Cost allocation

In order to complete costing calculations, and establish an appropriate level of overheads for a project, we must first understand how to divide a cost used by one or more projects. This is **cost allocation**.

Costs could be divided amongst different projects in a variety of ways:

1. Headcount
2. Time
3. Floor space
4. Expenditure

A simple example will help to make this statement clear.

Example 1: The Hospice

A hospice runs a drop-in counselling centre and safe shelter for young adults sleeping rough. These services occupy different parts of one building. Both services use electricity from the same bill and a social worker is on hand to provide counselling across both projects.

In order to appropriately cost the counselling centre project, we would need to allocate a fair proportion of electricity usage and the social worker's costs.

Electricity may be best allocated by floor area. We therefore include a cost allocation for electricity equal to the floor area the counselling centre occupies.

The social worker's cost may be best allocated by the time spent on each project. We therefore include a cost allocation for the social worker equal to the time spent on the counselling centre.

Imagine then that the total project costs for the counselling centre are £50,000 per annum, the electricity bill is an additional £1,000 and the social workers' wage plus NIC and pension contributions, is £25,000.

If the counselling centre takes 25 per cent of the floor area at the hospice and the social worker spends 50 per cent of her time at the centre, then the appropriate full costs for the service (including an appropriate level of overheads) is:

Costs		£
Project Costs		50,000
Overhead cost allocation		
Electricity Bill	25% x £1,000	250
Social Worker	50% x £25,000	12,500
Project Cost		62,750

Essentially it does not matter how you choose to allocate costs, as long as your cost 'drivers' e.g. floor space, time or headcount, are logical and clear. Much of the discussion with funders may centre on the appropriate basis for cost allocation. In fact, some funders will only allow certain bases and not others.

An appropriate model

Having established the basis for cost allocation, how would we calculate an overall project cost for a single project in a not-for-profit organisation?

To complete our full cost model, we finally need to understand how all costs in an organisation hang together, and what the applicable 'layers' of costs are.

Cost structure

Costs within an organisation can be looked at in four levels:

- Direct costs
- Direct support costs
- Indirect support costs
- Governance and strategic development costs

Direct costs are the costs of those activities that constitute the project itself e.g. the costs of hospice staff in the hospice example.

Direct support costs underpin the direct project work and can be directly identifiable as relating to the project e.g. the costs of the social worker in the previous example, who splits her time over several projects but who works directly on the counselling centre.

Indirect support costs are central costs such as the chief executive, computers, payroll, personnel, finance and accounting. These are all activities which support the service delivery, but which cannot be directly identifiable as costs against the project. An example here is that the hospice will use computers as will the chief executive, but how would we fairly allocate these costs?

Governance and strategic development costs are the costs associated with regulatory costs, engaging with trustees and identifying the strategic direction for the charity.

Typically, small charities would not have four levels of costs but would have three, combining direct and indirect support costs into one category as follows:

- Direct costs
- Support costs
- Governance and strategic development costs

It is this latter model that is proposed in the ACEVO template.

Budgets and forecasts

When making funding applications a charity is typically planning for the future. However, it will almost certainly base its cost estimates on historical financial information and from previous experience.

It may be more appropriate to use budget or forecast information in funding applications, especially where there will be a future change in funding requirements. One example is where a charity may be forced to rent more expensive premises in the next year. It is wholly applicable to pass this cost increase on to the funder, as this becomes the true cost of the project.

The key is to be able to justify your calculations and be transparent in your methodology. Completing proper, well constructed and well thought out funding applications will promote better communication between funder and funded and hopefully establish a more appropriate and sustainable level of overhead or core cost funding.

Count all costs

Many charities omit or 'cherry pick' costs to ensure that actual funding submissions equal known funding policies. An example is where a local authority is known to only fund up to 10 per cent overheads and, therefore, the charity's submission provides overhead costs to hit this figure. The shortfall will have to be found from somewhere – typically needing further fundraising cost or reducing free reserves.

It is vitally important that true costs are identified, and the real cost of the project presented in a transparent way. Core costs and overheads exist, and should not be hidden.

If the core costs and overheads are not being adequately funded you should bring this to the funders' attention. In an extreme case, this may lead to a charity saying 'no' to the new funding as this would adversely affect reserves, or be too costly in terms of new fundraising.

If the core costs and overheads are not being adequately funded you should bring this to the funders' attention.

Using a full cost recovery model

Having established a model, how would we use this to complete full cost recovery and ensure we receive a fair proportion of overheads for a project?

The best way to answer this question is to complete an example.

Example 2: The Hospice (continued from Example 1)

The Hospice in Example 1 (page 173) has a board of trustees, director, book-keeper and general office administrator. They all occupy the same building as the counselling centre and safe shelter.

The direct costs of the counselling centre have been previously identified as £62,750, including the electricity cost for the centre and the cost for the social worker's time.

The costs for the additional items are as follows:

Cost	£
Board of trustees	2,000
Director (Including NIC and pensions)	40,000
Book-Keeper (part-time)	12,000
Office Administrator (including NIC)	15,000
All other core costs	75,000

Overall, the counselling centre occupies 15 per cent of the director's time, and governance and strategic development costs for the centre are those represented by 30 per cent of the board of trustees and approximately 10 per cent of 'all other core costs'.

The safe shelter project costs (including electricity and social worker costs) are £188,250.

In order to identify the full costs for the project we will have to allocate a proportion of all overhead and core costs to the counselling centre, how would we do this?

Using our model we have the following structure:
- Direct costs
- Support costs
- Governance and strategic development costs

Direct costs are as previously established in Example 1, £62,750.

Governance and strategic development costs are represented by 30% of the costs for the board of trustees and approximately 10% of 'all other core costs'.

This figure is (30% x £2,000) + (10% x £75,000) = £8,100

Support costs are 15% of the director's time plus a proportion of all other costs.

We lack a basis to calculate the appropriate cost allocation for the book-keeper, office administrator and 'all other core costs'. Our best approximation will be project expenditure and it is this which we use as a default.

In this case the counselling centre takes 25% of all costs i.e. centre cost as a proportion of all project costs = £62,750 / (£188,250 + £62,750)

Example 2: The Hospice (continued)

Calculating the support costs then becomes:

Cost	£
Board of trustees (Already included under Governance)	
Director's time is 15% x 40,000	6,000
Book-keeper 25% x 12,000	3,000
Office administrator 25% x 15,000	3,750
All other central costs 25% x 75,000	18,750
Total support costs	**31,500**

Therefore the total overall project cost for the counselling centre is as follows:

Cost	£
Direct costs	62,750
Support costs	31,500
Governance and strategic development costs	8,100
Total costs	**102,350**

The cost allocation method used must be consistent with prior years and transparent.

Summary

In order to ensure full cost recovery you need to complete a two step process[3]:

1. Account for all costs – Ensure that no costs are omitted, and that you have appropriate information e.g. budgets and forecasts, with which to cost the project.
2. Allocate costs – Ensure that costs are allocated within a framework to appropriately cost direct project costs, support costs and governance and development costs, including a fair proportion of overheads.

The cost allocation method used must be consistent with prior years and transparent, such that open communication between funder and funded can be completed to ensure an appropriate level of overheads are funded.

Many organisations that have adopted a full cost approach have found that the true cost of providing a service or activity is greater than the funding being offered. This information enables the organisation's managers to be more assertive when negotiating with funders or taking the strategic decision to subsidise and/or fundraise to cover the loss.

Competitive bidding

Many charities are bidding for work in a competitive environment, what is the point in cost allocation and transparency in project funding here?

In this case, ensuring full cost recovery is just as important. By understanding costs, a charity will be able to calculate an appropriate cost for the bid, including a fair proportion of overheads.

A decision can then be taken to bid to receive a surplus or deficit throughout the life of the contract.

If the funding available is less than your cost of delivery, you have to make a choice:

Full cost recovery will help establish appropriate costs for the service and decide a strategic approach to bidding.

- either don't do the work; or
- fund the difference from another source.

Full cost recovery will help establish appropriate costs for the service and decide a strategic approach to bidding.

SORP Accounting Requirements

The cost allocation model shown in this section can also be used to allocate costs into the Statement of Recommended Practice (SORP 2005) categories.

By appropriately allocating costs and ensuring full cost recovery for projects a charity is better able to define:

- Costs of charitable activities (including support costs).
- Governance costs.
- Costs of generating funds (including support costs).

This will provide a consistent model by which costs can be allocated within the statutory accounts.

Activity based costing (ABC) and charities

To address these weaknesses, a system of activity based costing (ABC) has been developed and has gained some acceptance within the voluntary sector. At its simplest, ABC attributes the costs incurred by an organisation to processes or activities. It therefore cuts across the departmental boundaries that often appear in organisational charts. An example of such a process in a commercial company is order fulfilment: from persuading the customer to receiving their order, from fulfilling the order to receiving the cash, each process is performed in different parts of the company.

However, most business activities are organised not on the basis of processes but on a functional basis: for example, sales, accounts and legal. The same is true for voluntary organisations, which are divided into fundraising, accounts, personnel and so on. In accordance with this functional split, costs tend to be collected by department, and when appropriate may be allocated out to other departments as a general overhead. The reporting of costs to the department head is also usually by cost type: for example, salaries, travel, overheads and computer costs. Although this is important to the department head for internal budgetary control purposes, it gives no insight into the business processes which caused the costs to be incurred in the first place. It tells the management the 'what' but not the 'why'.

Take, for example, the finance department, which performs the functions of invoicing, payroll, general accounting, cash receipts and payments – all of them activities that exist as a result of other business processes. They are not an end in themselves, but a consequence of other activities. In most commercial organisations these costs are treated as overheads and may be reallocated to other departments.

However, as we have seen, the allocation is very arbitrary. Take the cost of running the payroll: a detailed analysis of how costs were incurred would probably show that it costs very little more to run a payroll for 200 staff than it does for 150. But a common basis for allocating payroll costs is the number of employees. As a

At its simplest, ABC attributes the costs incurred by an organisation to processes or activities.

179

result, a department employing 150 staff would receive a disproportionately higher charge than one employing only 50.

The critical difference under ABC accounting is that costs
should, if possible, be charged directly to the service or project in
such a way that the amount charged reflects as closely as possible
the actual cost of the service.

Despite the benefits it can bring, ABC does have a number of
problems associated with it. Some of these are peculiar to the
voluntary sector:

- When setting up the system it is easy to make it too complicated. Only the most important business processes need to
  be identified, and the components of those processes should
  be kept to a minimum. If for some reason more detail is
  required, this can be obtained by a one-off exercise, rather
  than by building it into the system.
- A balance needs to be struck between reasonable approxi-
  mations and excessive detail. This is particularly important
  when costs have to be allocated.
- Full implementation of ABC requires a sophisticated
  accounting system to collect and hold data.
- Maintaining time sheets to record how staff spend their
  time is commonly used as a basis for attributing staff costs,
  and some services, to the identified business processes or
  products. Maintaining such a system, with its associated
  complications, is an additional overhead that would need
  to be justified.
- Unlike their commercial counterparts, voluntary organisations often receive donations of time, goods and services
  that enable them to provide a much better service. How
  should these donations be valued, and how should they
  appear in management reports?
- To be effective, ABC needs the involvement and commitment of all staff, not just senior management. It may,
  however, be seen as a threat by staff, as business processes
  cut across departmental boundaries and challenge work
  practices or unproductive activities.

Although direct implementation of ABC across the voluntary sector
may not be appropriate, there are some organisations – in particular, the larger charities and those actively engaged in commercial
operations – that should seriously consider introducing it. ABC is
probably unsuitable for smaller voluntary organisations, however,
because it needs sophisticated computer systems to provide information on a regular basis. But such organisations should at least

think about conducting a one-off study to identify the business processes and determine what the real costs of each one are. There may be misconceptions about the true cost of a particular process, product or service that could have serious consequences for the future of the entire organisation.

5.4 Using costs for decision making

This section looks at using costs to help managers in their decision making activities; cost behaviour patterns; and different classifications of costs for decision making.

Cost behaviour patterns

The term 'cost behaviour patterns' is used to describe how costs behave in relation to the level of activity; essentially, it involves asking the question, 'Does this cost increase in line with activity or does it remain constant?' A variety of factors can cause costs to change – for example, inflation, scarcity in supply – but cost accounting focuses on how they change in response to the level of activity. Activity can be measured in a variety of ways, depending on the organisation, the type of costs being analysed and the reasons for analysing the costs. Common measures of activity might include the level of service provided (local, regional or national), the number of training courses run, the number of beneficiaries using the service, the number of employees, the number of telephone calls to a helpline etc.

Fixed costs

Fixed costs are those that do not vary with the level of activity of a project and remain constant for a reasonable length of time. If, for example, the rent of the premises is £10,000 p.a. then the total cost incurred in the period will be £10,000 for all activity levels, even at zero activity. In the short-term, therefore, an organisation will have to pay these costs even if activity drops to zero. Another term used to describe fixed costs is 'period costs'; this highlights the fact that a fixed cost is incurred according to the time elapsed rather than the level of activity. Drawn as a graph, fixed costs would be represented by a straight horizontal line.

Examples of fixed costs for a community centre operating a kitchen preparing food for homeless people on a contract basis would be:

- Rent and rates.
- Salaries of kitchen staff.
- Insurance.
- Depreciation of equipment.

> Fixed costs are those that do not vary with the level of activity of a project.
>
> Drawn as a graph, fixed costs would be represented by a straight horizontal line.

A fixed cost is therefore unaffected by changes within a relevant range of activity.

These costs will probably be unaffected by the number of homeless people served over a period. But there may come a point when demand for the service expands and more staff or bigger premises are needed. There will then be corresponding increases in salaries, rent and rates etc.

A fixed cost is therefore unaffected by changes within a relevant range of activity. If activity extends beyond this range, then the fixed costs change. The costs remain fixed for a certain range of activity. Within this range it is possible to serve more homeless people without needing extra staff, and therefore the salary cost remains constant. However, if activity is expanded to the critical point where another staff member is needed, then the salary cost moves up to a higher level. The cost then remains constant for a further range of increases in activity until another staff member is needed and another step occurs. The critical points are often referred to as 'break points'. This is referred to as 'stepped costs', because when represented graphically it resembles a set of steps or a staircase.

Out of a desire to serve as many beneficiaries as possible, voluntary organisations often increase their levels of activity beyond the relevant break point. This situation cannot be sustained in the long-term without affecting the quality of the services provided. Furthermore, it is seldom possible to obtain extra funding to allow for this expansion; a commercial provider, by contrast, is more likely to secure further investment. Identifying the relevant range and break point is, therefore, crucially important for voluntary organisations.

Variable costs

Variable costs are those that vary according to the amount of activity undertaken.

Variable costs are those that vary according to the amount of activity undertaken or goods produced. The higher the level of activity, the higher will be the cost incurred. When activity increases, the total variable cost increases in direct proportion: i.e. if activity goes up by 10 per cent, the total variable cost also increases by 10 per cent, as long as the activity level is still within the relevant range. Using the community kitchen as an example, the two costs likely to be variable are food and fuel.

Semi-variable costs

As levels of activity increase, a variable component is incurred in addition to the basic fixed cost.

Also referred to as 'semi fixed' or 'mixed' costs, this is a cost which contains both fixed and variable components, and is therefore partly affected by fluctuations in the level of activity. As levels of activity increase, a variable component is incurred in addition to the basic fixed cost. A typical example of a semi-variable cost is the telephone – there is a fixed standing charge and then a variable usage charge.

5.5 Breakeven analysis

The next section looks at a type of analysis that depends on an understanding of cost behaviour. Suppose the community centre was faced with the original decision about whether it should accept the fixed-price contract with the local authority to operate a community kitchen. One key factor in the decision will be: 'how many homeless people does the community centre need to attract in order to break even each month?'

Calculating the break even point

Suppose that you have produced the following estimates of your monthly costs:

Fixed costs £ per month

Rent and rates 800; Salaries 1,500; Insurance 100; Other 100; Total 2,500

Variable costs £ per person (average)

Food and drink 3; Laundry 1; Other 15; Total 19

The contract with the local authority will provide a fixed fee of £10 for every homeless person fed. It is now possible to calculate the break-even point. The first step is to calculate the contribution from each person. Every time the community centre serves a homeless person it receives £10 and has to pay £5 for food etc. The management accounting term for this difference of £5 is the 'contribution'. Therefore, the community centre gets a contribution of £5 per person:

contract income less variable costs = contribution (£10 − £5 = £5)

The contribution is so called because it literally contributes towards the fixed costs, which are incurred no matter how many persons are served. Therefore, if the community centre has one homeless person walk in, there is a £5 contribution towards the fixed costs of £2,500. If there are two customers, there is a £10 contribution towards the fixed costs of £2,500; and so on.

To break even, the community centre needs sufficient contributions to pay all the fixed costs. The centre will then have nothing left: no surplus and no deficit – the breakeven point will have been reached.

Limitations of break-even analysis

The example of the community centre shows that breakeven analysis can be useful for investigating the relationship between an organisation's costs and income.

However, it does have its limitations, most of which stem from its underlying assumptions:

- Costs are assumed to behave in a linear fashion. Unit variable costs are assumed to remain constant, and fixed costs are assumed to be unaffected by changes in activity levels. Breakeven charts can be adjusted to cope with non-linear variable costs or steps in fixed costs, but too many changes in behaviour patterns can make the charts very cluttered and difficult to use.
- Sales revenues are assumed to be constant for each unit sold. This may be true where, as in the community centre, there is a contract for services. But it may be unrealistic in situations where 'products' are sold, because of the necessity at times to reduce price in order to increase volume.
- It is assumed that activity is the only factor affecting costs and revenues. Other factors such as inflation and technology changes are ignored.
- The analysis can only be applied to a single product or service. Most voluntary organisations have more than one product or service, and the sale or take-up of each may be affected by the other.

5.6 Marginal analysis

We now look at a number of common decision-making situations to see how choices are made between alternative courses of action.

If alternative courses of action are being compared, there is little point in including data that is common to all of them. Management's attention should be focused on the costs and revenues which will differ as a result of the decision. In other words, the incremental costs and revenues should be highlighted. In many cases, the fixed costs will not be altered by a decision, since they are not incremental costs; they should therefore be excluded from the analysis. However, in some situations there may be a step in the fixed costs, and this extra, or incremental, fixed cost should be taken into the analysis. The following examples illustrate this.

Hamilton Care case study

Hamilton Care provides residential care for young people in need under contract from the surrounding local authorities. The contract price paid is on the basis of the number of young people cared for (i.e. spot purchase). Hamilton Care has the capacity to provide 100 beds in total. These facilities are available for 200 days of the year; at present, 80 beds are occupied for the full term (200 days p.a.). Extracts from their management accounts reveals the following:

Figure 5.13 Residential care facilities

		£
Contract Income for services		480,000
Variable costs	320,000	
Fixed costs	100,000	
		420,000
Surplus		60,000

A private sector competitor has recently gone out of business and Hamilton Care has been approached to take the competitor's place. The regional authority will refer 20 young people a year, but is only prepared to pay 75 per cent of the normal contract price per person.

Variable unit costs will not be altered by the proposal, but fixed costs would increase by £5,000, as extra staff would be needed to help with supervision.

Is it a worthwhile proposal from a financial point of view? Hamilton Care needs to determine the incremental costs and income that will arise from this proposal.

First calculate the number of 'bed nights':
Total days multiplied by current capacity 200 x 80 = 16,000
Then calculate the current 'spot price' per person: Contract income £480,000 = £30 per person.

Therefore the proposed contract price is: (75% x £30) = £22.50
The variable cost per 'bed night' = £320,000 = £20.00

A financial outline for the proposal has been prepared as shown:

The proposal would generate an extra £5,000 ((20*200)*(22.50-20.00)) and is therefore worthwhile from a financial point of view.

Closing a project

A national voluntary organisation, which provides support services and information for elderly people and campaigns on their behalf, has a chain of retail shops through which it sells donated goods. A financial review of the shops is currently under way, and three shops have been identified with a view to perhaps closing at least one of them. The results for the latest period are shown in Figure 5.14

Figure 5.14 Summary of financial results for shops

	Shop A	Shop B	Shop C	Total
	£000	£000	£000	£000
Sales revenue	78	120	21	219
Variable cost of sales	48	68	16	132
Contribution	30	52	5	87
Fixed cost	23	34	9	66
Profit/(loss)	7	18	(4)	21

	Shop A	Shop B	Total
	£000	£000	£000
Sales revenue	78	120	198
Variable cost of sales	48	68	116
Contribution	30	52	82
Fixed cost			66
Profit			16

The directors are considering closing down shop C because it makes a loss. But the fixed costs would be incurred even if this were done. The organisation's profit on its retail shops as a whole would fall to £16,000 per year if shop C is closed.

The £5,000 contribution from Shop C would be lost, and so this shop should not be closed, unless a more profitable

use can be found for the space it occupies.
The financial effect of closing shop C is shown below.

	Shop A	Shop B	Total
	£000	£000	£000
Sales revenue	78	120	198
Variable cost of sales	48	68	116
Contribution	30	52	82
Fixed cost			66
Profit			16

These examples have been evaluated on purely financial terms;
however, it is important to consider the non-financial consequences of such decisions as well. If, for example, a nursing home
for the elderly is closed, the emotional effects on long-term residents are impossible to calculate, but would certainly need to be
considered by the charity.

Relevant costs

Relevant costs are those that will be affected by the decision being
taken. In management decision making, all relevant costs should
be considered. If a cost will remain unaltered regardless of the
decision being taken, it is called a 'non-relevant cost'.

Non-relevant costs

Costs that are not usually relevant in management decisions
include:

- **Sunk or past cost.** Money already spent that cannot now be
  recovered: for example, expenditure incurred in developing
  a new fundraising campaign. Even if a decision is taken to
  abandon further work, the money cannot be recovered.
  The cost is therefore irrelevant to future deci-sions
  concerning the project. However, it should be noted that
  sunk costs are frequently anything but irrelevant psycho-
  logically; a manager who has expended a lot of time,
  money and effort in a project will be reluctant to admit
  that it was all effectively wasted and this tends to result in
  the organisation continuing with projects which should
  really have been abandoned.
- **Absorbed fixed overheads.** These will not increase or
  decrease as a result of the decision being taken; see the

example above on the closure of retail shops.

- **Expenditure that will be incurred in the future, but because of decisions taken in the past cannot now be changed.** Although this is a future cost, it will be incurred regardless of the decision being taken and is therefore not relevant. An example is expenditure on training material that has been delivered but not paid for; the organisation is obliged to pay for the material even if it subsequently decides not to proceed with the training courses. This is a variant on a sunk cost.
- **Historical cost depreciation.** Depreciation calculations do not result in any future cash flows. They are merely book-keeping entries designed to spread the original cost of an asset over its useful life.

Checklist – what have we learnt?

Attempt to answer these questions before checking the text:

1. What is the difference between output and outcomes?
2. Can ABC costing techniques be applied to voluntary organisations?
3. Describe cost behaviour.
4. Why should voluntary organisations undertake full cost recovery

Action points for your organisation

'Audit' your organisation by checking to see:

- ✓ Whether the trustees receive ratio analysis reports.
- ✓ Whether the organisation understands its costs!
- ✓ What method of apportioning overheads has been used.
- ✓ Whether ABC could be applied to your organisation.
- ✓ Whether projects are appraised using breakeven analysis.
- ✓ Is full cost recovery being applied to all contracts.

Women's Building Project

This case study looks at the use of marginal costing to help a voluntary organisation determine which projects should be accepted in order to ensure maximum contribution to core costs.

The Women's Building Project (WBP) is a recently-established charity that seeks to provide women who are disadvantaged (either because of low income or otherwise) with opportunities to gain new skills that can then be usefully employed within the construction industry. This is a unique project that offers training to reskill women, and initial information-gathering has identified a number of government and voluntary agencies that have indicated willingness to refer on to WBP.

WBP operates from premises in west London. The site was previously used as a warehouse storage facility and covers about 15,000 square feet. This has been modified by allocating 5,000 sq ft to office and administration functions and the remaining 10,000 sq ft to be used for training workshops.

WBP has applied to a well-known charitable trust set up by the construction industry for funding for both the running costs of the premises and the provision of free training to women. The trust agreed to provide £50,000 towards the core costs of running the premises, but no funding for the provision of training, which it argued should be self-financing through course fees. Further negotiations resulted in the trust agreeing to provide materials and trainers at heavily subsidised rates; however, WBP would still have to levy a charge to ensure that its costs were covered.

The training courses that WBP plans to offer are:

- *Utility installation*: this will provide the skills and knowledge needed to install electricity, water and gas supplies to new residential premises.
- *Woodwork and joinery*: this will provide women with the hands-on experience and skills they need to use different types of timber in the construction and decoration of residential premises.

- *Metal work*: this will provide women with the basic skills they need to use metal structures in the construction of industrial premises.
- *Brickwork*: this will provide women with the basic skills necessary to use brick materials in the construction of residential properties.

The training programmes are planned to provide as much hands-on experience as possible within a workshop environment. They will last for three months each, and will be repeated three times a year. The site will be closed for the remaining three months. To ensure maximum learning, the number of women allowed on to the training programmes at any one time will be restricted to 12.

Because of the workshop approach of this training, it has become apparent that only three of the planned programmes can be accommodated in the 10,000 sq ft space. Any unused space may be offered to another community organisation wanting office space at £5 per sq ft. Each training programme will require its own set of materials, to be used and facilitated by a skilled supervisor.

Detailed costings for each of the four training programmes and the premises as a whole are provided in figure 5.15. A unit of output has been defined as a 'training day' for the maximum of 12 women. For the nine months available in each year, the number of 'training days' will be 180 days per annum or 60 days per term. The costs for each training day will differ according to the type of training programme being run. For example, brickwork training requires more materials (cement, sand, bricks etc) than utility training.

Figure 5.15 Training programme costs

Per training day	Utilities £	Woodwork £	Brickwork £	Metalwork £
Materials	30	35	40	60
Supervisors staff costs	75	22	30	60
Consumables 1	5	10.50	10	20.00
Floor space required (sq.ft.)	2,000	2,000		3,000
	5,000			
Training course fees (per term)	£750	£700		£600
	£650			
Expected take-up rate (%)	90	80	75	95

The other fixed premises costs are estimated at £50,000 p.a. and indirect overhead costs are estimated at £30,000 p.a.

At the next trustees meeting, the management team needs to be able to recommend which training programmes to offer. An initial examination of the information has led the project manager to conclude that first priority should be given to utilities, then metalwork, and finally Woodwork, as these have the highest course fees and take-up rate.

The treasurer, who is also studying to be an accountant, has decided to take a more rigorous approach. He is particularly concerned that, in view of the restriction imposed by the available floor space, only those training programmes that maximise the contribution per square foot to the annual fixed overheads should be accepted. His calculations are shown in figure 5.16.

Figure 5.16 Training programme costs

	Utilities	Woodwork	Brickwork	Metalwork
Total variable costs per training day (a) (material+ staff+consumables)	£120	£67.50	£80	£140
Total variable costs per term (b) (a) multiply by 60 days	£7,200	£4,050	£4,800	£8,400
Expected variable costs per term (c) (b) multiply by take-up %	£6,480	£3,240	£3,600	£7,980
Expected course fees per term (total course fees (for 12) multiply by take-up %) (d)	£8,100	£6,720	£5,400	£7,410
Expected contribution per term (e) (d) minus (c)	£1,620	£3,480	£1,800	£(570)
Floor space required sq.ft. (f)	2,000	2,000	3,000	5,000
Contribution per sq. ft. (g) (e) divided by (f)	£0.81	£1.74	£0.60	£(0.114)
Treasurer's ranking	2nd	1st	3rd	not run
Project manager's ranking	1st	3rd	not run	2nd

As can be seen, the conclusions of the project manager and the treasurer are very different. The treasurer is recommending that the metalwork programme be dropped, whereas this was the project manager's second favourite.

The financial effect on WBP as a whole of the two proposals is shown in fig 5.17.
The information on fixed premises costs and indirect overhead costs will be the same for whatever course of action.

Figure 5.17 Financial results of the recommendations

	Treasurer's proposal	Project Manager's proposal
Contribution for year: ((e) multiply by 3 terms)		
1st: Woodwork	£10,440	
Utilities		£4,860
2nd: Utilities	£4,860	
Metalwork		£(1,710)
3rd: Brickwork	£5,400	
Woodwork		£10,440
	£20,700	£13,590
Remaining floor space available to rent	3,000 Sq. ft	1,000 Sq.ft
Rental income @ £5 per Sq. ft	£15,000	£5,000
Total contribution to overheads	£35,700	£18,590

Test Exercises

Exercise 5.1

The Captain Nelson Foundation has a residential services department, which runs three residential centres for disabled, elderly, former sailors. The details are:

Name of home	number of beds	actual beds occupied	staff establishment
Southways	40	30	8
Northend	40	20	8
Central	50	40	10

Health and local authorities pay the Nelson £3,500 per annum per resident in occupation. Variable overheads are £500 per annum per occupied bed. Fixed costs are staff whose average salary is £10,000 per annum each, and charity head office overheads at £200 per bed.

At a management team meeting reviewing the homes, the finance director states that the homes are currently running at a deficit. The charity can no longer afford these deficits, and so he informs the residential homes director that a revised budget is required which will, at a minimum, break even.

At a subsequent meeting of the heads of home to discuss options, the Central home head suggests that Northend be closed and the residents transferred to the other homes. The residential services director points out that two staff are shortly to leave. By reducing the establishment at Northend to six, it is suggested that this should resolve the problem.

Questions

1. Calculate the current residential homes department deficit by home.
2. What is the required number to break even?
3. Adopting the suggestion to lose two members of staff at Northend, what is the new position for the department? Assume the same occupancy, but a 10% rise in income and costs.
4. Discuss the advantages/disadvantages of the proposed solution. Are there alternatives?

Exercise 5.2

Understanding overhead costs in tendering to run a day centre.

Following reorganisation, Any Council now comprises two main urban areas at either end of its boundary, separated by countryside. One of the urban areas is the County Town which has an active and large Age Concern organisation – ACCT. In the other, smaller, Urban Town the services are still provided by the Council. The new Council has asked ACCT if it would like to run the same services in the Urban Town. It currently gives a grant of £80,000 to ACCT and it is proposed to offer a further grant of £45,000 to run the Urban Town's services. The Council will transfer its current building rent free to ACCT. There are no transfers or contractual problems for the existing staff as the council will re-deploy existing staff if ACCT takes over.

The current ACCT organisation has a large purpose-built building owned by the organisation, which accommodates 150 people daily in a variety of activities, advice, medical services etc. The building has an average 80 per cent capacity use. The Urban Town centre is half the size of the County town centre with 75 places and exactly half the running costs. The budget of ACCT for the current year is:

Income:

Council grant	80,000
Insurance/services	16,000
Donations	17,000
Catering profit	13,500
Total	126,500

Expenditure:
Staff   104,000
Costs   22,000
Total   126,000

Surplus   500

The director has made the following notes on the budget, with a plan for the take-over of the new service. They have proposed that both centres will be under their overall management assisted by the finance officer and catering manager all of whom would accept a 10 per cent pay rise to reflect additional responsibilities and time for managing both services. (All staff costs are inclusive of NI etc):

1. A director £25,000 – who has advised that the Urban Town centre will need a Centre manager at £22,000.
2. A secretary £15,000 – who has estimated that admin costs at the other Centre will be £7,500.
3. A finance officer £20,000 – who has advised that the urban centre will require a finance assistant at £10,000.
4. Service coordinators (both part-time at £10,000 each).
5. A catering manager £12,000 – who has advised they would need an assistant at the urban town centre at £10,000.
6. Service session staff £12,000; volunteers' expenses £4,000.
7. Building running costs £10,000, the new centre will be half in size.
8. Office, admin, audit £8,000. Admin costs at the urban centre will be £2,000.
9. Lunchtime meals are charged at £1.00 and two tea/coffee sessions at 25p per session. A profit of 30 per cent is made on catering. The centre and catering services are open for 250 days a year.
10. Donations and service income for the new centre will be equal in proportion to current ACCT.

From the perspective of ACCT would you take the council's offer and take over the new service? The proposed new management arrangements would mean moving from being one organisation on one site to being an organisation with a management team managing two sites. Prepare revised budgets for the new organisation.

6 Charity accounts and financial management

6.1 Who uses financial statements?

This chapter looks at the different users of charity financial statements and the types of information that will be particularly relevant to them.

The list of people who might need the information provided by financial statements is a key one. Some of them are directly connected with the organisation: for example, its employees and managers. Others are not directly connected, but may be affected by its management of finance or its financial stability: for example, the general public.

User groups who may require financial statements include (but are not restricted to):

- The trustees of voluntary organisations, governing bodies including any members.
- Managers, employees, prospective employees and volunteers.
- Donors and sponsors.
- Grant-making bodies.
- The beneficiary stakeholders using the services of the charity.
- Suppliers.
- Lenders and potential lenders.
- The government, including the Charity Commission, Companies House and Her Majesty's Revenue & Customs (HMRC).
- The public, including the media.

Trustees of voluntary organisations

The trustees are legally responsible for the financial resources entrusted to the organisation, and therefore need to ensure, not only that the financial statements comply with the charity accounting SORP (Statement of Recommended Practice), but also that they properly describe the voluntary organisation's activities and financial position.

Trustees are often unclear about how the information and figures in the management accounts – which they will be familiar with – become the annual financial statements. There are three key reasons for this:

1. The purpose of management accounts is monitoring and control, whereas the annual financial statements are for an external audience.
2. The format of annual financial statements is prescribed by the charity accounting SORP and other regulations, while management accounts should be in a format that informs the management of the organisation.
3. A number of adjustments may be needed to the management accounts – e.g. for accruals and prepayments – in order to arrive at a set of figures that comply with accounting principles.

It is important for the trustees of a voluntary organisation to be able to understand the annual report and financial statements, because it is the chair of the trustee board who signs the report, and, together with the honorary treasurer, the financial statements.

Managers, employees and prospective employees

The managers of a voluntary organisation need financial information to help them manage the business. They need past information to help them monitor the progress of the organisation (or their part of it), current information to carry out day-to-day operational management and control, and forecast information to plan activities in the future.

Employees and trade unions may consult the financial statements when they are negotiating pay and terms of employment. Current and prospective employees might be wise to examine the financial statements to assess whether the organisation is likely to grow and prosper, or whether it (and the job!) will have disappeared by this time next year.

Volunteers will be interested in how the organisation is doing, and may particularly want to see whether their work is being

The trustees are legally responsible for the financial resources entrusted to the organisation.

reflected. As the debate over valuing volunteers continues, it will be interesting to note how much more interest is taken.

Donors and sponsors

People and organisations who donate money to voluntary organisations, or who otherwise sponsor their activities, might use the financial statements to check that they are happy with the way the organisation is handling its funds.

Grant-making bodies

Many grant-making bodies will use the financial statements to obtain a better appreciation of what the organisation does and how it is managed. In particular, they can sometimes use the financial statements to determine the level of reserves available to the organisation, and on this basis decide whether funding will be granted.

For many voluntary organisations, restricted project funding may form a large part of their reserves as disclosed in the financial statements. However, since these project funds are restricted, they are not available for another purpose.

Grant-making bodies will also use financial statements to determine how well the voluntary organisation is managed. Although useful insights can be obtained by using key ratios, sometimes grant-makers have in the past paid too much attention to the figures for management and administration costs in isolation.

> Many grant-making bodies will use the financial statements to obtain a better appreciation of what the organisation does

The beneficiary stakeholders using the services of the charity

This group of users may be paying for services, or receiving them free of charge, but in either case they will want to use financial statements to assess how effectively and efficiently those services are being delivered. Their particular concern will be whether the voluntary organisation has sufficient resources, present and future, to support their continuing needs.

Suppliers

Potential suppliers want to know whether their customer will be able to pay for the goods and services supplied. Furthermore, many customer-supplier relationships are long-term and require a considerable investment of time and money. A supplier will want to be sure of the long-term viability of the other party before making the effort.

Lenders and potential lenders

Banks, Futurebuilders and others who lend money to voluntary organisations will need information about the organisation's ability to make interest payments in the short term and ultimately to repay the loan on its due date. They will also be concerned about the security for their loan: does the organisation have valuable items, or assets, that could be sold to raise the money to repay the loan if necessary?

The government, including the Charity Commission, Companies House and HMRC

HMRC (Her Majesty's Revenue & Customs, previously the Inland Revenue and HM Customs & Excise), for example, will need to consult the voluntary organisation's financial statements to determine whether there is a tax liability arising from any trading activities, and that the correct amount of VAT has been paid over or refunded. The Charity Commission in general will require financial statements and annual returns from registered charities as part of its monitoring activities. Companies House is the central government repository for all audited financial statements. Other government departments and agencies may require financial and non-financial statistics to monitor the state of the economy.

The public, including the media

Voluntary organisations rely to a large extent, upon the goodwill of the public in donating money to their causes, and are also able to take advantage of a range of tax concessions. As taxpayers and Council Tax payers, the public often use financial statements to decide whether to give to a particular charity or not, on the basis of how efficiently it is managed.

6.2 Introduction to the Charity SORP

Charity accounting changed in the 1990s with the official recognition that charity operations were very different from commercial companies. Previously charities had produced income and expenditure accounts, which in essence were the same as profit and loss accounts. In recognition of these differences – for example the object of a charity is not to make a profit but to spend money on its charitable objectives – the Charity Commission set up a working party to help improve the quality of financial reporting by charities, and to assist those who are responsible for the preparation of the charity's annual report and financial statements. An agreed Statement of Recommended

Practice for charity accounts, commonly known as the SORP was published in October 1995. It is subject to annual review, with two large revisions being issued, one in 2000 and more recently in March 2005. Although the word 'recommended' is used, the SORP is actually in the main mandatory, as the SORP forms the basis of the accounting regulations prescribed in the 1993 Charities Act and is supported by Statutory Instrument. Even for charities formed as companies its application is best practice.

Charity financial statements have come under scrutiny over the last few years and the setting up of various organisations, such as Guidestar, and the introduction of the Summary Information Return increase the emphasis. *Public Action, Private Benefit* issued by the Prime Minister's Strategy Unit in 2002 questioned governance, accountability and transparency. It stated: "public trust and confidence enable charities to thrive and prosper. But ... accountabilities to beneficiaries and donors can be unclear" and "in general the sector does not produce sufficiently accessible and relevant information to meet the public's needs". The issuing of the latest Charity SORP has sought to include, and improve, the types of information felt to be lacking within previous sets of financial statements.

Trustee report

In understanding a charity's financial statements, we firstly need to recognise that the responsibility for the financial statements is that of the trustees. The trustee report enables trustees to discharge their public duty of accountability and stewardship and provide an insight into the charity's activities and achievements.

While figures are the essence of financial statements accounts, our starting point in understanding charity accounts is with words. The revised SORP places far more prescriptive emphasis on the formal narrative in the trustees' report. The report now has to include information about the charity's structure, governance and management which involves giving details on the induction and training of trustees and risk management.

The trustee report includes the objects, aims and achievements, (what difference has the charity made) as well as its strategies for achieving those objectives and details of significant activities. Policies in respect of reserves, investments (including social or programme related investments) and grant-making should be given. A commentary on the financial position of the charity and information on volunteers must also be included.

Evolution of the Statement of Financial Activities (SOFA)

The traditional income and expenditure account treatment had, for some time, led to complaints that it did not reflect, or fully explain, all the financial activities of the charity. Therefore, it was considered that the very nature of the raising and using of charity resources required a different approach from that of the business community.

Charities, even those that are companies, do not usually have shareholders, so such matters as distributable profit (dividends) or the retention thereof do not arise. Moreover, those who provide the resources for charities do not usually expect a direct monetary return on their donations, but more of a 'warm glow', or, in the case of commercial donors, an enhancement of their brands or company image by the publicity normally associated with their support. However, the users of a charity's financial statements do need to be able to assess the services that the charity is providing, primarily through its charitable expenditure and its ability to continue to provide those services.

The financial statements should also show how the trustees have carried out their duties and ensured that their responsibilities have been met during the year. Whilst it may be that the bottom line, surplus or deficit, provides some of this information, any presentation which focuses only on the bottom line tends to ignore the fundamental differences between accounting for charities and for the business sector. What is the bottom line when there is in effect no bottom line?

Charities, except those that are trading (effectively), have not in the past been in the business of directly matching income and expenditure. Therefore, they are not working towards a particular year-end date. In other words, to place undue emphasis on the bottom line at a particular point in time can be misleading, as income and expenditure in any one period are not often directly linked; for example, grants received this year may be for projects to be carried out in the following year, or indeed over a number of years. SORP 2005 has extended the matching concept, as charities will now need to match, as far as possible, types of incoming resources with resources expended. However, charities do need to account in certain circumstances for income in advance of expenditure and vice versa.

Revenue and capital

Unfortunately, the traditional income and expenditure account with its distinction between revenue and capital, does not always adequately explain a charity's activities. Businesses primarily invest in fixed assets to generate future profits whilst, of course, a charity may be investing in fixed assets as part of its charitable activity (primary purpose), for example:

- equipping a cancer research laboratory;
- building a care home; and
- acquiring lifeboats.

This difference is extremely important to certain charities, where a significant proportion of their annual expenditure is of a capital nature.

In any particular year, a charity may use part of its income to purchase fixed assets for its charitable activities, since this expenditure is of a capital nature it will not be shown in the income and expenditure account. This could, therefore, lead to a surplus on the income and expenditure account and give a misleading impression, as the asset is written off over a number of years.

Disclosures

The SORP introduced the statement of financial activities (SOFA). This is a means of showing, in summary form for the year:

- All the charity's funds.
- All its incoming resources.
- All its revenue expenditure.
- All transfers between funds.
- All recognised and unrecognised gains and losses on investments.
- How the fund balances have changed since the last balance sheet date.

This comprehensive primary accounting statement should show what funds the charity has and how they have been used. Of course, it may be necessary to add appropriate additional information in the notes to the financial statements, wherever necessary, to bring out some special feature, for example, the equipping of a medical research laboratory or the effectiveness of a particular fundraising campaign or significant branch activities.

However, the SOFA is not as radical as it sounds. It essentially amalgamates the old-style income and expenditure account with the reconciliation and analysis of the movement of funds.

Reasoning

The SOFA recognises that charities do not usually have just one single indicator of performance which is comparable to the bottom line for business. As well as considering the changes in the amounts of the net resources of a charity, it is important to consider the changes in the nature of those resources. As a result, both the SORP and the regulations recommended a primary statement that records the resources entrusted to a charity and reflects its financial activities.

The SOFA is effectively divided into two parts:

- A statement of operations.
- A statement of other changes in net assets.

The SOFA moved away from giving undue emphasis to the bottom line based on matching and dropped the use of the words surplus and deficit. It focuses instead on the periodic measurement of the changes in both the nature and amounts of all the net resources of a charity.

Format

A columnar format is scheduled in the SORP 1995 and 2000 regulations and expanded in SORP 2005. The minimum requirement is:

- one column for unrestricted funds;
- one for restricted funds;
- one for permanent endowments; and,
- one for the total for the year.

Therefore, this requires separation of income and expenditure streams between the types of funds. There is also a fifth column, showing the comparative total for the previous period, but it is not a legal requirement to have to show comparatives for each type of fund.

However, where there have been no movements in any particular fund or the charity does not have that type of fund, then it is not necessary to include that column. In other words, columns will only need to be included where the actual funds exist and there has been movement on them. This columnar approach can be added to; for example, unrestricted funds can be split between general purpose funds and other unrestricted funds (e.g. in the case of a school wanting to distinguish its school fees from other general income). Whilst, of course, funds may be summarised in this way, if there is more than one restricted fund then details should be shown in the notes to the financial statements.

Prior to 1995 many charities either combined all funds together and just showed effectively what is now the total column, or produced separate income and expenditure accounts for each fund without any total for all funds. Both these methods of reporting have been effectively ruled out by the SORP, and SORP 2005 has developed the prescribed format further.

This format has been altered to introduce new standard headings for each row (i.e. line) such as:

Incoming resources from generated funds:
- Voluntary income
- Activities for generating funds
- Investment income
- Incoming resources from charitable activities
- Other incoming resources

Resources expended:
- Cost of generating funds (broken down between generating voluntary income, costs of goods sold, investment management costs etc)
- Charitable activities
- Governance costs

This has helped to make charity financial statements more comparable and transparent. Again, as the SORP makes clear, this information will always be required, but if there has been no movement on a particular heading in the year, or previous year, then that heading need not be included.

Under SORP 2005 there is now a new emphasis on analysis by activities. A clear link should now be established between incoming and outgoing resources. This may be difficult where there are a number of different sources of income supporting a charitable activity but where there is clarity – for example, the provision of care which can be linked with a local authority contract – then this should be reflected within the disclosures on the SOFA.

With the increase in contract culture within charities over the last few years special attention will need to be given to recognising income to the extent that the work has been done. This may require working with other parts of the organisation to establish how much of the work has been delivered. For example, in the case of digging wells overseas – how the contract has been structured and how many wells have been dug by the year end date will determine the accounting disclosure.

Similarly, with grants and donations the charity will need to ensure that all of the conditions have been fulfilled to enable income

Under SORP 2005 there is now a new emphasis on analysis by activities.

to be recognised. If income has been received in advance and all of the conditions have not been fulfilled, then a liability for repayment may need to be included within the financial statements.

Systems need to be included for recognition of material gifts in kind that the charity may receive. While these do not involve financial consideration, if they affect the users' understanding of the financial statements details should be given in the financial statements.

A large change in SORP 2005 has been the removal of management and administration costs and the substitution of governance costs – which look purely at the costs of operating the charity as a legal entity. Costs such as audit fees, legal costs in relation to the charity and strategic management costs should be included here, together with an element of support costs.

The requirement to disclose support costs within the notes to the financial statements has been expanded. These are the costs that do not produce a direct output, they do not constitute an activity in themselves but enable an activity to take place. The types of costs include management costs, finance, IT and human resources, and these should be allocated to the relevant cost category on a consistent basis based on usage, per capita, floor space or time spent. An example would be:

A large change in SORP 2005 has been the removal of management and administration costs.

Support cost (examples)	Fund-raising 1	Care home 2	Care home	Outreach project	Basis of allocation
Management	£10K	£5K	£5K	£10K	Time spent
Finance	£20K	£15K	£10K	£5K	Transactions processed
Information Technology	£15K	£5K	£5K	£10K	Number of computers/ software supported
Human Resources	£5K	£15K	£20K	£5K	Time spent
Head Office space	£30K	£10K	£10K	£5K	Floor space
Total	£80K	£50K	£50K	£35K	

All costs which directly relate to a specific SOFA cost category should be related to that cost. Detailed disclosure on a project-by-project basis can either be shown on the face of the SOFA or in the notes to the financial statements. The costs should break down whether expenditure is in respect of direct charitable activity or grant payments. The notes to the financial statements should also give details of support costs in a structure similar to the one shown below:

Activity or programme	Activities undertaken directly	Grant funding of activities	Support costs	Total
Care home 1	£150K	£-	£50K	£200K
Care home 2	£190K	£-	£50K	£240K
Outreach project	£50K	£60K	£35K	£145K
Total	£390K	£60K	£135K	£585K

Costs of generating funds should also seek to match the analysis of income. SORP 2005 has broken down further the analysis of the costs of generating funds (as noted above). The notes to the financial statements should now show where material costs have been incurred on start-up and recurring costs.

Any transfers between funds should be shown separately, outside of the incoming resources and resources expended sections. Transfers should be shown gross – not netted off and an explanation included within the notes to the financial statements.

Finally, the SOFA encompasses a statement of gains and losses covering both realised and unrealised gains and losses for investment assets but only realised gains and losses for tangible assets.

Any transfers between funds should be shown separately

Balance sheet

The balance sheet of a charity must show the state of affairs at the end of the financial year.

There have been many arguments about what a balance sheet is supposed to represent. As long ago as April 1993, the Accounting Standards Board (ASB) produced a discussion paper on 'the role of valuation in financial reporting'. There was a problem in UK accounting in that there was no consistency in valuation practice. This particularly affected the valuation of assets which may appear in the balance sheet at current revaluation, a previous revaluation or original historic cost. The ASB saw this as an unsatisfactory situation and suggested that a prescriptive approach should be followed, using one of three options.

The 1995 Charities SORP effectively moved well ahead of all of that debate and provided considerable guidance on balance sheet valuation, although it still essentially accepted general accounting principles, as do the 2000 and 2005 versions. It is perhaps worth bearing in mind that the only reference in the

The balance sheet of a charity must show the state of affairs at the end of the financial year.

regulations to the SORP occurs in relation to the valuation of assets and liabilities, where it clearly states that the SORP should be followed.

Presentation

The funds of a charity should be grouped together in the balance sheet according to their type, distinguishing between endowments, other restricted funds, designated and other unrestricted funds, as the SORP itself explains. Further analysis of major individual funds needs to be given, as appropriate, in the notes to the financial statements.

The assets of the charity should be analysed in the balance sheet between fixed and current assets. The fixed assets section should show separately those for charity use and those for investment, and for current assets these should be analysed between current and long-term elements, with the total (if material) of any provisions for liabilities or charges shown separately. The totals for both short-term and long-term creditors should be sub-analysed in the notes.

In addition, the assets and liabilities should be analysed in a way that enables the reader to gain a proper appreciation of their spread and character. The balance sheet must be approved by all the trustees as a body but need only be signed by one of them on behalf of all.

With the introduction of FRS 17 concerning defined pension scheme assets/liabilities, further disclosure is now required where a charity has such a scheme.

Guidance on the Statement of Recommended Practice on Accounting and Reporting by Charities (SORP) is available from the Charity Commission and on the Internet at www.charity-commission.gov.uk.

> The assets of the charity should be analysed in the balance sheet between fixed and current assets.

Statement of financial activities – example
Care Home Trust Limited
Consolidated statement of financial activities (including an income and expenditure account) for the year ended March 2006

Consolidated balance sheets
as at 31 March 2006

	Notes	Group 2006 £'000	Group 2005 £'000
Fixed assets			
Tangible assets	10	830	850
Investments	4	137	129
		967	979
Current assets			
Stocks	11	217	213
Debtors	12	290	287
Cash at bank and in hand		423	319
		930	819
Creditors: amounts falling due within one year	13	242	195
Net current assets		688	624
Total assets less current liabilities		1,655	1,603
Creditors: amounts falling due aftermore than one year	15	46	56
		1,609	1,547
Funds			
Unrestricted funds			
General	16	1,430	1,363
Designated	16	167	167
Restricted funds	17	12	17
		1,609	1,547

Approved by the board on 13 June 2006 and signed on its behalf by:

....

S.A. Bloggs, Chairman

6.3 Audit and independent examination requirements for charities

The 2005 Regulations/SORP detail the accounting and reporting requirements applicable to charities and are available from the same Charity Commission website.

For unincorporated charities the financial thresholds governing the type of accounts and what kind of external scrutiny is required are:

Annual gross income/ total expenditure	Type of accounts	Type of external scrutiny
Below £10,000	Receipts and payments option	None required
Above £10,000 but below £100,000*	Receipts and payments option	Independent
Above £100,000 but below £250,000 option	Accruals mandatory examination	Independent
Above £250,000	Accruals mandatory	Audit

* gross income only

All registered charities with an annual income in excess of £10,000 will have to submit a copy of their annual report and financial statements to the Commission.

In addition, charities with annual income of less than £1,000, and who do not have a permanent endowment nor occupy premises of their own, need not register with the Charity Commission. Those charities with annual income and expenditure of less than £10,000 i.e. the 'light touch' regime, need not submit a copy of their financial statements to the Charity Commission unless they are specifically asked for them. All registered charities with an annual income in excess of £10,000 will have to submit a copy of their annual report and financial statements to the Commission, together with a completed Annual Return for monitoring purposes.

Independent examination is a less onerous form of scrutiny than audit, both in terms of the depth of work to be carried out, and the qualification necessary to undertake such work. The examiner is not required to form an opinion as to whether the financial statements show a true and fair view, but reports instead, based on the examination carried out, whether reportable facts have come to his or her attention.

However, many charities will, because of their own constitution/trust deed, still require audit whatever their size. The audit rules applying to incorporated charities with an income under £250,000 are different, reflecting the lack of harmony between charity and company law. Incorporated charities with an income between £10,000 and £90,000 require no form of examination. Incorporated charities between £90,000 and £250,000 require an audit exemption report. All incorporated charities have to produce their financial statements on the accrual basis and show a 'true and fair view' to comply with company law. (Where a charity's income is below £250,000 and it has an audit requirement which is considered to be onerous the charity could consider changing its constitution – with permission from the Charity Commission.)

The charity legislation makes it clear that auditors and independent examiners are required to report certain matters directly to the Charity Commission (in the case of an unincorporated charity). The government believes that this obligation is essential to strengthen accountability, and public confidence in charities. The Auditing Practices Board has given guidance on what constitutes material or significant matters, which an auditor should report to the Commission. This is to avoid small or insignificant matters being reported which should be handled in a management letter to the trustees. The three main types of material or significant matter are:

1. A significant inadequacy in the arrangements made by trustees for the direction and management of a charity's affairs.
2. A significant breach of a legislative requirement in respect of the charity's trusts.
3. Circumstances indicating a probable deliberate misuse of charity property.

(Independent Examination is covered in more detail in Chapter 9, page 285.)

6.4 Converting management accounts to SORP financial statements

Converting internal management accounts, prepared on an income and expenditure basis, to a set of final year-end financial statements is essentially a process of apportionment.

The management accounts contain the income and expenditure results for the different departments of the organisation, reflecting the structure of the organisation.

These may be departments involved in the provision of charitable activities or departments that support the organisation as a whole: for example, the finance or human resource departments.

The expenditure within each of these departments must be identified and apportioned between the main expenditure headings identified in the SORP: direct charitable activities, costs of generating funds and governance costs (relative to ABC and apportionment status – see Chapter 5, page 155).

6.5 Interpreting published financial statements

The following 12 questions are a useful checklist to use when looking at a published set of financial statements.

1. Does the trustee report clearly show the aims and objectives of the charity?
2. Is the financial review in the trustees' report supported by the disclosures in the financial statements?
3. Does the trustees' report give an indication of future activities?
4. Are restricted funds properly identified and explained?
5. Are designated funds explained? Do you consider them definite commitments?
6. Are costs of generating funds properly identified?
7. Are support costs properly identified?
8. Are the trading subsidiary (if applicable) activities properly identified?
9. Do charitable expenditure headings properly describe the activity of the charity?
10. Are income sources properly identified, and where relevant tied into charitable activities?
11. Do the financial statements show a surplus or a deficit?
12. Is there a reserves policy?
13. Any other issues?

Learning points

- What would an external analyst make of your financial statements? Would a potential funder give you money?
- Does your charity comply with the regulations?
- Does your management team understand the financial statements – offer to run a training session on them if they don't.
- How do you present and explain the financial statements to the chief executive and the trustees?
- What type of external scrutiny does an incorporated charity with an income of £245,000 require?
- List the material or significant matters an auditor must report to the Charity Commission.
- Where do support costs appear in the SOFA?

Case Study

(This is a fictitious example to illustrate the production of a SOFA)

The Distressed Equine Animals in Disaster Relief Areas Trust was set up many years ago to rescue horses, donkeys and mules which were suffering from the effects of natural disasters.

For the last 20 years it had operated on a small but consistent scale; but in 2005, due to a highly emotive television programme which highlighted the plight of these animals following an earthquake in Elbonia, the charity has received greatly increased resources. During the 12 months to 31 December 2005 the following transactions occurred:

Transaction	£	Notes
Cash donations received	£375,000	Elbonia fund £250,000 Unspecified £125,000
Gift aid	£35,000	Received gift aid to date £30,000 Awaiting receipt of £5,000 re Elbonia Fund
Investment income from bank deposit account	£15,000	Elbonia Fund £10,000 interest Other £5,000
Gift of mobile veterinary clinic (for Elbonia)	£30,000	Expected life 3 years; straight line depreciation is used
Horse blankets (for Elbonia)	£8,000	£6,000 worth of these had been used by the year-end
Veterinary expenses	£115,000	Elbonia £50,000; Other £65,000
Costs of generating funds	£50,000	Travel in Elbonia in connection with assisting television production £20,000; £15,000 relates to charity dinner to be held in February 2006
Miscellaneous head office expenses	£50,000	Apportioned 60% Elbonia; 40% other

The charity operates from a building which was bequeathed to it many years ago. It was professionally revalued at £150,000 five years ago and the market value is now approximately £200,000. It is estimated to have a remaining useful life of 20 years. Since the revaluation £6,000 pa depreciation has been charged and the written-down value as at 1 January 2005 was £120,000.

The charity's furniture and fittings are fully written off, but during the year they have acquired six new motor vehicles – three pick-up trucks for use in Elbonia at £20,000 each and three Range Rovers for general use at £28,000 each. These are all to be depreciated over four years, charging a full year in the year of acquisition.

Accrued audit costs for the year were £5,000. No other costs have been incurred in respect of governance expenditure.

For the purposes of this example, the only items on the balance sheet as at 1 January 2005 were:

Buildings	£120,000
Cash	£80,000
Total	£200,000
Financed by:	
General Funds	£200,000

**Distressed Equine Animals in Disaster Relief
Areas Trust**

**Balance sheet
as at 31 December 2005**

	2005		2005
	£'000		£'000
Tangible fixed assets			
Building			114
Motor vehicles			108
Mobile clinic			20
			242
Current assets			
Debtors (gift aid)	5		
Debtors	15		
Cash at bank and in hand	141		
	161		
Current liabilities	5		
Net current assets			156
Total assets less current liabilities			398
Funds			
Restricted funds	170		
General funds	228		
			398

Workings:

Cash Summary

Receipts	£	Payments	£
Opening balance	80	Vet expense	115
Donations	375	Fundraising	50
Interest	15	HO	50
Gift aid	30	Motor vehicles	144
		Closing balance	141
	500		500

Exercise – Test your knowledge of the SORP

Answer all the questions – Circle the correct answers

1) Under the Charities Act 1993, charities must file their financial statements with the Charity Commission within a specific number of months from their year-end. Namely:

(a) 9 months
(a) 10 months
(a) 6 months
(a) None of the above

2) An incorporated charity with income of £260,000 and assets of £5m will require:

(a) an audit
(b) an independent examiners report
(c) a report by a reporting accountant
(d) no examination or report

3) In respect of investment property owned by an unincorporated charity, which statement is true:

(a) it must be re-valued professionally every year
(b) it must be re-valued professionally every five years
(c) it must be re-valued every year
(d) none of the above

4) Under the Charities Act 1993, which is the earliest year, an unincorporated charity does not require a full audit?

Year	Income	Expenditure
1	490,000	90,000
2	80,000	350,000
3	40,000	40,000
4	90,000	60,000
5	90,000	40,000
6	40,000	40,000
7	90,000	10,000

(a) year 2
(b) year 4
(c) year 5
(d) none of the above

5) Your charity has received a permanent endowment of £100,000. Half the money was invested in shares, which were worth £100,000 at the year-end and other half was left in the bank. Income received from the shares amounted to £5,000 (including tax credit) and gross bank interest received was £5,000. How much was the endowment fund balance at the year-end?

(a) £90,000
(b) £150,000
(c) £155,000
(d) £160,000

6) A charity is given a cottage as part of a legacy – probate value £100,000. The legacy was intended by the legatee to provide an income for the charity. The charity decides to use it as a holiday home and received rent of £30,000. The market value of the cottage was £130,000 at the year-end, based on its rental yield, but its insurance value was £125,000. The cottage has a useful life of 10 years. At what value would it be included in the financial statements at the year-end?

(a) £90,000
(b) £100,000
(c) £125,000
(d) £130,000

7) A charity has two funds: a general fund of £10,000, and a restricted fund of £40,000. The charity invested the funds in the same deposit account and earned interest of £5,000. The trustees decided to set up a designated fund with £5,000 of the unrestricted fund. What would be the total of the unrestricted funds held at the end of the period?

(a) £5,500
(b) £10,000
(c) £11,000
(d) £15,000

8) If the amount is substantial, how should help received by a charity from volunteers be disclosed in the financial statements?

(a)   no disclosure necessary
(b)   included in the SOFA in the same way as gifts in kind
(c)   included in the SOFA if the charity would otherwise have paid staff for the same work
(d)   not included in the financial statements but referred to in the notes or trustees report

Answers to exercise

1) b
2) a
3) c
4) c
5) b
6) d
7) c
8) d

7

Key issues

7.1 Introduction

This chapter introduces and explores some key financial and management issues in the voluntary sector.

The voluntary sector has seen a number of recent external influences and pressures brought to bear on it that seem far removed from the traditional financial accounting function. For example, registered charities are now required to undertake a risk assessment, and there have been greater calls for transparency and reporting on how well the charity has performed in meeting its objectives.

In addition, a voluntary organisation is now expected to manage its finances not just from an accounting good stewardship perspective, but to be proactive in seeking value for money and best value from its financial activities.

The finance officer now has an integral role in the organisation and is an important member of the management team, as well as a principal advisor on finance matters to the management committee.

Finance and financial objectives, as previously discussed, cannot be viewed in isolation from the objects of the organisation. A commercial organisation normally uses financial objectives to achieve clear financial aims – normally maximisation of shareholder value or annual profits – but a voluntary organisation needs to have effective management to achieve its non-financial aims, whether these are spiritual, as in a religious foundation, or material, as in the relief of poverty.

7.2 Risk management

The 2000 revised charity Statement of Recommended Practice (SORP) title evolved from 'Accounting by Charities' to 'Accounting and Reporting by Charities'. This was not a cosmetic title change but an important evolution, which has a major implication for charity trustees and senior staff. The original accounting SORP (1988) was intended to give accountants and auditors a framework to deal with a specialised area – other SORPs were issued by the Accounting Standards Board on areas such as pensions. After the Charities Acts 1992 and 1993, the Charity Commission became involved and the focus shifted to issuing charities with a prescriptive framework in which to prepare their accounts. The SORP was intended to ensure that the wide diversity of accounting practices would be eliminated and that a greater transparency to charity accounts would occur. The old (1988 and 1995) SORPs were primarily concerned with accounting principles. SORP 2000 resolves some accounting issues but focuses more on charities providing information about their affairs and in particular how they are meeting their objectives. This trend was further developed in SORP 2005

In 1998 the Charity Commission discovered that 74 per cent of the general public believed that 'there needs to be tighter control over the laws governing charity affairs'. The Charity Commission, which is charged with ensuring public confidence in charities, has in the past been criticised for not supervising the charity sector effectively. Since the late 1980s there has been a general decline in the public trust and confidence in institutions; caused in part by corporate and public sector scandals. Since 1992 a number of reports on improving corporate and public confidence have been published in response to these concerns, which have lead to good practice codes, some of which have had statutory enforcement (see also Chapter 1). Growing out of the corporate governance debate has been a growing interest in managing risk.

The charity sector does not exist in a vacuum and reflects what is happening in the wider environment. The new Charities Act in the early 1990s, and charity accounting SORPs, have introduced a greater prescription in the management of charity affairs. The Charity Commission has increased its supervision and monitoring function and, to support that role, SORP 2000 and now SORP 2005, has been expanded from being an accounting recommendation to a wider report. The addition of the term 'reporting' in the

SORP's title requires charities not only to demonstrate a greater transparency in their affairs, but to also ensure that the charity's trustees are managing their charity effectively.

To ensure charity trustees provide such information this narrative requirement has the mandatory enforcement of the SORP. Since 2000, charity trustees have been required to provide "a statement confirming that the major risks to which the charity is exposed, as identified by the trustees, have been reviewed and systems have been established to mitigate those risks". This requirement does not simply refer to insuring against traditional risks such as fire and flood. The risk requirement goes beyond ensuring that the charity has adequate insurance. The requirement is not just financial risk or internal control but concerns the wider concepts of business risk and, of particular relevance to charities – 'reputation risk'. These require more careful consideration, and insurance can be only part of the solution.

What do these terms mean and how can charity trustees and staffs ensure they are meeting this risk requirement? The following issues are explained:

- what is meant by risk in the context of charities;
- meeting the SORP requirement;
- developing a risk management process.

What is risk?

For charities, risk can be defined as 'any event or action that may adversely affect an organisation's ability to achieve its charitable objectives and execute its strategies'. This definition means that risk is not confined just to the financial affairs of the organisation, but to all areas of the charity's operations. Risk management and control was the focus of the Turnbull report and the following definition of effective risk management for charities can be adapted from the report:

risk is not confined just to the financial affairs of the organisation

> *A charity's system of internal control has as its principal aim the management of risks that are significant to the fulfilment of its charitable objectives, with a view to safeguarding the charity's assets and ensuring the charity is effectively fulfilling its objectives.*

Risk can be seen as having three components:

- Hazard – risk of bad things happening.
- Uncertain outcomes – not meeting expectations.
- Opportunity – exploiting the upside (i.e. the possibilities of

increasing investment returns with the Trustee Act 2000 which gives wider powers of investment but also a statutory duty of care. (See also later section on investment, page 227.)

Risks are either 'external' or 'internal' to the organisation. An example of external risk would be changes in economic conditions or public perceptions. The HIV/AIDS charities found in the middle of the 1990s that their income from government and public fundraising was in decline. An 'internal' risk could be a failure in operational or financial controls e.g. fraud. In addition, risk affects all parts of the organisation:

- **Strategic** – the risk of not meeting strategic objectives.
- **Operational** – failure in operation, which may in turn impact on charitable objectives – for example a fundraising campaign that fails to meet its target.
- **Financial** – not maximising returns or losing money – for example, leaving excess funds in a current bank account instead of a high return account.
- **Regulatory** – failure to meet regulatory requirements.
- **People** – failure to maximise performance or minimise loss.

Risk management does not have to be seen as a threatening or negative activity. Instead risk can be seen as an opportunity. For example, the Stakeholder Pension Scheme legislation requires employers, including charities, with more than five employees to designate a stakeholder scheme, provide access to it for staff and facilitate contributions direct from payroll. If employers show themselves to be uncooperative, fines will be levied. The risk for charity trustees not complying with the legislation is a potential fine of up to £50,000, which the Charity Commission could decide to seek direct from the trustees rather than from the charity's funds. While this is a risk, the opportunity is now to provide staff with pension plans, which means that the charity may retain good staff in an increasingly competitive employment situation. This example illustrates moving the perception of risk from being a defensive isolation activity to instead making risk management proactive. This involves identifying risks and having a strategy to deal with them which involves making a decision to do one or more of the following:

- Minimise the impact of risk – for example with contingency planning.
- Accept the risk.
- Transfer the risk (insurance).

- Reduce the risk (if complete avoidance is impossible or disproportionately expensive in time or money).
- Monitor the risk and potentially exploit the upside – e.g. environmental charities have traditionally seen landfill site operators as enemies, however, under the 1996 Landfill Tax Regulations such companies can divert a proportion of their tax liability to charities that have prevention of pollution of land as their purpose.

Underpinning proactive risk management is a sound internal control system, which:

- can respond to significant risks;
- is embedded in day-to-day processes;
- is capable of responding to external and internal changes;
- can immediately report major control weaknesses.

An *internal control system* will provide a trustee board with reports on:

- identification, evaluation and management of key risks;
- assessment of effectiveness of related controls;
- actions to remedy weaknesses, including considering costs and benefits;
- the adequacy of monitoring of internal control system;
- the process supporting reporting.

Having such information will not only meet the SORP requirements but will give comfort to the trustees that their charity is well run. The following examples of risk management implementations illustrate the point:

1. Board concerned about its overall risk strategy and compliance with the SORP: *Answer – potential full reviews of methods and processes organisation uses; recognise, manage and harness the power of risk to ensure compliance.*
2. Board concerned with potential level of fraud: *Answer – identification of potential areas of fraud and establishment of effective fraud prevention and detection function.*
3. Board of a children's charity concerned about confidentiality and security of data: *Answer – comprehensive review of IT security policy, including compliance with relevant legislation i.e. Data Protection Act.*

Meeting the SORP requirement

Charity trustees must meet the SORP compliance statement. SORP compliant examples are provided in book format from the Charity Commission and on their website: www.charity-commission.gov.uk. As a minimum, the statement in the trustees' report could say: 'The trustees have assessed the major risks to which the charity is exposed, in particular those related to the operations and finances of the trust, and are satisfied that systems are in place to mitigate our exposure to the major risks.'

This, however, is a very bland and uninformative statement which, even if complying with the letter of the SORP, goes against the spirit of openness of reporting. Also, in issuing such a statement the trustees, should certainly have supporting internal documentation that they have in fact undertaken a risk assessment, and would be advised to have this independently confirmed. A more expansive and helpful heading, 'Governance and internal control' might contain a statement outlining and explaining:

- the trustees' responsibilities;
- what they have done in the year to ensure the charity's objectives have been effectively met;
- what systems of internal controls are in place;
- how controls are reviewed; and,
- the adoption of a risk management process, which they have put in place with the assistance of their auditors.

Such a statement would then ensure that SORP 2005 is met which requires:

"A statement should be provided confirming that the major risks to which the charity is exposed, as identified by the trustees, have been reviewed and systems or procedures have been establsihed to manage those risks." (SORP 2005)

Developing a risk management process

Successful risk management frameworks have been found to have the following characteristics:

- aligned to the organisation's mission;
- supported by the trustees, management, staff and volunteers;
- communicated effectively throughout the charity;
- adaptable to environmental change;
- simple but structured.

Charitable organisations need to be clear about their key objectives and the risks associated with achieving those objectives. For example, objectives might be:

- To grow public donations by 10 per cent per annum.
- To meet the needs of our client group by 80 per cent within the next two years.
- To comply with legislation.
- To safeguard stakeholder interests.

Once identified two questions need to be answered:
1. What risks would prevent us from meeting these objectives?
2. What controls could we adopt to minimise risks to an acceptable level?

Inevitably this leads to balancing the charity objectives against the control objectives. Risk is inherent in all activity; it cannot be eliminated but it can be mitigated. For example, the following are key risks for charities:
- Loss of major funder.
- Regulatory breaches.
- Adverse public relations – reputation risk.
- Industrial action.
- Increased competitive activity for funds.
- Changes in economic conditions.

All of the risks can be managed if appropriate controls are in place. NCVO has been exploring risks for charitable organisations and what they can do to mitigate them. NCVO has formulated a ten-point plan based around the concepts of risk assessment, risk analysis and risk management, which voluntary organisations could follow:

Risk assessment:
- Develop/review your strategy.
- Highlight the potential risks.
- Research the evidence.

Risk analysis:
- Categorise the risk.
- Score and prioritise the risks.

Risk management:
- Devise a risk management strategy.
- Agree a plan of action.

- Communicate about risk.
- Monitor and evaluate.
- Review policies and procedures.

Risk management for charities is itself dependent on good internal control systems.

Risk management for charities is itself dependent on good internal control systems. The whole organisation must be involved in the process, and that process has to be led from the top of the organisation. The NCVO ten-point plan can be used as the basis for establishing a risk management process. Practically ensuring this is done will depend in part on the size and resources of the voluntary organisation. Where an organisation has an existing internal audit function it should take the lead. In smaller organisations a designated senior member of staff should take the lead.

Implementing risk management – a charity case study example

The charity Norwood (previously Norwood Ravenswood) established a working party chaired by a trustee, which comprised staff from all levels and aspects of the organisation. An external facilitator supported the working party. Over a period of three months the working party met and first established what they believed were the major risk issues facing the organisation. These were then scored on a matrix scale of 1–5 ranging from 1, meaning little risk, to 5 meaning very high risk, to the extent that the organisation could close down (the impact). The other side of the scale was based on probability of the event happening, ranging from 1, little likelihood, to 5, very likely to happen.

This can be represented as a grid on which to plot and highlight the risks and their likelihood of happening.

The staff on the working party then took back the identified risks to their colleagues and asked them to review them and either agree or score them differently.

The next meeting of the working party then reviewed the staff feedback and then plotted these on to a 'risk register' supplied by the charity's external auditors, identified what safeguards were in place and how effective these were.

Risk register

Area/activity:

_____

Risks identified: date/source

_____

Reported to trustees' meeting on [date]
by _____
Acknowledgement: Kingston Smith & Co

The safeguards were taken back again to the staff for evaluation and feedback. The third meeting of the working
party then fed back these observations. The risk register
was completed which also highlighted the major issues the
charity had to address. The trustee who chaired the
working party was able to present the register to his fellow
trustees and brief them. The trustees were then able to both
agree a programme of work and complete a risk statement
in their report to the Charity Commission.

7.3 Investments

This section will look at how to get the best out of financial
resources and maximise value in banking and investment, and
how to borrow and invest effectively.

All voluntary organisations require the services of banks to
hold funds and to pay expenses. Some voluntary organisations
occasionally have excess short-term funds that if left in a current
account actually lose money due to inflation. Some charities are
fortunate in having funds that can be invested for the long term,
out of which they pay grants to support their work. At the other
extreme some voluntary organisations need to borrow funds to
support their work. This section looks at how to maximise your
relationship with financial institutions to benefit the organisation
whether you are in surplus or need to borrow. Appendix B (page
251) lists some of the main types of investments.

Getting the best out of your bank

The banking industry has completely changed over the last ten years and with that change has come an increasing number of banks that are keen to develop their business in the voluntary sector. Charitable organisations should be reviewing their banking service in line with all other suppliers, including auditors etc., every three to five years as best practice – but how many do?

- When was the last time you reviewed your banking arrangements?
- Have you ever?
- Have you reviewed the charity-banking marketplace?
- Have you considered the competition that exists?

Once you have concluded that you should undertake a review the next step is to decide which banks to put on the shortlist to tender. Five points to consider while making this decision are:

1. Known abilities – specifically with your existing bank, but also with any previous experience as an employee or trustee.
2. Recommendation – a strong influence – from colleagues, members, affiliates, trustees, national and local umbrella support agencies.
3. Ethics – of increasing importance. Are the banks taking their corporate social responsibility seriously? What are their investment policies? Who do they lend money to? Are they solely profit motivated?
4. Suitability – does the choice suit the organisation's need? For example, an overseas aid charity undertaking regular foreign transactions will need to be confident that their bank has sufficient global coverage and expertise, to ensure funds reach their destination on a timely basis and at reasonable cost.
5. Press and satisfaction surveys – there are a number of charity publications which regularly review the banks and their services (e.g. Charity Finance magazine, annual banking survey).

The invitation to tender

A formal tender document should be prepared providing the tendering banks with the following information:

- An outline brief of your organisation.
- The organisation's legal status.
- Any known borrowing requirements – whether cash flow or capital.

Charitable organisations should be reviewing their banking service in line with all other suppliers

- Current banking terms.
- Breakdown of activity – number of transactions by cheque, cash, BACS, salaries etc.
- The past two years audited reports and accounts.
- The organisation's ethical statement/policy.
- Forecast monthly cash budgets for at least the next two years.
- Forecast income statements and balance sheets for the next two years.

The purpose of providing the transaction and balance information is that it tells the banks about the organisation, and gives them the opportunity to evaluate whether they can make a reasonable profit on your business. If they can, they will wish to tender; if they cannot then it is a wasted experience for both of you. Transactions cost banks money, some more expensive than others. The banks will calculate how much, according to the information you have given them, it will cost them to run your account. They will also estimate the organisation's average credit balances, as this gives them an opportunity to earn interest on funds deposited. This will then be taken away from the costs and the banks will determine the figure (within their own profit recovery margins) that they will charge for running the account. This is the 'hard' financial information for decision-making based on cost. However, the organisation should also consider other factors (e.g. ethical policies) before making a decision.

When tendering you should create an achievable timetable. You should also make sure that the selection process is to the satisfaction of the board.

When tendering you should create an achievable timetable.

The tender process
Ten useful points to remember when bank tendering:

1. When did you last review, if ever?
2. Which banks did you ask?
3. Are they known in the sector?
4. Trustees – whom do they know?

(At this point you can decide who to invite to tender.)

5. Create the timetable.
6. Draw up the tender document.
7. Invite visits from a 'long list' to enable the banks to understand your charity; do not ask them to quote 'cold'.

(At this point you will have enough information to create a 'short list'.)

8. Undertake the interviews.
9. Plan the transfer over a couple of months.
10. Develop the bank/customer relationship.

Borrowing

Charities in England have traditionally discharged their missions from custodial sources of funds – i.e. they could only function with funds for which they already have stewardship. Since their earliest days, they have depended on the generosity of wealthy and well-appointed benefactors and charitable trusts for their philanthropic operations.

However, the general perception is that fundraising is becoming increasingly difficult, with competition for funds (both within and without the sector) growing progressively critical and borrowing is therefore on the increase. And charities remain at a disadvantage in this area on two counts, both internal and external.

1. *Internal* (culture/ethos) – charities do not perceive them-selves as 'businesses'. Until very recently, the traditionally-held view that professionalism had no place, and was somehow harmful to the purity and idealism of the voluntary sector, constrained development and progression.
2. *External* – commercial banks conduct their business for optimum gain with minimum risk. Minimum risk is over-come with the security of collateral. Charities have little or no collateral to offer.

Both constraints are barriers to debt financing or borrowing. Whilst financing through borrowing is a common (and tradi-tional) practice in the corporate sector, it has not been widely adopted within the voluntary sector. Estimates of 'gearing' (the proportion of long-term finance which comes from borrowings) within the voluntary sector range between 3 per cent and 4 per cent in the UK, essentially confined to the larger charities. Compared with the for-profit sector, this is very low. But with increased gearing comes increased risk, as well as increased profitability. Charities need to weigh up the potential for under-taking income and surplus-generating projects on borrowed money, against the risk of insolvency should the expected cash flows not result.

Bank borrowing – practical advice and business practice

Before approaching a bank to seek finance, the first question to establish is: what is the financing need? Is the borrowing to:

- Undertake charitable purposes?
- Fund new developments?
- Fund core costs?
- Fund working capital?
- Fund capital expenditure?
- To do something now rather than later?
- To preserve investments?
- To maintain a reserves policy?
- To bridge the recipt of grant funding?

The purpose determines the type of finance and the time factor associated with each. The following types of finance are available:

Short term – maximum one year: to cover seasonal and short timing lags

- Overdraft.
- Factoring/invoice discounting.

Medium term: one to five years

- Leasing.
- Business development loan.
- Fundraising bridging loan.

Long term: over five years; to finance acquisitions of capital assets

- Mortgages – normally 70% of value, but some specialists can provide 100%.
- Sales and leaseback of property.
- Securitisation/bond issues.
- Social venture capital.

Other:

- Grants.
- Other support.

Before approaching a bank for finance the organisation should work up a finance proposal. This should set out the aims of the financing and in particular:

- What is to be achieved.
- At what cost.
- With what return.
- In what timescale.

Demonstrate what are the tangible and intangible benefits. In addition it should also answer the following points:

- Investment – is the amount identified sufficient?
- Can repayment be made?
- The proposal should be supported by financial forecasts of:
- Income and expenditure.
- Cash flow.
- Balance sheet (including effect on reserves).

These should be for a minimum of two years ahead.

Once this information is prepared, a formal proposal can be made to a bank. The proposal should be accompanied by a business plan covering the following topics:

1. Executive summary
2. Background
3. Management/governance
4. Services
5. The market (competition)
6. Method of operation
7. Public relations and fundraising
8. Implementation/timetable
9. Finance requirement and funding
10. Future prospects

Short term funds – cash management options

Introduction

'Cash' as an asset-class is often neglected. For many charities, cash is a passive asset class and typically consists of simple bank deposits or something similar (e.g. fixed-term money market rates). In our view this represents a sub-optimal use of cash. We believe cash should be viewed as an asset-class in its own right which should be actively managed whenever possible.

Cash should be viewed as an asset-class in its own right.

'Cash' on instant access represents a poor way to manage your cash and you are very unlikely to be making your assets work as hard for you as they otherwise might.

Your first step should be to identify, by means of a cash flow budget, the likely 'calls' (regular or one-off) on your cash holdings over the next couple of years. Once this has been done, you will be in a position to identify cash that needs to be kept on 'instant access' and which cannot afford to be tied up for any period of time. The cash flow budget will also identify how much can be locked up for certain periods of time e.g. one month, three months, six months, one year, two years etc. By locking cash up in, for example, term deposits, you would be aiming to achieve a higher return over the period of the deposit than you would achieve by simply keeping it on instant access.

In determining how to split the charity's cash holdings into the various 'liquidity pots', the main factors to bear in mind are (a) liquidity requirements (as identified above); (b) potential returns; and (c) the scale of investment to be made.

What should a charity do with cash that needs to be kept on 'instant access'?

Cash that has to be kept on instant access should be held in an account that will pay as high a level of interest as possible. However, you should be aware that banks or building societies with lower credit ratings sometimes pay higher interest rates. Credit rating is an important factor to bear in mind when choosing an institution to deposit cash with. In the UK, the Financial Services Compensation Scheme only serves to compensate depositors in relation to the loss of the first £35,000 deposited, up to a maximum payment of £31,700 (100 per cent of the first £2,000 and 90 per cent on the next £33,000). Any amounts deposited above this amount will be lost if the institution fails.

Credit rating is an important factor to bear in mind when choosing an institution to deposit cash with.

The other issue to be aware of is the fact that the institutions offering the most attractive rates at one point in time tend not to be amongst the best performers a few months later. This can be overcome (at least in theory) by continually chasing the best rates and being prepared to open and close accounts on a regular basis. In practice this requires an ongoing level of due diligence by keeping the rates (and credit ratings) available in the market under regular review. In addition, with deposit-takers becoming ever more strict with their account opening procedures (largely due to the tighter regulatory regime that governs them), this can become a fairly labour-intensive process.

One way around this is to deposit cash with institutions that are shown to provide consistently good rates. While these rates might not be the very best available in the market place at any one time, they tend not to be far below, and you do not have to go through the hassle of transferring cash from bank to bank on a regular basis.

What are the options for cash that can be locked up for longer periods of time?

There are various options available. Many charities simply use the term 'deposits' where the cash is to be locked up for a pre-specified length of time. Some make use of certificates of deposit (CDs), which are issued by banks. The main difference between term deposits and CDs is that the latter are tradeable in the secondary market. As identified earlier, it is important to bear in mind the credit rating of the deposit-taker/issuer in either case. While term deposits and CDs have their place, but they can represent a sub-optimal use of cash. An alternative are properly managed cash funds which can provide better returns with similar levels of risk.

Cash management funds invest in instruments that are available in the short-term bond and money markets e.g. government issues, corporate bonds, floating rate notes, callable bonds, CDs, commercial paper, eurobonds, asset-backed securities, deposits. Cash management funds tend to be benchmarked against LIBID (London Interbank Bid Rate), LIBOR (London Interbank Offered Rate), or some variant of either (e.g. 3 month LIBID is typical). The aim would be to beat whatever benchmark was set for the fund in question. It is worth noting, however, that relatively few bank accounts (or short-term deposits) will pay LIBID/LIBOR (and, to our knowledge, none do on a consistent basis). So if the fund merely achieves the benchmark return alone, this would represent a better result than one could reasonably expect from simply keeping cash on deposit.

Cash management funds tend to be managed within pre-defined sets of rules as set by the manager in question. These rules typically restrict credit ratings, liquidity, maturity and issuer/sector concentration. The aim is to ensure a well-diversified portfolio, whose overall credit rating is higher than that of many of the institutions commonly used by investors for cash deposits.

One advantage of using such funds is that, unlike term-deposits, there is no requirement to commit capital for a set period. This is because cash management funds deal regularly (normally daily or weekly) and settlement takes place shortly thereafter (typically three days later). However, it would be fair to say that this approach is best suited for 'strategically-held' cash that will not be drawn down on a very frequent basis. In other words, cash management funds should not be used for genuinely 'instant access' cash but are better suited for longer-term cash holdings. Precisely how long depends on the overall maturity/duration of the underlying portfolio of assets (which will vary from fund to fund and will depend to a large extent on the benchmark of the fund in question).

What are the risks associated with cash deposits?

In respect of cash deposits, the Financial Services Compensation Scheme provides limited protection in the unlikely event that a bank was to fail (as outlined previously). The key to ensuring the safety of cash deposits is the size and credit rating of the bank. The credit ratings of the major banks are set out in the table below.

AAA	AA+	AA	AA-	A+	A
Rabobank Nederland	UBS	Bank of Scotland Barclays Bank Lloyds TSB Bank	ABN Amro Bank of America Citigroup Deutsche Bank HBOS HSBC Bank Royal Bank of Scotland	Bank of Ireland Bank of New York Credit Suisse Goldman Sachs ING Group J P Morgan Chase Merrill Lynch Morgan Stanley	Allied Irish Banks Lehman Brothers Bear Stearns

Source: Standard & Poor's long-term credit rating – May 2005

The credit ratings used by two of the major credit rating agencies are set out below.

	Standard & Poor's	Moody's
Investment Grade	AAA	Aaa
	AA+	Aa1
	AA	Aa2
	AA-	Aa3
	A+	A1
	A	A2
	A-	A3
	BBB+	Baa1
	BBB	Baa2
	BBB-	Baa3
Non Investment Grade	BB+	Ba1
	BB-	Ba2
	B+	Ba3
	B	B1
	B-	B3

Source: Barclays Capital

No charity should deposit cash with an institution with a credit rating below A- (Standard & Poor's) or A3 (Moody's). The likelihood of an institution with a credit rating of A-/A3 or above failing is remote (although by no means impossible).

What about the risks of cash management funds?

These funds tend to be managed within pre-defined sets of rules as set by the manager in question. These rules typically restrict credit ratings, liquidity, maturity and issuer/sector concentration. The aim is to ensure a well-diversified portfolio, whose overall credit rating is higher than that of many of the institutions commonly used by investors for cash deposits.

The second risk relates to the possibility of capital losses in the short-term due to adverse market conditions. Cash management funds should not be used as overnight accounts as it is possible that the underlying instruments held within the fund can show a short-term fall in value in certain conditions. The possibility of such an event should be more than outweighed by the likelihood of higher returns over the short to medium-term. Finally, even the best planning cannot foresee all events. If a charity needed to access funds immediately and did not want to disturb its cash management holding for whatever reason, then it could always borrow, using the fund as collateral if necessary.

Summary – what are the differences between cash management funds and term- deposits?

	Cash management funds	Short term deposits
Rate payable	Should outperform the returns available from short-term deposits. (Fund price generally quoted in Financial Times so investors can easily keep track of performance).	Lock in a fixed rate for a defined period.
Time frame	Should be looking to invest for a minimum of (typically) six months at the outset (this depends to a large extent on the benchmark of the fund though).	Depends on the term of the deposit chosen.
Liquidity	Deals regularly (normally daily or weekly) and settlement takes place shortly thereafter (typically three business days later).	Can potentially be broken early but penalty costs will be incurred.
Credit Risk	Diversified credit risk. Overall credit rating likely to the same or higher than that offered by a bank or building society. However does not offer an identical level of security of capital to that provided by a bank or building society.	Concentrated credit risk. The security of capital will however vary depending on the credit rating of the bank or building society.

Longer term funds – entering the investment maze

The Trustee Act 2000 gave freedom of investment powers to trustees of all trusts, including trustees of charities. After many years of frustration of working within the 40 year old scheme of the Trustee Investment Act 1961 of 'narrow', 'wider' and 'special' ranges of prescribed investments, or needing to seek special orders from the Charity Commission, trustees may now make any kind of investment that they could make if they were absolutely entitled to the assets of the trust. However, as the Act further states, before exercising any power of investment, a trustee must obtain and consider proper advice about the way in which, having regard to the standard investment criteria, the power should be exercised. Trustees, and those advising them, should read the guidance provided by the Charity Commission – CC14 Investment of Charitable Funds.

The investment of charitable trust funds is one of the most important, and also one of the most difficult, duties requested of trustees and the finance officer. This is especially so if an individual has taken on the role of trustee because of the skill they hold relating specifically to their charity, e.g. a consultant physician on a medical trust, rather than any financial skills. Equally, most voluntary sector finance officers are unlikely to be appointed with investment training and experience, being more likely to come with an accountancy background. The trustees must be aware of the suitability of the investments currently held, or being considered, and be aware of the need to diversify their investment holdings. Clearly, for anyone unversed in financial matters, the need to seek advice is compelling and, under the Act, a duty.

> The investment of charitable trust funds is one of the most important duties requested of trustees and the finance officer.

Pooled versus segregated funds, or product versus service

Charities can choose between pooled funds or they can choose an individual portfolio service. One of the distinct and big advantages that the charity sector has over other investors is the existence of common investment funds, which enjoy the support of the Charity Commission. These special collective investment funds offer a number of clear benefits:

- they are well-diversified investment funds with clear objectives;
- there is a reasonably diverse choice of funds available;
- they are usually cheaper than unit trusts.

Common Investment Funds have set the marker for the rest of the charity investment sector. A segregated approach must either offer something unusual, or provide a better service at a similar cost. For smaller funds it is difficult to imagine how this can be done.

Segregated funds are usually tailored to individual client needs with individual holdings in cash, fixed interest securities and equities, both UK and overseas. The key deciding factor in the comparison with Common Investment Funds will be the minimum charge. On this basis, most charities which have funds worth less than £1m are probably better off using Common Investment Funds, while most charities with funds over £10m will be better off using a segregated approach. Funds between these two extremes will have to look at their distinct needs and cost. There are over 38 Common Investment Funds to choose from, ranging from equity (UK and overseas) to gilt fixed interest, mixed funds, property and hedge funds.

Choosing an investment manager – key factors

The selection of investment managers needs to be carried out professionally. Charities should go out to tender with the clear aim of matching the objectives of the trust to their investment policy. (Appendix A. Tendering for an Investment Manager suggests criteria.) Having appointed a fund manager, it will be necessary to monitor his/her performance in meeting the fund's needs, by holding regular review meetings with the manager and choosing an appropriate performance benchmark to assess their performance.

Review procedure

The normal procedure for a segregated fund would be quarterly reports supplemented by meetings with trustees. Often these meetings are quarterly as well, although once a fund is established with few major changes in its needs from quarter to quarter, the freqency may be reduced, although meetings should be held at least once a year. Trustees are required to have an annual review of investment performance from a longer-term perspective, including consideration of the appropriateness of the benchmark or the agreed investment policy.

Charities investing in pooled funds may well find less frequent reports more appropriate. Most pooled fund managers produce six-monthly reports, which are usually sufficient for trustees to keep in touch with developments. Even so, a formal meeting of the trustees to review the investments annually is still sensible. Where poor performance is an issue, the trustees will probably ask for the manager's comments prior to this annual review.

Performance measurement and targets

Measuring performance of investments is complex, but various measuring methods are available:

- **Measurement techniques which use quantitative tools and valuations.** However, charities are already a heterogeneous group with wide variation in investment policy and constraint. The use of comparisons to industry averages must, therefore, be treated with caution. It is unlikely that any single yardstick will provide an easy method of judging investment performance.
- **An independent performance measurement service for charities.** The strengths of this lie in the independent verification of returns and its analysis of the relative success in each asset category. Its weaknesses are the cost, which makes it inappropriate for funds of less than £1million and, more importantly, the fact that trustees may be tempted to assume its weighted average return represents a universally appropriate yardstick. It does not.
- **Bespoke benchmarking set by the charity.** This involves the trustees defining their investment objectives. In particular, they need to set clear income targets, defining precisely the constraints (including ethical issues) that will apply, and providing some indication of the degree of risk, which they are willing to incur. Limits can also be set as to how far the fund manager can deviate from the benchmark in response to shorter-term judgements of relative value. Once chosen, the benchmark needs to be regularly monitored.

Costs

The key driver of the recent changes in financial services has been the lack of transparency in fee charging. Charities should be aware of all the costs upon their funds, and should certainly consider the total costs when appointing new managers. The most common forms of charging are:

1. **Management fee:** a direct fee, usually charged as a proportion of market value on a sliding scale. This charge is very clear, easily verifiable, and is usually what trustees think of when talking about costs.
2. **Commissions on transactions:** a charge on each transaction based on a percentage of the market value of the deal, again usually on a sliding scale.
3. **Pooled fund charges:** pooled funds are subject to their own charges, including initial charges, annual fees and sometimes commissions.

4. **Bank interest deductions:** many firms derive revenue from the cash balances held by retaining a part of the interest rate charged. This is not always easy to identify, so it is sensible to compare cash rates earned with inter-bank rates at least annually.

5. **Administrative charges** – including charges for custodian services: many firms include these services in their standard charges, but those that do not may charge a fixed fee, a value based fee or a transaction charge.

6. **Third-party charges:** most firms pass on third-party charges to clients.

7. **Performance fees** have recently become very popular because they gear the manager's charges to the success of the fund. The manager may, for example, earn 50 per cent more if the fund outperforms by 2 per cent or more, but 50 per cent less if it under performs by 2 per cent or more. Whilst intuitively attractive, performance fees can be administratively cumbersome and their use is not conclusively proven.

While not an exhaustive list, this does cover the main charges. The trend, however, is towards fee structures where there is a single sliding scale, which covers most (if not all) of the manager's costs. Thus, the lower the sum invested, the higher percentage that fee will represent.

A final word on investments – ethical issues

Ethical investment has been debated within the voluntary sector for many years and is increasingly coming to the fore. Charities, unlike individuals, are constrained by law, which in this area is complex. Judgements tend to be against ethical investments with judges favouring the view that trustees are expected to act in the best interest of the beneficiaries. There are, however, some fairly clear areas – for example, cancer charities would not invest in tobacco company shares.

In setting a practical ethical policy on exclusions three points need to be addressed:

- What activities should be avoided?
- What constitutes a material involvement?
- Where will the information be obtained?

1. Activities for exclusion

Defining the activities for exclusion is the first step, but this is not always straightforward. For example, consider the exclusion of alcohol related investments. Should the exclusion apply to companies which manufacture alcoholic products, such as the brewers; or should it also apply to distributors and retailers? Adopting such a strict definition would exclude, for example, all the supermarkets. Trustees must come to an agreement as to precisely what activities to exclude and why these conflict with their charity's objectives. These decisions cannot be based solely on the trustees' own personal views.

2. Materiality

In principle, a company with any involvement in an excluded activity should be avoided. This poses a problem both in terms of the degree of exclusion and in obtaining information. In practice, therefore, some definition of materiality is normally applied. Such tests can include proportions of sales, profits or numbers of employees.

3. Obtaining information

The final problem is obtaining information. This is particularly problematic when a strict materiality test is used. For example, a fund manager will clearly know when a company earns 50 per cent of its profits from alcohol but may not if only 0.5 per cent is so derived. Annual reports and accounts can be informative, but of course accentuate the positive and bury the negative. The most effective screening service is provided by specialist ethical services, of which the leading exponent in the UK is the Ethical Investment Research Service (EIRIS).

Other practical issues which need to be considered, are whether to use an ethical pooled fund or a segregated approach. The disadvantage with pooled funds is they tend to be expensive, using a segregated approach requires being very clear on the issues we have raised previously in this chapter. The other practical issue is long-term consequences, and these fall into two main areas:

- monitoring of performance; and
- cost.

Monitoring of performance

There is no conclusive evidence for or against ethical investment on long-term performance grounds. There is clear historical evidence that ethical restrictions can have short-term implications, with such constraints meaning that some opportunities have been lost. It is also possible for fund mangers to shelter behind the ethical constraints when defending poor performance.

> There is no conclusive evidence for or against ethical investment on long-term performance grounds.

Cost

An ethical portfolio will cost more to manage than a conventional one as an additional workload is involved in vetting ethical restrictions, either by the fund manager or through purchasing an independent screening service. For large funds such costs, however, will be a small additional amount.

7.4 Performance

Meeting the need of SORP 2005 and the Standard Information Return

Context

The charity sector does not exist in a vacuum and reflects what is happening in the wider environment. The new Charities Act in the early 1990s, and charity accounting SORPs, have introduced a greater prescription in the management of charity affairs. The Charity Commission has increased its supervision and monitoring function and, to support that role, SORP 2000 and now SORP 2005, have been expanded from being an accounting recommendation to a wider report. The addition of the term 'reporting' in the SORP's title requires charities not only to demonstrate a greater transparency in their affairs, but to also ensure that the charity's trustees are managing their charity effectively.

Voluntary organisations have a variety of different stakeholders; some internal to the organisation, for example management committee members, and others external, for example funders. In addition, for charities having to comply with the Charity SORP there are new requirements requiring not just factual data, but also information about the achievements of the organisation. The often under-resourced finance office may find servicing and providing information to these different stakeholders a problem. There are a number of possible reasons for this:

- The training and experience of the finance staff is usually in financial accounting not management accounting.
- The finance department is often a single or two person function which focuses on 'getting the books right' and does not have the time in reality, or in priority, to produce information for various groups.
- The finance officer fails to see that different groups require different information and produces just one set of information – this is not a case of 'one size fits all'.

These problems can be resolved by the finance officer working on communicating effectively by adopting a customer focus function, by:

1. Identifying who the stakeholders are, both internal and external.
2. Establishing what are the particular needs of those stakeholders, for example timing of reports – it is pointless producing a budget report two months after the end of the budget!
3. Recognising that there is a 'hierarchy' and segmentation of information demand. By this we mean that departmental type managers require budgetary control information only about their department – hence the importance of establishing a financial accounting system that reports on cost codes and budget centres – whilst more senior managers, notably the chief executive officer, are going to require an overview of the entire organisation.

As well as providing timely and relevant financial management information within the organisation, the finance department is also required to produce information to a variety of external stakeholders. The production of end of year accounts is not the final stage in the process, in some respects it is the beginning.

The annual report in many voluntary organisations has to date ranged from some text about the organisation placed before the accounts, to a glossy fundraising-type publication with a page of summarised information devoted to finance. In the future neither of these reports will be acceptable.

Voluntary organisations are increasingly going to see the issue of providing information about their performance, not just for public relations, but for those registered as charities as a statutory requirement, both through the Charity SORP and the Standard Information Return. The RNID (Royal National Institute for the Deaf) were in the vanguard of these developments by producing an annual report that identified targeted activities and measurable performance targets to prove whether it has achieved them.

The role of the finance department in producing this information will be crucial, both in assisting the organisation to produce quantifiable data and being able to convert such data into meaningful, value for money analysis. This will mean using benchmarking techniques, where actual performance can be compared against predetermined targets or budgets. Such processes will be measured over time and involve both internal and external (comparison with similar organisations) analysis.

Developing benchmarking means that the organisation has to understand what it is doing, and can lead to challenging questions of why a service is delivered in a certain way, as well as opportunities to improve.

THE SORP Requirements and the Standard Information Return

SORP 2005 and the Standard Information Return for registered charities are at the forefront of making charities explain not just their aims and objectives but also the strategies and activities they are following to achieve them. In essence if the charity does not have a strategy with measurable targets how can the charity know if it is achieving its objectives?

SORP brackets the information required in the trustee annual report as follows:

- **Administrative details** – which includes the name of trustees, the chief executive and other relevant persons and principal advisors, banks etc.
- **Structure, governance and management** – SORP 2000 introduced a requirement for a statement on risk which we covered earlier in this chapter. This section has now been expanded to enable the reader to understand how the charity is constituted and its organisational structure. An important new addition is to explain how charity trustees are recruited and new ones inducted
- **Objectives and activities** – this is a new section and requires the charity to explain both what the aims and objectives are and what strategies it has in place to achieve the stated objectives. Significant activities during the year should also be reported, relating to the type of charity activities, for example a grant-making charity detailing its grant making policies
- **Achievements and performance** – another new section, which links to objectives and achievements. What the charity has achieved during the year should be reported and how it compared against the objectives that have been set. This section also asks for disclosure on fundraising or investment performance and for comment on factors within and outside its control which are relevant to the achievement of those objectives which could include employees and users.
- **Financial review** – as well as describing the charity's principal financial management policies this section should also include the reserves policy, principal funding sources and if investments are held whether any social, environmental or

ethical considerations have been taken into account.
- **Plans for the future** – this section links back to the aims and achievements section, but for future periods and should set out key objectives for the future and what plans exist to achieve them. Note that the links as future plans become the following year's report on what was achieved.

The Standard Information Return

Larger charities (£1million plus) will also have to complete for the Charity Commission an expanded Standard Information Return. Charities that have adopted the SORP reporting requirements should have no problems completing the Information sought by the return which asks questions such as:

Larger charities will also have to complete for the Charity Commission an expanded Standard Information Return.

- What does your charity aim to do?
- Who are your beneficiaries?

It reflects the SORP's focus on objectives, activities, outcomes and impact.

How to pro-actively meet the SORP requirement – an overview of some useful techniques:

1. The balanced scorecard

'Nonprofits and governmental agencies should consider placing an overarching objective at the top of their scorecard that represents their long-term objective: for instance, a reduction in poverty or illiteracy, or improvements in the environment … For a nonprofits agency, financial measures are not the relevant indicators of whether the agency is delivering on its mission'. Kaplan and Norton (2001).

The balanced scorecard seeks to measure performance against organisational strategy, by creating a set of linked, measurable indicators. This is best introduced by turning organisations into strategy-focused organisations. These organisations have five principles which define them:

- Translate the strategy to operational terms.
- Align the organisation to the strategy.
- Make strategy everyone's everyday job.
- Make strategy a continual process.
- Mobile change through executive leadership.

Using these principles they then suggest that organisations build strategy maps. These maps link strategies within the perspectives of the balanced scorecard system to a top-level overall vision or strategy. For voluntary organisations they suggest that these high-level visions are not financial measures, as they are for corporations. This gives the balanced scorecard a key position in providing managers with a tool to measure their overall strategy and not just those financial areas.

Although measurement still needs to be numerical, the use of non-financial measures within the scorecard enables managers to clearly link the measurement of outcomes, inputs and therefore to report on effectiveness.

2. The excellence model

"The excellence model is a framework of continuous improvement that has a proven track record, with thousands of organisations currently using it to improve their operations and performance." Sauve and Bell (2000).

The excellence model is underpinned by some fundamental concepts:

- Results orientation
- Customer focus
- Leadership and constancy of purpose
- Management by processes and facts
- People development and involvement
- Continuous learning, innovation and improvement
- Partnership development
- Public responsibility

The model consists of nine criteria, each representing an area of activity which contributes to an organisation's success. By regularly reviewing activities and results in these areas, organisations can test their progress towards excellence.

The nine criteria of the model are:

1. **Leadership** – how leaders develop, facilitate and implement the mission, vision and values required for long-term success. This includes their personal involvement in ensuring that the organisation's management system is developed and implemented.
2. **Policy and strategy** – how an organisation implements its mission and vision through a clear stakeholder-focused strategy, supported by relevant policies, plans, objectives, targets and processes.

3. **People** – how an organisation manages, develops and releases the knowledge and full potential of employees (including part-time, temporary and contract employees and volunteers) at an individual, team-based and organisation wide level in order to support its policy and strategy and the effective operation of its processes.

4. **Partnerships and resources** – how an organisation manages its external partnerships and internal resources to support its policy, strategy and effective operation of its processes. Internal resources include financial resources, buildings, equipment and materials, technology, information and knowledge.

5. **Processes** – how an organisation designs, manages and improves its processes to support its policy and strategy and fully satisfy (and generate increasing value for) its customers and other stakeholders. A process is a sequence of steps that adds value by producing required outputs from a variety of inputs.

6. **Customer results** – what an organisation is achieving in relation to its external customers or service users.

7. **People results** – what an organisation is achieving in relation to those individuals employed by the business, including part-time, temporary and contract employees, and volunteers.

8. **Society results** – what an organisation is achieving in relation to local, national and international society.

9. **Key performance results** – what an organisation is achieving in relation to its planned performance in both financial and non-financial terms.

These nine criteria can be grouped into two broad areas: 'how we do things' (enablers) and 'what we target, measure and achieve' (results).

The model is not prescriptive. It does not tell an organisation what to do; instead it provides guidelines that enable the organisation to pursue excellence on its own terms, taking into account its own circumstances, and at its own pace.

3. PQASSO

"PQASSO is a quality assurance system that has been designed specifically for small and medium-sized voluntary organisations. Designed as a work pack, it is simple and straightforward to use, offering a flexible and staged approach to implementing quality." Charities Evaluation Services (2000).

PQASSO covers 12 quality areas and promotes continuous improvements through self assessment. It helps staff and management committees identify what the organisation is doing well and what needs to be done in order to improve. The areas are:

1. Planning for quality
2. Governance
3. Management
4. User-centred services
5. Staff and volunteers
6. Training and development
7. Managing money
8. Managing resources
9. Managing activities
10. Networking and partnership
11. Monitoring and evaluation
12. Results

PQASSO can assist with organisational development and improved services in many ways including:

- Demonstrating accountability, through the use of a well-recognised quality assurance system.
- Bringing people together to work for improvements.
- Facilitating discussion within an organisation, to ensure all stakeholders are aware of organisational policies, procedures and plans.
- Focusing effort on what really matters.
- Motivating people by making progress more visible.
- Providing a clear, shared language for negotiating with funders.

4. Social audit

Social accounting and auditing is a way of measuring and reporting on an organisation's social and ethical performance. An organisation which takes on an audit makes itself accountable to its stakeholders and commits itself to following the audit's recommendations. A foundation standard – AA1000 – has been developed by Accountability:

"AA1000 is focused on securing the quality of social and ethical accounting, auditing and reporting. It is a foundation standard, and as such can be used in two ways: as a common currency to underpin the quality of specialised accountability standards; and as a stand-alone system and process for managing and communicating social and ethical accountability and performance.

AA1000 should be viewed as a complement to existing tools, but it is also a process that aims to support organisational learning and overall performance. The standard is underpinned by the principle of accountability to stakeholders."

Conclusion

We have provided an overview to some current performance techniques – suggested further reading and support for these various techniques are at the end of the book. There are many other management techniques, as well as traditional sources of information retrieval, for example surveys and oral histories. The important learning point is for the voluntary organisation to communicate (thereby demonstrating it has gone through a process) to stakeholders that it both understands its aims and purpose, and has clear objectives with a plan to achieve them which it monitors to ensure that it is meeting those purposes effectively.

Appendix A

Tendering for an investment manager – a suggested questionnaire
1. Introduction.
2. The fund's investment objectives.
3. Details of the investment firm, which should include:

- The firm's ownership, financial strength and structure.
- The size and number of funds under management, including an analysis by client type and growth in funds under management during the last three years.
- Charities for whom they act.
- The number of staff involved in investment management, research and administration.
- Details of the investment managers who would manage funds, how many other funds they currently manage, their experience in investment management, length of service and other responsibilities.
- Details of who would be making investment decisions and dealing with the charity and advise if these persons would be available to report directly to the trustees.
- Indication of turnover of fund managers and administrators over the last three years.

4. Services available – this should indicate the range of fund management services the firm provides for charities, showing which services are offered to clients of different sizes and stating any minimum segregated portfolio size.

5. Investment process – this should provide a brief overview of the firm's investment philosophy and process for charitable funds including:

- Investment philosophy and how investment strategy is drawn up.
- Internal decision-making process for stock selection.
- Definition of risk and what techniques are used to quantify it.
- Constraints placed on total investments at stock and stock levels and checks made on adherence to client and house guidelines.
- Policy towards the use of pooled funds.
- Research capacity and methodology.

6. Performance – tables comparing the firm's charities returns for the last five years against a suitable index for example:

- Unconstrained discretionary portfolio against WM unconstrained Charity Index.
- Charity fixed interest, UK equity and overseas equity total returns, comparing results with the FT All Gilts Index, FTSE All Share Index and the FTSE World Index (ex–UK) respectively.

7. Fees – this should ask for:

- A description of the charging structure identifying all fees, commissions, initial charges and other charges derived by the firm and on what basis fees are calculated
- Provide a full pro-forma example of the fees they would expect to charge in a full year
- Estimate the costs of transferring the present account

8. Administration and reporting – this should seek to discover the custody arrangements, administration and reporting service provided and an outline of the administrative arrangements which they would supply.

- How regularly reports and valuations will be provided and what information they would contain (ask for an example).
- Whether the service includes custodial facilities where appropriate, and if so on what basis of charging
- How, and with whom is uninvested cash deposited, and on what basis this facility is charged for

9. General – this should invite the firm to bring to your attention any additional information they think adds value, for example their knowledge of the charity sector.

10. Who will be coming to the presentation?

Appendix B

Common types of investment

Deposit account with bank or building society
These give immediate access, or they may be on seven-day or longer notice periods.
- Rate of interest will usually increase as the amount invested and the period of notice increases.
- Be wary of depositing large sums with less well-known financial institutions.

Common deposit fund
This is a special deposit fund available only to charities in England and Wales. It uses a system of pooling cash deposits, so that the amount available for investment is increased and the return improved. The fund manager will invest these funds with several different banks or deposit-takers so that the risk is spread.

- Immediate access.
- Interest is paid gross.

Equities
These are shares in quoted companies.

- Dividends usually paid twice yearly, with no guarantee of how much.
- Market value can go up as well as down.
- Risk can be diversified by investing in companies in different market sectors.

Bonds

These are fixed interest securities, such as government stocks (gilts), corporate bonds, debentures and preference shares issued by central and local government.

- Risk of losing the principal capital is negligible, hence the rate of return is low.
- Investment portfolios may well include gilts because they are a way of balancing the overall risk profile.

Unit trust

A pooled investment fund that invests in quoted shares.

- Allows the charity to enjoy the benefits of more diversification than it would otherwise be capable of, as the portfolio will comprise fixed interest and equities.
- An entry and exit charge, as well as annual management charges, are usually levied.

Common Investment Funds (CIFs)

Pooled funds are similar in many ways to unit trusts, but with additional benefits to charities. CIFs have the same advantage of diversifying investments across different stocks and shares. They are approved by the Charity Commission and are themselves registered as charities.

Property

An investment suitable only for voluntary organisations with large investment portfolios and governing documents that give them the power to do so. They are long-term investments and cannot readily be sold should the organisation require quick access to resources.

- There are costs associated with managing and maintaining the property.
- Trustees are likely to need professional advice on the long-term growth and income prospects of property.

8 Taxation

8.1 Introduction
8.2 Charities and direct taxes
8.3 Donor relief
8.4 Charities and VAT

8.1 Introduction

The first point to be made is that tax law does not recognise voluntary organisations; it only recognises charities, as defined by case law. This chapter will therefore discuss only charities. Responsibility for determining whether an organisation is charitable or not is the responsibility of the Charity Commission in England and Wales (in Scotland the Revenue makes this decision). The second point to make is that each tax has its own concepts and philosophy and these should normally not be used in relation to a different tax, otherwise error and confusion will result. An example is the income tax concept of trading; this does not apply to VAT which has its own concept of 'business activities'.

Sections 8.2 and 8.3 begin by examining direct taxes; income tax, corporation tax, capital gains tax, inheritance tax and stamp duty. Section 8.2 will discuss the impact of direct taxes on charities themselves, and Section 8.3 will discuss reliefs aimed at donors, and their effects on donors and the charities that receive the donations. The final section will discuss the impact of VAT on charities.

It should be emphasised that this chapter is very much an overview, and should not be used as a replacement for professional advice. All areas of taxation are extremely complex, and the financial cost of a bad decision could far outweigh any savings on professional fees. Many decisions and contracts cannot be restructured for tax purposes once set in train, and it is therefore essential to get competent advice to ensure that you get it 'right first time'. Most problems occur for a charity when its circumstances change. Most large firms of accountants have specialist charity tax departments; you should consult them whenever you think there may be a problem. This guide can only indicate where the tax 'landmines' might lie.

> All areas of taxation are extremely complex, and the financial cost of a bad decision could far outweigh any savings on professional fees.

8.2 Charities and direct taxes

Charities benefit from a very favourable regime in relation to income/corporation tax, as long as they are careful about how they arrange their affairs. The rules for income tax and those for corporation tax are more or less identical; charitable trusts are subject to the income tax rules, *companies limited by guarantee* and *unincorporated associations* are subject to those for corporation tax.

The rules for income tax and those for corporation tax are more or less identical

> The supreme rule is that as long as the charity income in question is applicable for charitable purposes only, and actually applied for charitable purposes, then much of it is exempt from income tax.

The following is a list of types that are exempt.

Rent or other receipts from rights over land

This applies whether the charity is located in the UK or elsewhere. In addition, there is another condition, that states that the income must: "arise in respect of rents or receipts from an estate, interest or right vested in any person for charitable purposes". This appears to mean that the property must be held for charitable purposes and not, by implication, for investment or fundraising purposes.

The legal definition of land in the **Interpretation Act 1978** states: "*Land includes buildings and other structures, land covered with water, and any estate, interest, easement, servitude or right in or over land ...*" The type of income taxed will be principally rent, but will include feu duties, lease premiums, and income from the letting of sporting rights.

Profits from the development of land are not covered by the exemption. On first sight such profits may appear to be capital items and as such outside the scope of income tax. Prior to the introduction of capital gains tax, such profits would have escaped tax altogether if it were not for two strategies of the tax authorities. First, such profits could be regarded as 'an adventure in the nature of trade' and therefore taxable as trading profits; or secondly, they could be caught by a specific piece of anti-avoidance legislation and treated as taxable. The basic message is to take care when developing land, and where possible place any such profits in a trading subsidiary (see below).

Interest received by charities

This includes bank interest and loan stock interest, governmental and commercial, arising both in the UK and abroad. Where UK income tax has been deducted at source this is reclaimable from the Revenue by the charity, though most types of interest received by charities will be paid gross.

Tax-effective donations

This applies to donations made under the Gift Aid scheme since 6 April 2000. A donation which is not made under the Gift Aid scheme is ignored by income tax. This might appear to be good but it is not. A donation that is ignored by income tax cannot be subject to a reclaim from the Revenue, and cannot reduce higher rate tax for the donor. So, if the donation fulfils the requirements of the Gift Aid scheme (see below), the charity can reclaim 28p in every pound (22/78 of the net amount received) from the Revenue. The reason is that the tax system treats the donation as already having had basic rate tax, currently 22 per cent, deducted from it. Because this income is exempt from income tax for a charity, the charity can reclaim this tax deducted. The scheme is curious, but it means effectively that tax relief is shared between the charity, which gets the basic rate tax; and the donor, who can deduct the donation from their higher rate tax bill. This is dealt with further in Section 8.3, Donor reliefs, page 258.

Company donations

Donations to charities by companies are treated in a different way, in that the charity does not make a tax reclaim on them. They therefore need to be kept separate in the charity's records. Donations received under the payroll giving scheme are also not eligible for a tax reclaim.

Dividends

Formerly, charities could obtain a refund of the tax credit from HMRC, but this is no longer possible. The dividend income itself is still tax-free for charities, whereas it would be taxable if received by an individual.

Profits from trading

The final major category of charity income which is eligible for income tax relief is profits from trading. There are pitfalls here, however, because not all trading is exempt. This is a summary of types of trading that are eligible for relief, which will be explained in more detail later:

- Primary purpose trading.
- Trading ancillary to primary purpose.
- Trading carried out by the beneficiaries of the charity.
- 'Small' trading as defined by statutory guidelines.
- Trading falling under extra-statutory concession C4.

Taxable trading

Trading carried out by a charity, which does not fall under one of these categories, will be taxable; and, if profits are made, the charity could end up paying hard-earned charity funds over to HMRC. An example would be trading purely for fundraising purposes and which is on a material scale. Any trading like this should not be carried out in the charity itself but should be placed in a non-charitable trading subsidiary. The subsidiary then donates the profits under the Gift Aid scheme back to the charity, meaning that what were taxable profits are now exempt as a tax-effective donation. This rather arcane system ensures that no trading profits suffer corporation or income tax, but does need to be followed properly. The Charity Commission offers assistance in ensuring that the paperwork is correct, and the Revenue's publication IR2001 offers an excellent explanation of tax-exempt trading.

Primary purpose trading

Primary purpose trading occurs when a charity has to trade to fulfil its reason for existence, as it is within its objects. Some examples are:

- Fee-paying schools.
- Sale of tickets giving admission to shows staged by theatrical charities.
- The provision of residential accommodation by residential care charities in return for payment.
- An institution selling learned journals.

Ancillary trading

Profits from trading which is ancillary to the primary purpose are also exempt from income tax. Examples are:

- Sales of text-books to students by a school or college.
- Sales of food or drink from a café to art gallery visitors.
- The sale of confectionery and flowers to patients and visitors by a hospital.

Care needs to be taken where some of this trading ceases to be ancillary and becomes trading in its own right. This could occur, for example, if the café in the art gallery becomes dominated by customers who do not visit the art gallery. HMRC has tests to ensure that such trading is not material. Currently, to comply the trading needs to be small and less than 10 per cent of the turnover. Small means turnover of less than £50,000, but does not include fundraising activities as such. These tests are distinct from the 'small' trading rules laid down by statutory guideline.

Beneficiary trading

Beneficiary trading is also eligible for relief. Examples of trades where the trading is carried out by beneficiaries of the charity would be sales of goods manufactured by disabled people who are the beneficiaries of the charity. Another would be a restaurant run by students as part of a catering course at a college.

'Small trading'

There is one other statutory exemption for charity trading and that is 'small' trading. The definitions are a little complex, but in effect state that profits are exempt if the turnover is less that £50,000, or 25 per cent of the charity's total gross income. This is aimed at non-primary purpose, non-ancillary, activities which would otherwise have to be put in a trading subsidiary. They can remain in the charity as long as they continue to fulfil the requirements.

Extra-statutory concessions

Finally, there may be trading which cannot benefit from any of the previous statutory exemptions. Extra-statutory concession C4 is aimed at certain fundraising events carried out by charities. The tax authority's main concerns are that those attending are aware they are at a charity event, and that the events do not compete with commercial activities. In theory, the exempt events are supposed to be 'one-off', but in fact up to 15 such events at the same venue within one year can be exempt. Examples are barbecues, auctions, festivals, concerts, balls and discos. All income from such an event is covered, including sponsorship and sales of goods before, during and after the event.

Business sponsorship

There are some types of activity where particular care needs to be taken, such as business sponsorship. The key here is the nature of the relationship between the charity and the sponsor, and who is getting what out of the arrangement. On the one hand, a simple acknowledgment of assistance in a theatrical programme is treated as a simple donation, on the other hand, the selling of a list of donors to a commercial body is considered to be straight trading and should be put through a trading subsidiary to protect the profit from tax.

One final point on trading. The sale of donated goods in charity shops is regarded as an indirect donation rather than trading and as such is not taxable.

Capital taxes and charities

When a charity disposes of an asset it owns, such as a parcel of shares, it will not be subject to Capital Gains Tax (CGT), as long as the gain is applied for charitable purposes only. Inheritance tax is not payable by charitable bodies, but is payable only by individuals and certain non-charitable trusts.

Conclusion

Charities should not pay direct tax as long as they arrange their affairs properly. All the time, the exemptions are subject to the requirement that income and gains should not be spent on non-charitable objectives. If they are, then the exemptions are withdrawn and tax becomes payable. An example of a non-charitable objective would be a loan to a person that is not a beneficiary or employee.

> Charities should not pay direct tax as long as they arrange their affairs properly.

8.3 Donor reliefs

This section will look at the following donor reliefs in terms of the detailed requirements for each to be successful:

- Gift Aid.
- Corporate giving.
- Gifts in kind and loan of employees.
- Share gift relief.
- Payroll giving.
- Halfway house charities/personal charitable trusts.
- Interest free loans.

- Capital Gains tax relief.
- Inheritance tax (IHT) relief.

First, a few words about *covenanted giving*. For many years this was the only tax-effective way of giving, and its administration was supervised in a highly formalistic way by the Revenue; by which we mean that wording and dates had to be absolutely exact, otherwise the Revenue would refuse to recognise tax-effectiveness. The introduction of Gift Aid in April 2000 removed the need to set up the legalistic rigmarole of a deed of covenant.

Gift Aid

Tax-effective single donation giving was introduced by the Finance Act (FA) 1990, and prior to April 2000 an individual could donate at least £250 cash as a one-off payment each year to a charity, as long as it was accompanied by the appropriate paperwork.

The introduction of the current Gift Aid scheme removed the minimum amount. Individual donors can give as little or as much as they like, and these donations will be tax-effective in the same way as in the old systems, as long as the donor completes either a written or an oral declaration. Charities still reclaim basic rate tax from the Revenue.

Lower rate taxpayers are treated less harshly, but non-taxpayers will still have to pay the tax to cover the amount the charity reclaims. This can be either by income or capital gains tax.

Companies no longer have to pay the basic rate tax to HMRC and charities can no longer reclaim this amount.

The key document from the charity's point of view is the Gift Aid declaration. Before a charity can reclaim tax on donations by individuals it must have received a Gift Aid declaration from the donor containing seven pieces of information:

1. A confirmation that the donation is to be treated as a Gift Aid donation.
2. The donor's name.
3. The donor's address.
4. The charity's name.
5. A description of the donations to which the declaration relates.
6. A note explaining the requirement that the donor must pay an amount of income tax or capital gains tax equal to the tax deducted from his or her donations. (Declarations can be given orally, of which more below, and these do not need to contain this item.)

7. The date of the declaration.

There is no requirement for a declaration to contain the donor's signature.

Oral declarations need to cover the same items as above. The donor has entitlement to cancel the notice, and it is not effective unless/until the donor is sent notice.

Confirmation by the donor that the donations are to be Gift Aided can be in various forms. The Revenue gives the following suggestions:

- I want my donations to be Gift Aid donations
- Please reclaim tax on my donations
- Tick here if you want us to reclaim tax on your donations

A new 'gift aid it' logo promoting the Gift Aid scheme was developed by the Giving Campaign in 2002, with the aim of raising awareness of the scheme amongst charities and their donors. Declarations can be backdated to cover all donations received since 6 April 2000, as long as tax has been paid covering those donations.

Charities need to ensure that they have a record-keeping system that is able to store indefinite records of the declarations. Once a declaration is in place the charity will need to ensure that the donor remains a taxpayer. HMRC will periodically inspect charity gift aid claims. This is done on a statistical basis. If declarations are found to be missing, they will ask for repayment back to April 2000 of a proportion of the gift aid where any errors/omissions are found.

HMRC will periodically inspect charity Gift Aid claims.

Benefits

In theory there should be no benefit provided in return for a donation. But in practice this often happens, for example, reduced admission charges for those donors who donate via Gift Aid. There are, therefore, rules about the maximum level of such benefits. If these limits are breached then the donation is no longer a tax-effective donation and becomes trading income. The limits are as follows:

Amount of donation	Value of benefits
£0 - £100	25% of donation
£101 - £1,000	£25
> £1,001	2.5%

These limits apply to each donation. The value of benefits is also accumulated for each donor during the tax-year, and if the value exceeds £250 then cancellation of Gift Aid ensues for the total donations for that donor for that tax year. This rule means that charities will need to keep a cumulative record of donations per donor. Benefits are valued on a market-value basis. From the charity's point of view, the mechanism for reclaiming tax, after receipt of the payment, is to complete the new reclaim form and send off to HMRC. Careful calculations are needed where large donations are made by the same person e.g. at a charity auction.

Higher-rate taxpayers can claim the difference between the basic and higher rate for themselves (currently 18 per cent). Donors can now get higher-rate tax relief in a previous year, and tax repayments can be passed on directly now by HMRC under Gift Aid.

Corporate giving

Since the Finance Act 2000, corporate donations are not subject to tax deducted at source, so the charity cannot reclaim any tax on them. The company treats the amount paid as a charge on income, deductible from profits chargeable to corporation tax.

> Corporate donations are not subject to tax deducted at source.

The question of benefits to non-close companies (a close company is usually small, and frequently a family company) in return for such payments is a little more complex than in the case of an individual. If the company was to make a donation to a charity which was local and could be seen to provide some benefit to the company, say to a benevolent fund from which the employees could benefit, or to a local hospital, then such payments are likely to be allowable as a normal expense wholly and exclusively incurred for the benefit of the company. They would not be treated as charges on income and tax would not need to be deducted and accounted for to HMRC. Similarly, a sponsorship payment to a charity where the company is benefiting from association with the good name of the charity is a business expense. On the other hand, a pure donation to a charity which is not providing any benefit to the company could not be regarded as a business expense and so has to be treated as a one-off charge and tax deducted.

Gifts in kind and loan of employees

The Finance Act 1983 introduced the concession whereby businesses could lend an employee to a charity temporarily and continue to treat the employee's remuneration as a proper business expense. The business does not have to be incorporated. The Finance Act 1987 extended this concession by allowing businesses to second their employees to educational establishments run by local education authorities, or approved educational establishments, and continue to deduct the costs of the employee.

Share gift relief

The Finance Act 2000 introduced a new relief whereby donations of quoted shares to charities would be treated as a charge in the tax computation of the donor at the shares' market value, thus giving full relief at the donor's marginal rate of tax. The donor will also be exempt from capital gains tax on the gift. This now also covers freehold and leasehold property. Charities must give written acceptance of gifts of shares (in case they do not want them). Individuals can claim a deduction of the gift against their income for income tax purposes and companies can claim a deduction from corporation tax.

It is good practice for the charity to keep records of the date of transfer of the shares to help the donor if necessary. If the charity offers any consideration to the donor for the gift of shares the value of the consideration must be deducted from the amount of the relief.

Payroll giving

Another extension in flexibility of giving was introduced by the Finance Act 1986, whereby employees can have their donation deducted from their gross salary by their employer, who then passes the money to an agency charity, which acts as a clearing house. The funds are passed by the clearing house agency to the charities previously chosen by the employee. There is no need for reclaim of tax by the agency or the final destination charity because the donation will be made gross out of the employee's income before tax. From the charity's point of view this saves on administration. The effective cost of the donation to the employee is 78 per cent of the committed amount for a basic rate taxpayer and 60 per cent for a higher-rate taxpayer. (Earnings for National Insurance purposes are not reduced by payroll giving.)

No long-term commitment is necessary by the employee, only the signature of a simple deduction agreement is required. As the scheme is bolted on to PAYE, only employees whose employers have agreed to offer a scheme will be able to take advantage of payroll giving. There are currently government grants available for employers with up to 500 staff to join the scheme, ranging up to £500. The government will match donations up to £10 per month for up to the first six months. This was because originally only selected larger employers had set up schemes. Donors cannot receive benefits under the scheme.

The main agency charity acting as a clearing house is the Charities Aid Foundation, which handles 75 per cent of payroll giving schemes. Others include a scheme run by Barnardo's; and a consortium of animal charities.

Half-way house charities

Such charities include the Charities Aid Foundation (CAF) and personal charitable trusts. The key point about using a half-way house strategy is that it requires more planning; in other words, a donation strategy.

The Charities Aid Foundation, and similar agency charities, act as collecting agencies for Gift Aid payments from individuals and companies. The agencies reclaim the tax from HMRC, and pay out to the charities chosen by the donors. Such a scheme gives more flexibility for the donor than a deed taken out directly with one charity. The donor can pick and choose charities. The charities will receive the donation gross and so will not have to reclaim tax. There is no charge on the handling of deed payments, but an administrative charge of 2 per cent of gross value is deducted from gift aid payments. Interest on funds held is retained by CAF to cover overheads.

Personal charitable trusts

How do personal charitable trusts work? A donor sets up his or her own grant-making charitable trust. The trust deed can be so worded that grants can be made for the full range of charitable purposes. This would enable the trust to make grants to recognised charities and to non-charitable bodies where the fund will be used for a charitable purpose.

The trust will need to be registered with the Charity Commission, and can be funded by gifts of capital, such as legacies, or payments under deeds of covenant, or payments under Gift Aid. The trust will reclaim tax on such payments and hold them for gross distributions for charitable purposes.

Control of the trust can be secured by the donor being a trustee, and retaining the power to appoint new trustees, or it can be written into the trust deed that the trustees shall distribute the money in accordance with the wishes of the settlor. Care needs to be taken with the wording. Care also needs to be taken in realising that the property in the trust is no longer the settlor's; it is now held for charitable purposes only, and the money can only be distributed for charitable purposes, not private purposes.

The main agency charity acting as a clearing house is the Charities Aid Foundation

The main advantages of such a trust for the donor include:

1. The donor can support a range of charities without having to enter into a long-term commitment to them.
2. The donor can respond to emergency or disaster appeals promptly and with funds which have already received tax relief.
3. Payments can be made to individuals and bodies not registered as charities, thus increasing flexibility of charitable giving, as long as the money is spent solely on a charitable object. It has been suggested that relief of poverty could be achieved by supporting a grandparent in an old people's home, provided that he or she is genuinely in poverty.

The downside to the trust is the cost of establishing it in terms of legal fees, and then ongoing administrative overheads, though both of these need not be excessive.

The attraction of such trusts to wealthy individuals, and to companies, is obvious. It should be noted that such trusts may accumulate funds, as long as it is in their trust deed, to build up a capital fund, the income from which will be used for charitable purposes; or for a specific future capital charitable legacy, say the purchase of a building to be used by a charity.

Interest free loans to charities

These do not bring any tax benefits to the donor, but they can be very helpful for charities when they need to fund a capital project, or to cover a shortfall in funds. The interest which arises on the funds, if they are invested, will be the charity's and therefore tax-free. For this to occur, the lender has to give up the right to determine how the funds should be invested.

Capital gains tax relief

The original capital gains tax legislation introduced by the Finance Act 1965 did not contain any relief for donors to charities. This relief was introduced in 1972 and the section containing it has not changed materially since. The relief is given where a disposal to a charity is made 'otherwise than under a bargain at arm's length', in other words is a gift, or is for lower than market value.

There are two situations to consider: first, where the asset is either given free to the charity or is sold at less than cost to it; second, where the asset is sold to the charity at an amount higher than cost but lower than market value.

In the first situation, the deemed value of the proceeds will be such as to produce neither gain nor loss for the donor. In other words, the deemed proceeds will be equal to the allowable deductions plus indexation allowance. In this way no charge accrues to the donor, and also no allowable loss occurs. In the second situation, there will be a chargeable gain for the donor to the extent that actual proceeds exceed allowable deductions, with indexation allowance taken into account.

Inheritance tax relief

From the days of IHT's predecessor but one, estate duty, gifts to charity were treated favourably: the fall in value of an individual's estate as a result of a gift to charity was not taxable, whereas most other gifts were. This is still the case: when the value of a person's estate is calculated on death, assets to be given to charities are excluded, thus leaving them free from tax. IHT is otherwise charged at 40 per cent on the value of the estate currently over £275,000.

Conclusion

The UK now has a very generous tax regime in relation to charitable donations. It is up to the sector to take advantage of this, by producing attractive tax-effective donation products in the way that the US non-profit sector has.

8.4 Charities and VAT

Value-added tax (VAT)

VAT is not a tax on profits; it is essentially a tax on transactions, which is ultimately borne by the final consumer, at least in theory. The actual distribution of the tax burden differs from this where there are anomalies in the types of supply organisations make, as we shall see with charities, and this can mean that the effective incidence of the tax stops short of the final consumer. VAT is a European consumer tax which is now being administered by the newly formed HMRC.

VAT is not a tax on profits; it is essentially a tax on transactions

VAT is a tax which is levied on turnover, calculated on the value, actual or deemed, of the supply of goods and services known as 'taxable supplies', which are supplied by the registered taxpayer. Taxable supplies are supplies of all types of goods and services other than those which fall within the exemption list. These supplies have to be made 'in the course or furtherance of business'. The definition of 'business' has been drawn widely in the relevant case law and can catch activities not necessarily confined to commercial or profit-making activities. The leading case decided that the provision of accommodation for pupils of a school was a business activity.

It is not just a matter of knowing whether an activity is regarded as business, but also whether its outputs should be standard-rated, zero-rated or exempt. Clearly there may well be an advantage for a charity if it has an activity which is standard-rated because some, at least, of the charity's input VAT will be recovered.

The variety of types of income received is growing with the development of more and more ingenious fundraising schemes, and with more and more charities embracing trading opportunities. Also, another important development contributing to this variety is the advance of the so-called 'contract culture'. The extension of competitive tendering of services previously run by local authorities has created a market within which charities can, and do, compete for contracts, for example, in the provision of care. The consideration for the provision of such services will be business and standard-rated, unless the type of supply qualifies for exemption or zero-rating. By contrast, a grant which is made to a charity without the requirement of service provision would be outside-the-scope as a form of donation.

VAT is blind to whether an activity is for charitable purposes – unlike direct taxation as discussed above. Estimates vary on the cost to the sector as being between £400 million and £1 billion. VAT is charged on taxable supplies of goods and services ... by a taxable person. The term person includes individuals, partnerships, trusts, companies and charities. If a person is making taxable supplies, then the value of these supplies is called the taxable turnover. If a person's taxable turnover exceeds certain limits, known as the registration threshold (for the current threshold check with your local VAT office or accountants), then they are a taxable person and should be registered for VAT. For charities, a good rule to follow in defining whether activities fall within VAT or not, is to assume business activities as falling within the scope of VAT and non-business activities as falling outside its scope. However, if in any doubt take professional advice. A taxable supply is a supply of goods and services other than an exempt supply. A taxable supply is either standard rated – currently 17.5% – zero-rated – 0% – or exempt, which means that the supply is not chargeable to VAT.

The following example illustrates the differences:

If in any doubt take professional advice.

Charity:	A	B	C
	Standard Rated	Zero rated	Exempt
	£	£	£
Inputs	80,000	80,000	80,000
VAT	14,000	14,000	14,000
Outputs	120,000	120,000	120,000
VAT	21,000	0	0
Pay (reclaim)	7,000	(14,000)	0

Zero-rated means that no VAT is chargeable, but a registered person may recover the input on related expenses (as charity B). In addition, voluntary organisations may make supplies that are zero-rated – these include books, periodicals and other publications, certain aids designed for use by disabled people, the sales of donated goods and distribution of goods overseas.

To help the reader determine further which activities are classified as 'business', and whether they are standard-rated (SR), zero-rated (ZR) or exempt (EX) see figure 8.1 (page 269). Non-business activities will be outside the scope of VAT (OS). It draws partly on **VAT Leaflet 701 Charities** and aims to provide a summary. It starts with general activities and then delves into more specific aspects of charities, the VAT treatment of whose income may be less obvious.

This list is clearly not exhaustive but should include the most important. Many charities will have a mixture of outputs in all three categories (SR, ZR and EX) plus outside the scope income (which is not an output). As previously mentioned, VAT recognises taxable persons, not taxable activities, as its focus of attention, which means that all the activities of that person are taken together for the purposes of registration.

VAT recognises taxable persons, not taxable activities.

Concessions

There are three concessions specifically for charities in relation to income, that is, in VAT terminology, supplies by them:

- zero-rating for the sale of goods donated to a charity;
- zero-rating for the donation of any goods for sale or export by a charity;

- the possibility of exemption of all income which would otherwise be standard-rated from a fundraising event.

There are of course other concessions which charities can take advantage of in relation to their income as included above, in particular, the exemption of education, and health and welfare, but these are not specifically aimed at charities.

Goods donated to a charity

How does the first concession benefit a charity? Firstly, that in the absence of the concession, part of the proceeds of sale would go to the Treasury rather than the charity. Secondly, that all VAT incurred on the costs of disposing of donated goods is fully recoverable.

Prior to 1990 only certain classes of charities selling donated goods were allowed to zero-rate sales. Following the 1991 Budget, the provision was extended to allow all charities and their trading subsidiaries to benefit from zero-rating. Any goods which are purchased and then sold must be standard-rated, unless they are zero-rated goods such as books. The legislation says nothing about any concession for goods bought below market value so one must assume that the sale of these should also be standard-rated. Goods which are purchased for resale and which would be zero-rated in a normal commercial situation will remain zero-rated, for example, books and pamphlets.

> Any goods which are purchased and then sold must be standard-rated, unless they are zero-rated goods such as books.

Goods donated by a charity

The second concession, although it appears to relate to income, has its beneficial effect in relation to inputs, whereby charities are allowed to reclaim the VAT on goods to be given away abroad by them. This is achieved by allowing charities to treat this activity as a zero-rated business activity. If the concession did not exist the charities would not have been able to recover VAT paid when these goods were purchased.

Fundraising events

The third concession will benefit the charity in that part of the takings which would otherwise have gone to the Treasury remain with the charity, but has the disadvantage that any VAT incurred will be locked in and become a cost to the charity. The rules are now the same as for extra statutory concession C4 in relation to income tax (see above).

Once the concession is available, all types of income directly connected with the event which would otherwise have been standard-rated are exempt, including admission charges, catering, sales of merchandise, sponsorship and the sale of advertising space. It is important that sponsorship and advertising are directly connected with the event. The downside of this exemption is that any VAT incurred on the costs of mounting the one-off event will be irrecoverable. The availability of the exemption from VAT has no effect on the direct tax status of such events and whether, for example, the sale of entrance tickets represents trading income.

Figure 8.1 VAT treatment of activities

	Business	Non-business	Treatment
General fundraising		Donations, including covenants, Gift Aid, legacies, flag days	OS
		Selling bequeathed property	OS
	Concerts, galas, performances Admission charges to premises		SR
	– unless 'one-off' events		EX
	Sales of donated goods		ZR
	Sales of bought-in goods excl. books		SR
	Sales of bought-in books		ZR
	Sponsorship where benefits provided		SR
		Sponsorship where acknowledgement only	OS
	Affinity card sponsorship		SR
		Affinity card donation	OS
	Selling advertising space: equal to or more than 50% commercial		SR
		Selling advertising space: less than 50% commercial	OS
	Lotteries		EX
Central/local government funding	Grants with services rendered as condition		Dependent on type of service
		Grant with no service condition	OS
Financial income	Interest		EX, but effectively ignored
		Dividends	OS
		Profits from share dealings	OS

Letting charity property	To another charity		EX
	Community building to local groups etc		EX/SR (option to tax)
	To businesses		EX/SR (option to tax)
	Sale of farm produce		ZR
Voluntary services		If provided free as part of charitable purpose	OS
Relief aid	Export of goods by gift overseas as part of charitable purposes		ZR
Churches		Fees for rites, e.g. weddings, funerals	OS
		Offerings from congregation	OS
Clubs, associations	Subscriptions giving benefits		SR
		Subscriptions giving voting rights only	OS
Sports clubs	Subscriptions to play at a club or use sports facilities only		EX
Welfare charities applying services not for profit	Provision of care for the sick, elderly etc.		EX
	Protection of children		EX
	Spiritual welfare		EX
		Relief of the distressed below cost, i.e. recipient pays less than 85% of cost	OS
Approved hospital	Provision of care or medical treatment and goods in connection therewith		EX
School		Education provided free, or for a fee less than cost by a local authority	OS
	Education for a fee at or above cost by D.E. approved school		EX
	Education for a fee at or above cost by other institution e.g. playschool		SR
	Sale of educational materials in class		EX
	Sale of education materials in school shop		SR

University		HEFC grant	OS
	Educational courses		EX
	Research activities		EX
	Sporting, recreational courses		SR
	Business consultancy		SR
	Secondment of staff		SR

Sponsorship

Sponsorship can sometimes cause VAT problems for charities. Sponsorship can be a genuine donation, a trading transaction, or a mixture of the two. Clearly, if anything is supplied, or deemed to have been supplied, in return for financial support, then a taxable supply has been made for VAT purposes. Customs do, like the Revenue, accept that a payment where only an acknowledgement has been given can be treated as a donation and therefore outside the scope of VAT. If a contribution is made to the charity on the condition that a company's name or trading style is advertised or promoted, then this constitutes advertising, and is a standard-rated supply by the charity. Furthermore, if the company receives some other benefit in return, for example, tickets to a concert which is not an exempt one-off event, then this is a standard-rate supply by the charity. Where there is an element of donation in the payment it may be possible to split the amount, putting the vatable supply through the charity's trading subsidiary, and the non-vatable element through the charity. If this is not possible, it is advisable to put the complete transaction through the trading subsidiary.

Affinity credit cards

The income from affinity credit cards has, via a non-statutory concession, become capable of being split into two parts. One part relating to payment for services provided by the charity, such as use of logo and mailing list, and another part which is a donation for which the charity provides nothing in return. The normal split would be 20 per cent for services, 80 per cent donation, but the split would need to be negotiated and carefully drafted in each particular case. The contracts would need to be approved by Customs and the Revenue in advance.

Income from branches or fundraisers

An important point to determine is how far the income of branches or fundraisers apparently independent of the charity should be included within the charity's own activities. Branches and fundraisers which are under the control of the main charity should be included; branches and fundraisers which are effectively independent should not. It is up to the charity to work out where, between those two points, each branch lies. The decision should be based on where the real power of decision-making and control of assets lies. If a branch is judged to be independent it may have to register in its own right. If Customs suspects that an organisation is being broken down into separate units to keep below the registration limits they may apply the disaggregation provisions, which give them power to treat the whole entity as a single taxable unit.

Irrecoverable VAT

The major problem in relation to charities and VAT is irrecoverable VAT. Much of the income of the sector is either exempt from VAT or outside-the-scope. This means there is no output VAT to set input VAT on purchases against. The input VAT cannot be passed on and comes to rest in the charity as an additional cost. Some charities have a mixture of income, which renders them partially exempt if they are registered for VAT because of their mixture of outputs. An organisation is partly exempt when it has a mixture of taxable and exempt income. The main objective will be to minimise the size of the irrecoverable VAT charge which has arisen, because not all the input VAT incurred by the organisation can be set against taxable outputs. There are various ways in which this can be done, and it is sensible to consult professional advisers in order to maximise recovery.

It is sensible to consult professional advisers in order to maximise recovery.

It was recognised by the government during the 1980s, after lobbying by the charity sector, that charities had a problem with irrecoverable VAT. The government's response has been to extend the concessions whereby charities receive the benefit of zero-rating on certain purchases they make. These concessions are unusual in the context of VAT's basic concepts, in that entitlement to the benefits of zero-rating depends on the status of the recipient, whether donee or purchaser. Usually, zero-rating of a transaction depends on the status of the supplier, as with the concession for charities selling donated goods. Some of these concessions date from the origin of VAT, but most were introduced piecemeal during the 1980s in response to specific pressures from charitable organisations. Most of the zero-rate concessions are in Schedule 8 **VATA 1994**. They include:

- Charity advertising.
- Goods connected with collecting donations.
- Purchase of radios and talking books for use by visually impaired people.

- Supply of buildings for charitable use.
- Lifeboats.
- Various types of equipment for disabled people.
- Medical equipment.

VAT planning and maximising recovery

Tax planning is important for voluntary organisations, and particularly registered charities. Organisations which are not compulsorily required to register for VAT may still consider doing so under what is called voluntary registration. This is because it may allow a partial recovery of VAT incurred. Such a decision requires being able to answer the following questions:

- Will the VAT the organisation is able to recover exceed that which it will have to declare to Customs on standard-rated activities?
- Will the organisation's customers be able to bear the cost of VAT that will now be charged – this should not be a problem for commercial organisations?
- Will the costs of setting up the financial system to record and claim VAT be covered?

Voluntary organisations should always be seeking to recover as much VAT as possible. Because voluntary organisations have a mixture of supplies that are taxable, exempt and outside-the-scope, there are issues as to how much of their costs can be recoverable and how much is irrecoverable. Issues, particularly around the expenses attributable to head offices, where some of these costs can be recovered require careful planning and negotiation with Customs and Excise. Professional advice from a specialist charity VAT expert may be required. This does not mean the charity having to incur direct fees. Many firms of accountants with specialist charity departments have charity VAT experts, who will base their fee as a percentage of the amount of VAT they can recover and will also cap their fees to an agreed amount.

> Voluntary organisations should always be seeking to recover as much VAT as possible.

Many firms of accountants with specialist charity departments have charity VAT experts who will base their fee as a percentage of the amount of VAT they can recover and will also cap their fees to an agreed amount.

As the following case study demonstrates:

Case Study

A charity, whose objectives included the funding of research and provision of welfare to children who had a particular disease, had remained unregistered for VAT since its formation. The taxable income it generated had been historically low, as its main sources of income were research grants (outside the scope), donations and legacies (outside the scope) and fundraising activities (mainly exempt). The opportunity to register for VAT arose when it decided to open a charity shop selling goods donated by the public (specifically zero-rated). The shop was very successful and soon the charity had five shops with a turnover of £250,000.

On speaking with professional charity VAT advisers, VAT registration was sought retrospectively from the date the first shop was opened (retrospective voluntary registration can be sought up to three years from the date of application). This ensured all VAT incurred during this period attributable to the shops could be fully recovered, a healthy proportion of overhead VAT. In addition, all VAT incurred on the annual ball and other fundraising events was fully recoverable as it fell below the partial exemption de-minimise limits.

The charity enjoyed a one-off windfall of £75,000 and an enduring annual VAT recovery of circa £12,000. As the majority of taxable income is zero-rated there is little VAT to pay on income. The professional advisers charged a one-off fee of 10 per cent of the windfall received plus VAT (which was fully recoverable!).

A charity registering will need to be mindful of the administrative requirements that accompany registration. Once registered, a charity will need to complete regular returns, keep adequate books and records to support such returns and be prepared for potential VAT inspections.

A charity registered for VAT will need to take advice, as it may be able to claim back an element of its residual VAT on expenditure which is not specifically allocated to either a business or non business activity. This is referred to as the POT recovery method and can be calculated using a variety of methods that will need to be agreed with HMRC.

Conclusion

The sector, through various lobbying groups, has tried many times to convince the government that the best solution to irrecoverable VAT would be for charities to be able to reclaim its cost from the tax authorities. Such a scheme already exists in relation to local authorities. The proposals have been consistently rejected by each Chancellor who has considered them. The battle is not over, however, and research is now underway to assess the true size of the sector's VAT bill.

Final remarks

The direct tax regime treats charities very favourably, and also contains several useful reliefs aimed at encouraging donations to the sector. The regime now is as generous as any country across the world. There are also several useful reliefs in relation to VAT, but the main problem for the sector is still irrecoverable VAT.

Illustrative exercise – appraising a charity's tax position

In this exercise we review a charity's operations from the perspective of reducing the burden of tax. Direct taxation implications are discussed first. The answer then appraises the indirect tax position:

> Wretched of the Earth is a charitable trust that was registered in 1962. Its purpose is to relieve poverty, distress and suffering in any part of the world.
>
> The charity operated from a building just off Soho Square, which was donated to it 15 years ago. On the ground floor, there is a 'restaurant' which offers frugal meals supposed to replicate the inadequate nourishment suffered by much of the world's poor. The restaurant is surprisingly popular, many of its clientele being overweight workers in the media industry located nearby.
>
> The charity was formerly a quiet operation, which had concentrated on convincing the Department for International Development (DFID) to give it a grant. Now, however, Harry Flashpoint, who was brought in by the trustees to give the charity a higher profile, runs it. Harry feels that his conspicuous lifestyle should be partly funded by the charity because the charity is benefiting.
>
> On Friday nights, there is a 'rave for the poor' at the charity's premises. This has become massively popular due to the presence of trendy disc jockeys and various glitterati. The very high entrance fee means that only those with a

large disposal income can get in, which increases the exclusiveness of the event.

Part of the premises is used by the charity as a shop, from which goods made by artisans in Africa are sold, together with donated goods and a small range of bought-in-jewellery.

The charity's income and expenditure for 200X/XX is as follows:

INCOME	£
Collecting tin donations	1,500
DFID grant	227,000
Other donations	7,000
Legacies	12,000
Net profit on restaurant	75,700
Net profit on raves	125,000
Proceeds of sale of donated goods	12,000
Net proceeds of artisan goods	500
Net proceeds of bought-in-goods	7,500
Total Income	468,200

EXPENDITURE	£
Setting-up irrigation project	200,000
Costs of shop	8,000
Central charity administration	40,000
Clothes, meals, for Harry	50,000
Roll Royce hire for Harry	16,000
Harry's salary	50,000
Total Expenditure	364,000
Surplus	104,200

Answer to exercise

Wretched of the Earth
A) Direct Tax

1. Charity has trading activities: restaurant
   shop
   bought in goods
   raves

These activities will probably be taxable. A possible answer to rectify the situation would be to set up a trading company (ies) which gift aids its profits. Are the trading activities profitable? From the information supplied the relevant income is:

Restaurant profit	75,700
Raves	125,000
Bought in goods	7,500
Artisan	500
	208,700

Issues of direct expenditure and the allocation of overheads as previously discussed in this guide would then have to be considered and a business plan drawn up.

B) Indirect tax

VAT treatment of income and expenditure:

INCOME

Collecting tin donations	OS
DFID Grant	OS
Other donations	OS
Legacies	OS
Restaurant turnover	SR
Entrance fee to raves	SR
Proceeds of donated goods at shop	ZR
Sales of artisan goods	SR
Sales of bought-in-goods	SR

EXPENDITURE

Setting-up of irrigation project	OS
Costs of shop	SR
Central charity administration	SR
Clothes, meals, for Harry	SR
Rolls Royce hire for Harry	SR
Harry's salary	OS

Other points

This standard-rated trading activity, if its turnover exceeds the allowance in the Finance Act (currently £60,000) will have to be put in a VAT-registered trading subsidiary to avoid income tax. If possible as much of the input tax on administration should be put through the subsidiary for recovery of VAT.

Code

EX = Exempt
OS = Outside the scope of VAT
SR = Standard-rated
ZR = Zero-rated

Checklist – what have we learnt?

Questions – Answers are in the text, but have a go at these before checking them:

1. What is required to be in place to ensure that Gift Aid can be claimed on a donation?
2. What are the major tax concessions that a charity should be aware of?
3. What is a taxable person?
4. Define standard-rate, zero-rate and exempt.
5. List which voluntary sector income sources are outside the scope of VAT.
6. What factors need to be considered in deciding whether VAT voluntary registration is appropriate?

Action points for your organisation

Audit your organisation to see if:

✓ It is maximising VAT recovery. For example: when was the last time the organisation had professional advisers assessing the tax position of the organisation?
✓ The trading subsidiary is profitable and keeping to its business plan?
✓ The fundraisers are fully briefed on tax effective giving?
✓ The fundraising department has plans for maximising tax effective giving among the charity supporters.
✓ The charity's fundraising material is creating a tax liability or restricting funds in an appeal.

Exercise

St Mungo's Monastery is located just outside Eastry in Kent and was established in the late 19th century with a number of endowments from a wealthy individual. It is a registered charitable trust. The monks are subject to the disciplines of the Order of the Sacred Veil and are not generally allowed out of the monastery.

The monks are a very active group, engaged in a number of activities. The monastery owns a vineyard that produces 'tonic' wine which is usually strong and is very popular. The monastery owns a large acreage, some of which has been turned over to market gardening, again carried out by monks. They also run a residential home for elderly men (who are not monks) attached to the monastery. There is also a public house, 'The Laughing Abbot', owned by the monastery but staffed by outsiders. All the activities of the monastery are carried out by the charitable trust.

Income and expenses are as follows:

	£
Local authority contract for residential home	500,000
Set-aside funds from the European Commission	75,000
Grant from the local authority	120,000
Sale of bar meals in the pub	65,000
Sale of drinks in the pub	250,000
Hire of rooms for functions	15,000
Collections at services in the monastery church	175,000
National Lottery grant for repair of church	200,000
Monks' salaries donated	350,000
DSS Income Support and State Pensions of elderly gentlemen	91,000
Sale of wine to wholesalers	1,200,000
Sales of produce from market garden to supermarkets	750,000
Monks' salaries paid	330,000
Salaries to full-time outsiders	510,000
Wages of part-time staff	60,000
Payments to freelancers and consultants	145,000
Redundancy payment to outsider	40,000
Repairs to church	300,000

Business rates	34,000
Council tax	6,250
Various materials used in manufacture of wine	350,000
Living expenses of monks	55,000
Donation to archdiocese	150,000
Advertising of tonic wine	30,000
Fundraising from bazaars, jumble sales, etc	133,000

The part-time staff is paid out of petty cash with no deductions for income tax or National Insurance. At least one of the so-called freelance staff has duties that hardly differ from an employee.

Answer the following questions

1. HMRC is planning to visit the charity to ensure that PAYE has been properly deducted. What precautions should be taken by the charity?
2. State how the VAT system would treat each of the monastery's activities.
3. What recommendations would you make in relation to the monastery's activities in order to reduce the liability to pay direct taxes?

Answer to exercise

1) What precautions should be taken if an HMRC PAYE audit is imminent?

Part-time staff

Depending on the level of pay, part-time staff should have income tax and NICs deducted in just the same way as full-time staff. A calculation should be made of the liability going back as far as necessary if tax and NICs have not been properly deducted. This is a liability of the charity, not employees. Penalties amounting to a maximum of the tax/NIC may also be payable, which cannot properly be borne by the charity and so must fall on its trustees personally. These will reduce depending on the level of cooperation with HMRC, so be cooperative. Proper pay deduction records should be maintained from now on, and the correct form issued at the end of the tax year.

Form P46 (or P38S for students) should be signed by each part-time employee and retained for HMRC to inspect.

Freelancers and consultants

HMRC will endeavour to treat as many of these as employees as they can, so evidence of the proper self-employed status of each should be sought. If in doubt, they should be treated as an employee and subjected to the PAYE scheme. This will upset the consultant, but this is less damaging than using charity funds to pay their tax/NICs. HMRC will use the following tests:

Control and work performance

Employees will not be able to decide in general where, when and how the work is performed.

Self-employed people have the power of delegation and do not have to work certain hours.

Financial risk

Employees do not risk their own personal capital if the work is not up to standard.

Equipment

Employees do not usually use their own equipment to carry out the work.

Holidays and sickness

Self-employed people do not get these.

Exclusivity

In general, employees will work for the one employer. Not so with the self-employed.

If the Revenue has granted the particular consultant self-employed status and issued a 'Schedule D number' this should be obtained, but it is not conclusive evidence.

Redundancy payment

This should be non-contractual. Care needs to be taken in this area for the payment to qualify for the £30,000 exemption. The remainder of it is taxable and tax should be deducted under PAYE. Any ex-gratia payment will be a breach of trust, unless consent is obtained from the Charity Commission.

2) **State how the VAT system would treat the monastery's activities.**

Local authority contract for the residential home	EX
Set-aside funds from the European Commission	OS
Grant from the local authority	OS
Sale of bar meals in the pub	SR
Sale of drinks in the pub	SR
Hire of rooms for functions	SR
Collections at services in the monastery church	OS
National Lottery grant for repair of church	OS
Monks' salaries donated	OS
DSS Income Support and State Pensions of elderly gentlemen	OS
Sale of wine to wholesalers	SR
Sale of produce from market garden to supermarkets	SR
Monks' salaries	OS
Salaries to full-time outsiders	OS
Wages of part-time staff	OS
Payments to freelancers and consultants	see note 1
Redundancy payment to outsider	OS
Repairs of church	SR
Business rates	OS
Council tax	OS
Various materials used in manufacture of wine	SR
Living expenses of monks	SR
Donations to archdiocese	OS
Advertising of tonic wine	SR
Fundraising from bazaars, jumble sales, etc	EX

Note 1. Depends on whether the consultants are registered for VAT.

Code

EX = exempt
OS = outside the scope of VAT
SR = Standard-rated
ZR = Zero-rated

3) What recommendations would you make in relation to the monastery's activities and direct taxes?

A trading subsidiary should be established. The trust deed should be checked to see whether to invest in such a subsidiary would be ultra vires. The deed may need adjusting and this should be cleared with the Charity Commission.

If the subsidiary is to be financed partly by loan capital, the loan should be properly documented and treated as if it was on an arm's-length basis, with security, interest and repayment terms made explicit.

If the following activities remain in the charity they will become taxable, (unless they can be classed as 'ancillary') as Schedule D Case I, profits unless they fall within the Revenue's exemptions for small traders because they are not for the primary purpose of the charity, i.e. the advancement of religion:

- Running of the pub and hire of rooms.
- Production and sale of wine.
- Sale of farm produce.
- Running of residential home.

Other points

The VAT regulations should be complied with. The trading subsidiary will be making the taxable supplies and VAT should be accounted for on the normal basis. Record-keeping rules should be complied with.

The residential home has exempt income and any input VAT relating to this activity is not reclaimable.

9 Accounting for smaller voluntary organisations

9.1 Introduction

This chapter introduces the regulation and accounting requirements for smaller voluntary organisations, which we define as having an income of less than £250,000. Many smaller voluntary organisations will be unincorporated charities with income above the threshold of £10,000 a year, and these are now subject to greater scrutiny and accountability than in the past. Please note Chapter 6 (see page 197) considers the regulatory framework that unincorporated charities work under. Charities that are constituted as a charitable company will operate under a different regime. The chapter also discusses the requirements of an independent examination, an alternative to having a full professional audit.

9.2 Accruals accounting for the smaller charity

The Charity Commission updated its guidance on accruals accounting for the smaller charity in August 2001, with CC65 *Accruals Pack: explanatory notes*. This is a guide for unincorporated charities with gross income for the year of £250,000. Charities with any other reporting requirements, for example a registered social landlord, cannot report under these guidelines.

The accruals pack

The pack includes forms, which if a charity chooses to complete will be sufficient to produce their annual report and accounts, together with specific guidance. Alternatively the forms can be used as a workbook or checklist of items that must be included.

Unincorporated charities with income under £100,000

Unincorporated charities with income under £100,000 have the option as to how to show their accounts. They can show their accounts under the accruals method or under the receipts and payments method.

Incorporated charities

The incorporated charity has to account under the accruals method. It does not have the option to show its accounts under the receipts and payments method, irrespective of its level of income.

The smaller unincorporated charity, unless preparing its accounts under the receipts and payments method, can also follow the Financial Reporting Standard for Smaller Entities (FRSSE), except where it conflicts with SORP 2005, in which case SORP 2005 should be followed. The incorporated charity must follow SORP 2005.

The incorporated charity must follow SORP 2005.

The accounts should include a Statement of Financial Activities (SOFA) in place of a profit and loss account, the principles of fund accounting should be adopted and investments should be shown at market value.

Accounts structure

The accounts structure follows the normal structure of accounts under the accruals accounting method and would include a statement of financial activities, a balance sheet and notes to the accounts.

The statement of financial activities will in most cases be the same as a traditional income and expenditure account, with the addition of the balance brought forward from the previous year. Charities can choose between analysing their resources expended by either the functional classification recommended by SORP 2005 or by natural classification.

The balance sheet should explain in general terms how the funds may, or because of restrictions imposed by donors, must, be utilised.

Also charities do not need to state whether the accounts have been prepared in accordance with any applicable accounting standards and statements of recommended practice, or give particulars of any material departure from those standards and statements of practice and the reasons for doing so.

Emoluments of employees earning more than £60,000 need to be disclosed. In bands of £10,000, transactions with trustees and other connected persons also need to be disclosed.

The accruals method for SORP accounting for charities with

income under £250,000 does not differ materially from the treatment of larger charities preparing their accounts under the SORP accounting method.

Trustees report

The accruals pack also provides a minimum framework for the completion of the trustees' annual report. Trustees may choose to provide additional information, but will include reference and administrative information, structure, governance and management, objectives and activities, achievements and performance, financial review and funds held as custodian trustee.

9.3 Receipts and payments accounting

In October 1995 the Charity Commission issued *Guidance on Accounting for the Smaller Charity*, which contains simplified extracts from the SORP, as it was the Charity Commission's opinion that many of the SORP's recommendations were suitable mainly for large charities, or those with complicated finances. The receipts and payments account is a relatively simple form of account, suitable for smaller charities with income up to £100,000, and consists of a summary of money received and paid during the financial year concerned. The statement of assets and liabilities is a straightforward schedule of information, which does not require the accountancy knowledge needed to prepare a balance sheet. Incorporated charities, however, cannot benefit from this and must produce accrual accounts. A charity will need to ensure that its governing document does not prevent it preparing accounts on this basis.

In 2001 the Charity Commission published a booklet *CC64 SORP 2000: Receipts and Payments Accounts Pack.*

The practices described in this pack will meet the requirements of the law and Appendix 5: Accounting for Smaller Charities, SORP 2005 5.1.5. Charities are advised to follow the recommendations, since they represent best practice, but are not obliged by law to do so. The accounts will not claim to show a true and fair view of the charity's financial activities and state of affairs. Accounting standards do not generally apply to such accounts. However, the accounts should be prepared on a consistent basis from year to year, and if asset valuations other than cost are provided they should be reasonable, relevant and reliable.

> The statement of assets and liabilities is a straightforward schedule of information, which does not require the accountancy knowledge needed to prepare a balance sheet.

What are the legal requirements?

In England and Wales, s42 (3) of the Charities Act 1993 applies. This allows a charity to prepare a 'receipts and payments account' for the year and a 'statement of assets and liabilities' at the year-end, instead of preparing full accounts for a particular financial year. This is on condition that in that financial year the charity's gross recorded income from all sources was £100,000, and it is not a company, is not required to prepare accruals accounts and has no subsidiary or associated companies. There are no statutory requirements as to what must be contained in the receipts and payments account or the statement of assets and liabilities.

In Scotland, the Charities Accounts (Scotland) Regulations 1992 apply. This allows a recognised body to prepare a 'receipts and payments account' for a particular financial year and a 'statement of balances' as at the year-end, if in that financial year the charity's gross receipts amounted to £25,000 or less. The receipts and payments account and statement of balances must contain the information listed in Part 2 of Schedule I to the Charities Accounts (Scotland) Regulations 1992 Part 2 of Schedule II to those regulations, lists the information which must be given in notes to the accounts.

In Northern Ireland and the Republic of Ireland there are no regulations governing either the form or the contents of charity accounts.

Annual report

The trustees of all registered charities in England and Wales are required by s45 of the Charities Act 1993 to prepare an annual report containing the information required by the Charities (Accounts and Reports) Regulations 2005. In Scotland, each recognised body must produce a report containing the information specified in Part 3 of Schedule I to the Charities Accounts (Scotland) Regulations 1992. In Northern Ireland and the Republic of Ireland there are no legal requirements to prepare annual reports.

> The trustees of a charity are responsible for preparing the accounts and annual report.

Trustees' responsibility for annual report and accounts

The trustees of a charity are responsible for preparing the accounts and annual report. Whether or not trustees delegate the preparation of accounts to others (perhaps to their accountant, treasurer or employees), the trustees remain responsible for ensuring that the accounts and report comply with the law. The legal requirements for producing and laying accounts before the annual general meeting, and for allowing other trustees access to the accounts with a reasonable amount of time before the

> The trustees remain responsible for ensuring that the accounts and report comply with the law.

accounts are approved, hold for both the smaller charity and the larger charity. The accounts have to be approved in the same way as for a larger charity and accounts must be delivered to the Charity Commission. The accounts of an unincorporated charity not exceeding £10,000 gross income and total expenditure for the year will not normally be required to be audited or independently examined, nor will they need to be submitted to the Charity Commission. Members of the public are entitled to request copies of the accounts.

Members of the public are entitled to request copies of the accounts.

Charity Commission CC64(a) receipts and payments accounts

For England and Wales, the Charity Commission has prepared a standard pack for use in preparing a charity's receipts and payments accounts and statement of assets and liabilities. No charity is obliged to use the pack CC64(a) but its use or adaptation for use is recommended by the Charity Commission as an alternative. The pack contains notes and instructions for trustees on how to complete the accounts in accordance with the law and is designed to meet minimum levels of accountability. The pack includes four documents. Three of which are to be prepared by the trustees: trustees annual report, one or more receipts and payments accounts and a statement of assets and liabilities. The fourth is the independent examiner's report. Copies are available without charge from the Charity Commission. The format is readily adaptable by umbrella bodies to suit their particular needs.

9.4 Independent examination

This section expands on an area already covered in chapter 6. Whether a charity needs an audit or independent examination depends on its size. To meet the requirements of the Charities Act 1993, all charities with an income in excess of £250,000 will require audit – whether independent examination is required or not depends on the legal status of the charity, i.e. whether it is incorporated or unincorporated. Those unincorporated charities with an income between £10,000 and £250,000 will require, as a basic minimum, an independent examination. Incorporated charities fall under the auspices of the Companies Act 1985 in respect of the requirement to audit and the preparation of an accountant's report.

Some charities may still require an audit due to governing documentation, a requirement under another statutory or regulatory regime or funder's requirements.

What is independent examination?

This is a less onerous form of scrutiny than audit, although the level of assurance given by independent examination is higher than that given under the exemption report regulations for companies. It is primarily based on a review of the accounts and consideration of any unusual items or disclosures identified. It indicates whether certain matters have been brought to the reviewer's attention. The examination must be carried out in accordance with the directions issued by the Charity Commission. The examiner is not required to form an opinion as to whether the accounts give a true and fair view.

The level of assurance provided by independent examination may be lower than that provided by audit, but it can be a very attractive option. This is particularly true where a charity's accounts have traditionally been 'audited' to satisfy members or the terms of a charity's trust by an individual without formal auditing qualifications.

If the accounts are prepared on an accruals basis, then the independent examiner must check them for compliance with the regulations in terms of format and content, review accounting policies, and enquire about post-balance sheet events. The examiner must also compare the accounts with the trustees' report to make sure the two are consistent with each other.

Who can do an independent examination?

An independent examiner is defined as 'an independent person who is reasonably believed by the trustees to have the requisite ability and practical experience to carry out competent examination of the accounts'. The Charities Act 1993 went on to define independent as having 'no connection with a charity's trustees which might inhibit the impartial conduct of the examination'.

The independent examiner will need to have good analytical and communication skills in order to be able to raise questions and to interpret and challenge responses. Also, the individual chosen should have practical experience, which should be indicated by involvement with the financial administration or independent examination of similar charities.

Although the independent examiner should be familiar with accountancy methods, they need not be a practising accountant. Someone with a professional qualification, especially a qualified accountant, however, is strongly recommended by the Charity

---

The level of assurance provided by independent examination may be lower than that provided by audit

The independent examiner should be familiar with accountancy methods, [although] they need not be a practising accountant.

Commission, particularly for a larger charity or cases where accruals accounting is adopted.

Independent examiner's report

The content of this report is determined by the regulations and it should be signed by the independent examiner personally, not on behalf of his/her firm, and must state any relevant professional qualifications or professional body of which he/she is a member. Examiners should avoid making positive statements of opinion or belief that could only be substantiated by carrying out an audit. The examiner should report clearly and unambiguously where the charity's accounts appear to be in order.

The examiner should report clearly and unambiguously where the charity's accounts appear to be in order.

The carrying out of an independent examination – directions and guidance notes

In March 1996, the Charity Commission issued the first set of guidance on the carrying out of an independent examination. The guidance covers examination requirements, the question 'what is an examination?', the selection of examiners and the examiner's report. CC63 Independent Examination of Accounts under SORP 2000: Directions and Guidance Notes version 10/02 is the current guidance issued by the Charity Commission.

Whistle-blowing

This additional role given to the auditor or independent examiner of an unincorporated charity of reporting certain facts directly to the Charity Commission is designed to increase public confidence. However, a similar obligation does not exist where the charity is incorporated. This duty occurs where the auditor or independent examiner has reasonable cause to believe that the matter is, or is likely to be, of material significance in relation to the charity, requiring the Commission to implement its functions under Section 8 (general power to institute enquiries) or 18 (power to act for protection of charities) of the 1993 Act (Regulation 6(5) of the 1995 Regulations (England & Wales)).

Auditors and independent examiners should not have to change the scope of their work to discover whether or not reportable issues exist. A duty arises if something is discovered whilst carrying out the audit/independent examination which in their opinion is judged to be of 'material significance', and assists the Commission in its supervisory functions relating to the investigating and checking of abuses within charities. If evidence of misuse is discovered the auditors are asked to extend their work.

The APB practice note currently sets out the three particular types of issues likely to be reportable:

- significant inadequacy in the arrangements made by trustees for the discretion and management of a charity's affairs;
- a significant breach of the legislative requirement in respect of the charity's trusts;
- circumstances indicating a probable deliberate misuse of charity property.

The APB requires that the auditors discuss concerns with trustees as part of the process of forming a judgement, unless the matter casts doubt on the integrity of the trustees, as to whether a particular issue needs to be reported directly to the Charity Commission. It is not intended that the auditor/examiner should report on insignificant issues, particularly where such issues have been satisfactorily resolved.

The regulations provide rights of access to all documents relating to the charity and which the auditor/independent examiner properly considers necessary to inspect. This includes the right to require information from past or present trustees, officers or employees.

A report to the Commission must be made in writing. Failure to report a matter could result in disciplinary procedures by the relevant professional body. The revised Practise Note 11 has extended its guidance on SAS 620: The auditor's right and duty to report to the regulators in the Financial Sector, together with Appendix 8 which gives examples of matters that would be routinely investigated by the Charity Commission.

The regulations provide rights of access to all documents relating to the charity and which the auditor/ independent examiner properly considers necessary to inspect.

Exercise 9.1 – test your knowledge

Answer all the questions – ring the correct answers

1. The main obligation in preparing a charity's account is to show a true and fair view of its incoming resources, their application and its state of affairs; except in the case of:
   (a) small charities which elect to prepare a receipts and payments account
   (b) charitable companies
   (c) charities with branches
   (d) charities financed from permanent endowments

2. An incorporated charity is promised a grant of £200,000 in the year to 31 March 2006 (the charity's year-end) for the salary costs. The grant was not received until May 2006. Actual income received in the year was £90,000. On what basis would the charity be required to prepare its accounts for the year to 31 March 2006:
   (a) a receipt and payments basis and would require a reporting accountants report
   (b) a receipt and payments basis and would require an audit
   (c) a full accruals accounting basis and would require a reporting accountants report
   (d) a full accruals accounting basis and would require an audit

3. The value of resources accruing to a charity should be recorded in the SOFA:
   (a) when the financial year ends
   (b) only when the cash has been received
   (c) as soon as it is prudent and practical to do so
   (d) even if the conditions for receipts have not been met

4. Under the Charities Act 1993 it states that the accounting records must:
   (a) show the solvency of the charity at any time
   (b) show the financial position at any point in time
   (c) disclose the financial position at the end of the financial year
   (d) be written up on a daily basis to show the current financial position

5. A non-incorporated charity expects income of £30,000 for the year ended 31 March 2005 and has had this level of income for the last five years. In the past it had an audit because its trust deed required an audit and the trustees thought it was necessary. When can this charity take advantage of the new charity regulations to avoid the cost of an audit?
   (a) only after changing the trust deed
   (b) as soon as the trustees inform the existing auditors
   (c) immediately
   (d) as soon as the existing auditors have resigned

6. In response to an appeal, your charity has received a gift of shares worth £20,000 and cash of £50,000 to be used for relief in Cuba. During the year the shares have produced income of £15,000 and the sale of 50% of the shares generated proceeds of £25,000. At the end of the year the charity spent £60,000 on Cuba. How much is the fund balance at the year-end?
   (a) £30,000
   (b) £35,000
   (c) £40,000
   (d) £45,000

7. A non-incorporated charity prepares its accounts on a receipts and payments basis to the 31 March 2006. It received £95,000 in the year. In addition it has claimed back Gift Aid of £10,000 on its donations. This money was received after the year-end. Assume that the trustees do not wish to change the basis of accounting unless this is required. In this case, the accounts should disclose:
   (a) income of £395,000 and be prepared on a receipts and payment basis
   (b) income of £105,000 and be prepared on a receipts and payment basis
   (c) income of £105,000 and be prepared on an accruals basis
   (d) either income of £95,000 or £105,000 depending on whether the tax refund is received before the accounts are approved

8. A small charity producing a receipts and payments accounts
   (a) need not distinguish restricted funds from general funds
   (b) may produce a statement of assets and liabilities instead of a balance sheet
   (c) must file their accounts within nine months of the financial year end
   (d) must have the accounts independently examined

9. A charity sells donated goods through its subsidiary which raised income £100,000 and shop expenses were £40,000 giving a profit of £60,000. The charity's consolidated Statement of Financial Activities should show:
   (a) income of 100,000 under trading income
   (b) income of 100,000 under donations
   (c) net profit of 60,000 as a single line
   (d) none of the above

Answers to exercise

1. a
2. d
3. c
4. b
5. a
6. c
7. a
8. b
9. b

Overseas charity
Receipts and payments account
For the year ended 31 March 2004

	Unrestricted	Restricted	TOTAL 2004	TOTAL 2003
INCOMING RECEIPTS	£	£	£	£
Donations – child sponsorship				
(CSP) and gifts	22,848	-	22,848	24,052
Donations – monitoring visits	5,000	-	5,000	5,000
Grants and corporate donors	6,340	8,125	14,465	-
Fundraising events	13,943	-	13,943	-
Interest received	311	-	311	103
Other receipts	820	-	820	-
Tax reclaim	2,628	-	2,628	4,208
Total receipts	51,890	8,125	60,015	33,363

PAYMENTS
Direct charitable expenditure

	Unrestricted	Restricted	TOTAL 2004	TOTAL 2003
Child sponsorship programme				
(CSP)	25,584	-	25,584	16,104
Monitoring visits and associated				
costs	3,728	-	3,728	3,776

Other Expenditure:

Fundraising costs	3,106	1,616	4,722	-
Printing, postage & stationery	869	515	1,384	1,004
Travel & subsistence	234	-	234	5
Telephone, Internet and website cost	1,237	-	1,237	1,487
Marketing, entertainment and related expenses	66	153	219	309
Office rent	1,728	-	1,728	1,728
Insurance	183	-	183	182
Purchase of computer & printer	-	576	576	1,084
Repairs & maintenance	-	-	-	267
Conference cost	326	380	706	-
Sundry	223	-	223	-
Bank charges & interest	168	-	168	90
Total payments	37,452	3,240	40,692	26,036
Net receipts for the year	14,438	4,885	19,323	7,327
Cash Fund balances at 31 March 2003	22,428	-	22,428	15,101
Cash Fund balances at 31 March 2004	£36,866	£4,885	£41,751	£22,428

Overseas charity

STATEMENT OF ASSETS AND LIABILITIES

As at 31 March 2004

			2004	2003
MONETARY ASSETS:				
	General Purpose Funds	Restricted Funds	TOTAL	TOTAL
	£	£	£	£
Bank & cash balances:				
Bank current account	9,858	4,885	14,743	3,757
Bank deposit account	26,960	-	26,960	18,671
Petty cash	48	-	48	-
Total	£36,866	£ 4,885	£41,751	£22,428

Restricted Funds:

Building project	4,675	
CAF	210	
	£4,885	(see Note 4)

Other Monetary Assets:

		2004	2003
		£	£
Debtors:	Tax credits	3,563	791
	Deposit – rent and keys	270	270
	Overseas currencies held	240	155
	Petty cash	-	28
		£4,073	£1,244

Approved by the trustees on 31 August 2004 and signed on their behalf by:
J Smith

Overseas charity
Notes to the financial statements for
the year ended 31 March 2004

1. Accounting policies
The financial statements have been prepared under the historical cost convention and are in accordance with applicable accounting standards, and the Charities Accounting Statement of Recommended Practice (SORP).
(a) Income is accounted for on a receipts basis. This includes donation, interest and tax reclaim.
(b) Direct charitable expenditure includes the direct costs of the charity's activities.

2. Trustee remuneration
The trustees received no remuneration in the year.

3. Staff remuneration
No salary or allowance was paid to the two volunteer staff.

4. Restricted fund
Restricted funds are for the following purposes:

Building project:
The grant has been awarded for the building project which is due to take place later on in the year.

CAF:
Charities Aid Foundation (CAF) grant was for trustees and staff to attend selected fundraising courses forming part of The Fundraising Programme run by the Directory of Social Change. Since the year-end the unexpended amount of £210 has been repaid.

Glossary

accounting systems
The series of tasks and records of an organisation by which the transactions are processed as a means of maintaining financial records.

activity classification of costs
An 'activity classification of costs' is the aggregation of costs incurred in pursuit of a defined activity (e.g. provision of services to elderly people or counselling), and is achieved by adding together all the costs (salaries, rents, depreciation etc.) relating to that specific activity.

advanced corporation tax
An amount payable in respect of the final corporation tax liability arising whenever a dividend is made by a company.

annual report and accounts
A set of statements which may comprise the trustees' report and the financial statements of the charity.

audit threshold
This is the threshold (which may include income, expenditure and asset limits) above which a charity will be required to have a statutory audit.

balanced score card
A management method which seeks to find a balance between: financial results, customer satisfaction, process performance, and competence level.

branches
'Branches (which may also be known as supporters' groups, friends' groups, members' groups etc.) are entities or administrative bodies set up, for example, to conduct a particular aspect of the activities of the reporting charity, or to conduct the activities of the reporting charity in a particular geographical area. They may or may not be legal entities which are separate from the reporting charity.

break-even point
The level of activity at which there is neither a surplus nor a deficit: total income equates to total cost.

budget
A quantitative statement, for a defined period of time, which may include planned income, expenses, assets, liabilities and cash flows. A budget provides a focus for the organisation, helps the coordination of activities and facilitates control.

budget forecast
A prediction of future income and expenditure or receipts and payments for the purpose of preparing budgets.

budget profiling
The assignment of annual income and expenditure figures to relevant months in the year when the income or expenditure is likely to be receivable or incurred.

budget variances
The difference, for each expense or income element in a budget, between the budgeted amount and the actual expense or income.

budget worksheets
Standard templates used for the preparation, update and consolidation of budgets; often produced using a spreadsheet package.

budgetary control
The establishment of budgets relating the responsibility of individuals or departments to the requirements of a financial policy, and the continuous comparison of actual with budgeted results.

charity
A 'charity' is any institution established for purposes which are exclusively charitable.

charity trustees
'Charity trustees' has the same meaning as in s97(1) of the Charities Act 1993, that is the persons having the general control and management of the administration of a charity regardless of what they are called.

conflict of interest policy
A statement which seeks to identify instances when the judgement of trustees of a charity may be unduly influenced by their connections with other persons or bodies.

controllable costs
A cost that can be influenced by the budget holder.

cost accounting
The establishment of budgets, standard costs and actual costs of operations, processes, activities or products; and the analysis of variances, social use of funds.

cost centre
A service location, function or activity for which costs are accumulated.

costs of generating voluntary income
Costs of generating voluntary income comprise the costs actually incurred by a charity, or by an agent, in inducing others to make gifts to it that are voluntary income.

current liabilities
Liabilities that fall due for payment within one year.

direct cost
Expenditure that can be identified and specifically measured in respect of a relevant activity.

emolument
a salary, fee or benefit from employment or office

endowment funding
An endowment is a special type of restricted fund that must normally be retained intact and not spent.

equities
Shares in a company. Equity shares normally entitle the holder to a dividend and are traded on an exchange.

exempt supplies (VAT)
Supplies which do not attract VAT, but no input tax is repayable.

external environment
Key factors that have their origins outside the voluntary organisation, but may affect its activities and the fulfilment of charitable objectives.

extra-statutory concession
The practice of the HM Revenue & Customs of allowing certain minor items to avoid tax, even though taxable under a strict interpretation of the law. Normally done to avoid a multitude of disputes about trivial amounts

financial procedures manual
A document outlining the key responsibilities of trustees, management and staff, and the controls in place to regulate financial activity.

governance
A function of trustee boards or directors boards who are concerned with the fulfilment of strategic objectives.

governance costs
These are the costs associated with the governance arrangements of the charity which relate to the general running of the charity as opposed to those costs associated with fundraising or charitable activity. The costs will normally include internal and external audit, legal advice for trustees and cost associated with constitutional and statutory requirements and strategic advice.

governing document
The instrument that defines the reasons why the charity exists and how it is to conduct its internal affairs; may be in the form of a written constitution, memorandum and articles of association or deed.

grant
A grant is any voluntary payment (or other transfer of property) in favour of a person or institution.

income
Money that the organisation is legally entitled to receive. The accounting records will recognise this by recording an entry as soon as legal entitlement exists. To be distinguished from receipts, which are recorded when the money is actually received.

incremental budgeting
A method of budgeting that uses the previous period's results and inflates these by a fixed amount to account for increase in retail prices, for example.

indirect costs
Expenditure on labour, materials or services that cannot be directly identified with a specific activity.

input tax (VAT)
Is the tax paid by the organisation on goods and services purchased. It is offset against output tax, and the balance paid over to, or reclaimed from HM Customs & Excise.

internal audit
An independent appraisal function established with an organisation to examine and evaluate its activities as a service to the organisation. The object of internal auditing is to help members of the organisation to discharge their responsibilities effectively.

investment assets
Assets held by a charity for the purpose of deriving income and/or capital growth: for example, property and equity shares.

investment policy
A statement that defines the objectives for holding investments; will therefore include details of what type of investments are to be held, in what proportions, and the expected returns.

investment portfolio
A basket of investment assets held collectively with the intention of reducing the risk that would arise if these assets were held separately.

irrecoverable VAT
The proportion of VAT that is incurred and relates to non-business activities and therefore cannot be reclaimed.

joint venture
A project undertaken by two or more persons or entities joining together with a view to profit, often in connection with a single operation.

liquid assets
Cash and other assets readily convertible into cash: for example short-term investments.

liquidity
Condition in which assets are held in a cash or near-cash form.

longitudinal study
Research which follows a selected number of individuals or organisations for an extended period.

mission
The fundamental principles by which an organisation exists and operates.

non-profit organisations
Any organisation whose primary objective is not exclusively orientated towards the maximisation of wealth for its owners and/or profit. This need not be a registered charity.

outcomes
Used in performance measurement. Outcomes or impacts are difficult to identify and measure, but might be considered as the desired end results from the outputs of the organisation. However, it can be difficult to prove that a cause and effect relationship exists.

outputs
Not always measured in money terms, but represent some delivery, service or result of special interest.

outsourcing
The buying in from a third party of services or goods that had previously been produced internally. The day-to-day management of the process is also delegated to the third party.

output tax (VAT)
Is the VAT due on taxable supplies made by the organisation.

relevant costs
Costs appropriate to a specific management decision.

reserves
Income available to be spent at the trustee's discretion in furtherance of the charity's objects but which is not yet spent, committed or designated; in other words, 'free' reserves.

restricted fund
A fund subject to specific trusts within the objects of the charity (for example, by a letter from the donor at the time of the gift or by the terms of a public appeal). It may be a capital fund which cannot be spent but must be retained for the benefit of the charity;

or it may be an income fund which must be spent on the specified purpose within a reasonable time.

shareholder value
The maximisation of economic value for shareholders, as measured by share price performance and flow of dividends.

stakeholders
Any group of people (either internal to the charity or not) or organisations externally that may be affected by the decisions and policies of the charity.

standard rate of VAT
The main rate of VAT (currently 17.5%) on the cost of goods or services.

static budget
The original budget that has been approved by the trustees and is not changed to reflect either changes in the underlying assumptions used to prepare the budget or inaccurate forecasts.

strategic planning
The formulation, evaluation and selection of strategies for the purpose of preparing a long-term plan of action to attain objectives.

support costs
Support costs are those costs that, whilst necessary to deliver an activity, do not themselves produce or constitute the output of the charitable activity. Similarly, costs will be incurred in supporting income generation activities such as fundraising, and in supporting the governance of the charity.

taxable person (VAT)
An individual or organisation etc. which is or ought to be registered for VAT because their taxable supplies are above the current limit.

tax point (VAT)
The date at which a taxable supply of goods is treated as taking place.

taxable supplies
Are supplies made in the UK which are not specifically exempted.

treasury management

The handling of all financial matters, the generation of external and internal funds for an organisation, the management of currencies and cash flows.

trustee board

A collective body of trustees responsible in law for the activities of the charity, whether officially designated as trustees or not.

VAT (value added tax)

A tax collected by H.M. Customs & Excise (not the Inland Revenue) charged on supplies of goods and services.

vendorism

The practice of charging fees for the provision of services or activities which the organisation exists to supply.

venturing

Non-related commercial activities whose sole rationale is to raise money for the agency.

virement

The authority to apply savings under one subhead of a budget to meet excesses on others.

working capital

The capital available for conducting the day-to-day operations of an organisation; normally, the excess of current assets over current liabilities.

zero-based budgeting

A method of budgeting which requires each cost element to be specifically justified as though the activities to which the budget relates were being undertaken for the first time. Without approval, the budget allowance is zero.

zero rate of VAT

A supply which is taxable but the rate is 0 per cent. Relevant VAT on the inputs can be reclaimed.

Further reading and resources

There are now some excellent books on voluntary sector finance. It is also worth being on at least one of the accounting firms/investment firms' charity mailing lists to get regular newsletters and updates on issues such as the budget and how it affects charities.

Given the recent changes to the Charities SORP make sure that you have editions of books updated for SORP 2005, if they cover accounting matters.

Accounting, Tax and Investments

Butterworth's Law (2000) *Tolley's Charities Administration Handbook*

Butterworth's Law (2002) *Tolley's Charity Investigations*

Butterworth's Law (2001) *Tolley's Tax & Accountancy Directory*

Butterworth's Law (2000) *VAT for Charities and Other Voluntary Organisations*

Charities SORP – Charity Commission

Charity Finance Director's Group *Charity Finance Yearbook*, Plaza Publishing Limited

Elliott, G (2005) *VAT for Voluntary Organisations: A step-by-step guide*, NCVO

HM Customs and Excise, *VAT leaflet 701/1*, at www.hmce.gov.uk/forms/catalogue/catalogue/.htm#700

Palmer P, Meakin R, Whitefield J, and Scanlon, C *Socially Responsible Investment*, Key Haven Publications

Randall, AJL andYoung, F (2005) *The ICSA Guide to Charity Accounting*

Scott, M (ed) (2000) *Butterworth's Charity Law Handbook*, Butterworth's Law

Vincent, R (ed) (2005) *Charity Accounting and Taxation*, Lexis Nexis

Wood, C (2003) *The Good Investment Guide for the Voluntary Sector*, NCVO

Charity governance and related matters

Adirondack, S (2002) *The Good Governance Action Plan for Voluntary Organisations*, NCVO

Akpeki, T (2004) *Best Behaviour: Using trustee codes of conduct to improve governance practice*, NCVO

Akpebi, T (2005) *A Chair's First 100 Days: A practice guide to the basics of board leadership*, NCVO

Akpeki, T and Brown, A (2001) *Enhancing Trusteeship Through Mentroring*, NCVO

Akpeki, T (2005) *The Good Governance Action Plan Workbook*, NCVO

Akpeki, T (2004) *A Polished Performance: Findings from NCVO's Leadership Programme for chief executives and chairs*, NCVO

Akpeki, T (2001) *Recruiting and Supporting Black and Minority Ethnic Trustees*, NCVO

Barclay, J and Abdy, M (2001) *Quality Matters*, NCVO

Blake Ranken, W (2005) *The Good Employment Guide for the Voluntary Sector*, NCVO

Cornforth, C (2001) *Recent Trends in Charity Governance and Trusteeship*, NCVO

Dalton, D (2005) *The Board's Responsibility for Appraising the Chief Executive*, NCVO

Dalton, D (2005) *Recruting a New Chief Executive: A guide for chairs and trustees*, NCVO

Dyer, P (2003) *The Good Trustee Guide*, NCVO

Forrester B, Akpeki T, and Maretich, M (2004) *Living Policy*, NCVO

Harris, J (2002) *The Good Management Guide for the Voluntary Sector*, NCVO

Jas, P (2000) *Charitable giving in theory and practice*, NCVO

NCVO (2003) *The Adoption and Use of Quality Systems in the Voluntary Sector: Literature Review*

NCVO (2004) *The Adoption and Use of Quality Systems in the Voluntary Sector: Research Report*

NCVO (1999) *Approaching Quality: A guide to the choices you could make*

NCVO (2005) *Better Communication = Better Governance*

NCVO (2005) *The Board Answer Book*

NCVO (2002) *Developing Trustee Board: A manual for trainers*

NCVO (2000) *Excellence in View: A guide to the EFQM excellence model for the voluntary sector*, NCVO

NCVO (2004) *Getting Ready for Quality: Learning from experience*

NCVO (2003) *Governance in the Information Age: A trustee's guide to information and communication technology*

NCVO, (2004) *Tools for Tomorrow: A practical guide to strategic planning and voluntary organisations*

Waterhouse, G (2001) *Evaluating Quality in the Voluntary Sector*, NCVO

Academic journals, which cover finance, particularly reporting on reseach

Financial Accountability and Management, Blackwells, Public Money, CIPFA

Journal of non-profit and voluntary sector marketing, Henry Stewart Publications

Managerial Auditing Journal, *MCB University Press*

Magazines

VS Magazine (formerly Voluntary Sector) is read by charity profesisonals and all those working with the voluntary and community sector. It keeps you informed of new legislation, provides detailed analysis of policy developments, features exclusive interviews with key figures, contains examples of best practice and case studies, plus up-to-the-minute briefings. Its practical mix of news and features provide everything you need to know about the sector in one monthly round up, including: government policy, finance, fundraising, trustee issues, campaigning, recruitment and training, volunteering, and ICT.

Charity Finance

Charity Times

Professional Fundraising

Third Sector

Websites

Charity Commission: www.charity-commission.gov.uk

NCVO: www.ncvo-vol.org.uk

The Inland Revenue publishes useful information online: www.inland revenue.gov.uk/charities/index.htm

VAT: Frequently Asked Questions, Guides from Customs and Excise with useful links: www.hmce.gov.uk/business/vat.charityfaqs.htm

Free resources

Campbell, B (2004) *Making Giving go Further: A fundraiser's guide to tax-effective giving*, The Giving Campaign

Unwin, J (2005) *Fruitful Funding: A guide to levels of engagement*, NCVO

Action Points for Public Services, (2005) based on reearch carried out by NCVO

Common Aspiration: The role of the VCS in iomproving the funding relationship with government, (2005) research undertaken by NCVO for the National Audit Office

Inside Research: The 17th Annual Voluntary Sector Salary Survey (2005)
The full survey published by Renumeration Economics has been produced in association with NCVO

Charitable Giving and Donor Motivation – ESRC Seminar Series: Mapping the public policy landscape, (2005)

Voluntary Sector Added Value: A discussion paper, (2003)

For more information on any NCVO publication visit www.ncvo-vol.org.uk or call 0845 458 9910